DARFUR
THE AMBIGUOUS GENOCIDE

Crises in World Politics

TARAK BARKAWI
JAMES MAYALL
BRENDAN SIMMS
editors

GÉRARD PRUNIER
Darfur: the Ambiguous Genocide

MARK ETHERINGTON
Revolt on the Tigris

FAISAL DEVJI
Landscapes of the Jihad

AHMED HASHIM
Insurgency and Counter-Insurgency in Iraq

GÉRARD PRUNIER

Darfur
The Ambiguous Genocide

Cornell University Press
Ithaca, New York

Originally published in the United Kingdom by
C. Hurst & Co. (Publishers) Ltd, London.

First published 2005 by Cornell University Press

ISBN 0-8014-4450-0 (cloth: alk. paper)

Printed in the United States of America

Librarians: Library of Congress Cataloging-in-Publication Data are available.

Cornell University Press strives to use environmentally responsible suppliers and materials to the fullest extent possible in the publishing of its books. Such materials include vegetable-based, low-VOC inks and acid-free papers that are recycled, totally chlorine-free, or partly composed of nonwood fibers. For further information, visit our website at www.cornellpress.cornell.edu.

Cloth printing   10 9 8 7 6 5 4 3 2 1

CONTENTS

PREFACE AND ACKNOWLEDGEMENTS

During the spring of 2003 people who were professionally involved in East African matters began to hear strange rumbles coming out of a little-known part of western Sudan called Darfur. Apart from some ethnologists and historians, few people had a clear picture of the place. But among those with some familiarity with the Sudan it was known that Darfur had lived in a state of endemic insecurity since the big 1984–5 Sahelian famine. Recurrent clashes between nomads and sedentary peasants had taken place in the region throughout the 1990s. But this time the violence seemed more threatening—the reports had a more sinister ring to them. It seemed that an insurgency against the government had started and that this was being countered by extreme means including, strangely, raids by groups of horsemen who massacred peasants and burnt whole villages. Ethnic clashes had occurred before in Darfur, but apparently never on such a scale. Or was it just ethnic clashes? The attackers were shouting that "the Blacks" had to go, that "the land now belonged to the Arabs". The few members of the international community who were professionally engaged in dealing with the region were confused: were not the Islamist Sudanese government and its enemies, the Southern Christian guerrilla insurgents, engaged in a promising process of negotiation in Kenya? Was not the long-lasting Sudanese civil war finally about to end? And how could a new conflict be developing in a province wholly populated by Muslims when it was known by everybody that the war in the Sudan was a religious conflict between the Arab Muslim North and the African Christian South?

What had at first seemed like a bizarre anomaly began to develop into a serious concern. Advocacy NGOs, whose *raison d'être* was to look at such problems with a probing eye, began to sound alarm bells. The titles of their reports mirrored the mounting seriousness of the emergency: *Sudan: Looming Crisis in Darfur* (Amnesty International, July 2003), *Darfur Rising* (International Crisis Group, March 2004) and finally *Darfur in Flames* (Human Rights Watch Africa, April 2004). By the late spring of 2004 the world media began to suspect that the "real story" in the Sudan might not be the languishing peace talks in Kenya but the exploding violence in Darfur. By the summer the biggest and most sinister word that could be applied to such a situation, "genocide", had been uttered. A shock went through the world opinion: ten years after the Rwandese genocide, when commemorations of the 1994 horror filled the newspapers and TV screens, could the same nightmare be occurring again in another part of the African continent? Was Africa cursed? Or was the international community guilty of blindness and neglect? Or perhaps both?

Suddenly everybody got frantic. The international community panicked at the thought that the long and difficult peace negotiations between North and South might abort; Washington, which had an electoral interest in seeing them come to a successful termination, began applying massive pressure to the various players on the world diplomatic game in order to bring Khartoum to its senses without having to divert its own interest from Iraq to Sudan; the Sudanese government, fearing that it might trigger a military intervention on its territory, began desperately struggling to convince the world that Darfur was simply a case of ethnic conflict gone out of control; the humanitarian community rushed on to the scene and began massive aid programs; the UN began to worry lest it be dragged into something it could not handle, given the exaggerated prudence of the member states; and the media and the NGOs began proclaiming that this was Rwanda over again and that the world had learnt nothing. Then in quick succession came the Christmas holidays, a killer tsunami in Asia and the final signature of the Sudan Peace Agreement in Kenya on 9 January 2005. The Darfur crisis suddenly went limp. The word "genocide" disappeared from the headlines, news of the massacres stopped, and Sudan was only mentioned in the media inconnection with the "peace at last" announcement in Nairobi.

Did this mean that the crisis was over? Not in the least—in fact it had become even worse. Now confident that the world had turned its back on what it was doing in Darfur, the Khartoum government had launched new offensives to sweep the guerrillas clear from the ground, at a massive cost in the lives of civilians. The resulting insecurity prevented the UN and NGOs from working normally and the number of war victims who could be helped dropped drastically. Mortality rates shot up and a state of quasi-anarchy developed. Meanwhile a UN Commission of Inquiry gave its answer as to whether the Darfur horror deserved to be called a genocide and the answer was negative; it was merely a routine matter of some war crimes and assorted violations of human rights. In any case the people responsible for these violations were the very ones who had signed the Nairobi Peace Agreement a few weeks before. How embarrassing it would be to have to prosecute them before an international court of justice when they were supposed to implement "peace" in their country. This fragmentation of peace into watertight segments was hard to swallow, but after all was it not the task of diplomacy to handle such paradoxes for the general satisfaction?

At the time of writing the massacres and the slow deaths of the refugees and displaced persons continue. The attention of the world has wandered elsewhere and the crisis has reverted to the attention of the "specialists". This seems to be the inescapable fate of African political problems fifteen years after the Cold War ended. There are no big political, economic or security stakes for the developed world in these conflicts—just the deaths of human beings. The element which could draw wider attention to the problem, the fear of Radical Islam, is not even there. Muslims killing Muslims—it is not a subject to arouse passions, because in spite of the rhetoric which accompanied the demise of the Cold War, our culture has not undertaken a Human Rights revolution or embraced humanity as one. It has simply developed a specialised task force to take care of such things, and tragedies like Darfur remain a job for the humanitarians. Or perhaps for rock singers with faltering careers, even if that particular line of public relations seems to have largely gone into eclipse since *we were the world* twenty years ago in Ethiopia.

But beyond the shock and the emotions there remained an essential task: trying to understand. If I can be allowed to quote myself, I have written elsewhere about another genocide that "respect for the dead does not preclude an effort at understanding why they died."[1] I would argue that on the contrary trying to analysing the causes of their tragic fate is an essential form of respect for the victims. Darfur is little known, and it is often not realized how specific and distinct its history is from that of the rest of the country. Many people do not even know that for several centuries it was an independent country and was annexed to Sudan only in 1916. The nature of the problems and the contradictions which developed there after independence, particularly during the last twenty years, is also often overlooked because most analysis of Sudanese politics has had to do either with the core areas of the North or with the

[1] Gerard Prunier, *The Rwanda Crisis: History of a Genocide*, London: Hurst, 1995, Foreword.

North-South conflictual relationship. Darfur, like the other "marginalized areas" of the Sudan (the Beja country, most of Blue Nile Province, the Nuba Mountains) has received proportionally much less attention than either the "true North" or the South, and any writing about it tended to be from the viewpoint of the anthropologist or the historian rather than from that of the contemporary social scientist. A major armed conflict was not expected in Darfur, which is probably why its repression turned so horribly violent. The ruling élite in Sudan had for many years been accustomed to considering the South as its main problem and it did not expect a sudden uprising of the poor western relatives. The North-South conflict has been in many of its aspects a colonial conflict, while the Darfur uprising was from the beginning much closer to a genuine civil war. And civil wars are often the most relentless forms of conflict because they involve relatives. In Khartoum the government panicked because it suddenly felt that the Muslim family was splintering, potentially with enormous consequences. The violence of the response was directly linked to the magnitude of the fear. That fear has not yet abated, and it could well prove justified since "the North" could unravel from Darfur, leading to a complete reassessment of the distribution of power and financial resources in the country. The fate of the so-called "Peace Agreement" signed in Nairobi on 9 January 2005 could well hinge on what happens in the "marginalized areas" of Sudan for which Darfur could prove to have been the vanguard.

Acknowledgements

For obvious reasons of confidentiality I cannot acknowledge the help and information received from many people in Sudan, Ethiopia, Europe and the United States. So my special gratitude goes to those who not only helped me with this book written in a state of personal emergency but also allow me to thank them: first my publisher Michael Dwyer, who convinced me of the importance of undertaking this work in spite of other pressing professional commitments; then my wife Widad Mustafa el-Hadi, for whom the Sudan has turned into a dark night of the soul. And then Ahmed Ibrahim Diraige, former Governor of Darfur; Jemera Rone of Human Rights Watch Africa, Ambassador David Shinn, Thomas Ofcansky, Ali Hassan Taj ed-Din, Rashid Said Yakoub, Issam Akrat, Jean-Hervé Bradol, Douglas Johnson, Jean-Christophe Bélliard, Casimiro Jocundo, François Piguet, Medhane Tadesse and John Young. Their support does not make them responsible for the opinions expressed in this book whose shortcomings are inescapably mine.

Addis Ababa, June 2005   G. P.

GLOSSARY OF ARABIC TERMS

This glossary is intended as a practical tool for use in the book. Linguists will object to its transliteration, and its inclusion of *aamiya* (i.e. colloquial Sudanese Arabic terms) may shock purists. But its relevance is in its practicality: these terms are in common use. The letters *q.v.* appear after words found elsewhere in the glossary.

'ajam   "barbarians", people whose mother tongue is not Arabic, who speak a *rottana* (*q.v.*).

amir   a political and military title of leadership. In the Sudan it was particularly used for the "generals" of the Mahdist movement.

awlad al-beled   lit. "children of the country". The name given to themselves by the riverine Arabs to pride themselves of their "true Sudanese" credentials. Syn. *awlad al-Bahar* or "children of the river".

awlad al-gharb   "children of the west". Name given to the Westerners by the *awlad al-beled*. This appellation is given to all Westerners, whether *zurug* (*q.v.*) or "Arabs" and contains an implicit racial slur.

baggara   lit. "those of the cow". A common name given to a number of cattle-raising tribes living in Darfur and southern Kordofan. As arabized Africans they are a prime example of Western Sudan's ethnic ambiguities.

bahharia (hist.)   name that used to be given in the 19th century to those *awlad al-bahar* hunting for slaves and elephants in Bahr-el-Ghazal.

bazinger (hist.)   slave soldiers in the armies of 19th-century Sudan.

dajjal   in popular Mahdist tradition, the anti-Christ whose coming will herald the End of Time.

damra   nomad settlement. Its provisional natural is markedly different from the more settled *dar* (*q.v.*).

dar   "country". Used in Western Sudan to refer to the local Sultanates, i.e. Dar Fur or Dar Massalit. Later used by the British administrators of the Anglo-Egyptian Condominium to designate the tribal homelands (including those of the nomads), whether they were a Sultanate or not.

dar al-harb   "the domain of war", i.e. the lands inhabited by non-Muslims, where war could be waged freely, either for the purpose of booty and slave capture or in order to convert the *kuffar* (*q.v.*).

dar al-Islam   "the domain of Islam", i.e. the lands populated by Muslims where war is not allowed.

darb al-arbayn   "forty days road" (by camel). The traditional pre-colonial road going from northern Darfur to Assiut in Egypt.

effendi (Turkish)   name given to the educated bureaucratic élite in the Turco-Egyptian regime. Most of the *effendi* later became civil servants in the British colonial administration. Regarded with some amusement by the Sudanese, and generally as objects of irritated spite by the Sudan Political Service administrators who judged them to be both "soft" and subversive.

failaka al-Islamiya   Islamic Legion, name given to the "international brigade" created by Colonel Gaddafi in the mid-1980s to fight for the Arabization and Islamization of at least The Sahelian marches, or perhaps even of the whole of Africa. It had members of various nationalities, but most were Chadian and Sudanese.

faris (pl. *fursan*)   horsemen, with an implied notion of "knight" in the traditional pre-1874 Darfurian context. After 2003 often used as a synonym for *janjaweed* (*q.v.*).

fellata   name given to *muhajirun* (*q.v.*) from West Africa. By extension the name also applies to a *baggara* (*q.v.*) tribe of the same origin.

fiqi or *faqi* (pl. *fuqara*)   "holy men". Often poorly educated, they tended to propagate fiercely millenarian and obscurantist forms of Islam.

ghazzua   a rapid military raid carried out in enemy land, usually to capture stock and/or slaves.

hakura (pl. *hawakir*)   in the old Darfur Sultanate days, a domain conceded to a person by the Sultan. The word has been used in more recent times for pieces of private property carved out of the collective property of a *dar* (*q.v.*) and "sold", given or grabbed by people with good political connections.

haraba   banditry. A term commonly used in the Darfur Special Courts prior to the February 2003 insurrection to prosecute acts of armed resistance by "Africans".

hizb   a political party.

idara al-ahliyya   lit. "administration of the people". A term used to describe the tribal administration of Darfur as set up during the Anglo-Egyptian condominium, later suppressed and re-instated several times during the post 1956 period.

ikhwaan al-Muslimin   the Muslim Brothers, a radical politico-religious organization started in Egypt by Hassan al-Banna in 1926 and now possessing branches all over the Muslim world. The Sudanese branch has been legal since 1953. After operating in Sudanese politics under a variety of names (Islamic Charter Front, National Islamic Front), the *ikhwaan* came to power in the Sudan in 1989 through a military coup. They then renamed themselves *al-mutammar al-watani* (the Patriotic Congress) to try fudging their radical Muslim origins. A small politically marginal group, which is in rather bad terms with the mainstream Islamist group, still uses the name "*al-Ikhwaan al-Muslimin*".

Inqaz al-watani   "national salvation", name given to itself by the radical militant Islamist group which took power in the Sudan on 30 June 1989. Often shortened simply to "*al-inqaz*".

ittihadiyin   "those who support the Union"; in Sudan name given to the members and supporters of *hizb al-ittihadiyin*, the Unionist Party.

jallaba   lit. meaning "procurers". Initially given to the Arab slavers from Northern Sudan operating in the South, the term was later extended to mean any riverine Arab trader plying his trade in the South or the West. The word has retained from its origins a pejorative sense among non-riverine Arab tribes, with a meaning more or less akin to "colonialists".

Janjaweed   from *jinn* ("spirit") and *jawad* (horse). Could be roughly translated as the "ghostly riders" or "evil horsemen". Name given to the "Arab" militiamen who started to operate in Darfur in the 1980s and whom the government unleashed to commit the 2003–4 genocidal attacks.

kaffir (pl. *kuffar*)   unbeliever, a strongly derogatory word in Islam. Technically the only *kuffar* are polytheistic "pagans". Christians and Jews are *ahl al-kitab* ("people of the book", i.e. monotheists) and therefore *dhimmi*, i.e. living under a statute of protected subservience (see *kufr*). But in common parlance *kuffar* is often used to refer to all non-Muslims.

khalwa   native school, particularly during the Condominium period.

khawadja   from the Turkish name meaning "sir", this typically Sudanese word was initially applied to the Ottomans between 1821 and 1885 and later, with the British colonization, came to mean all pale people, i.e. Europeans.

kufr   state of unbelief. Dissident Islamic groups are at times accused of *kufr* for maximum propaganda effect.

mahdi   in popular Islam, an inspired holy man who will come towards the End of Time to fight evil and bring Islam back to its original glory. In Sudan Mohamed Ahmed "al-Mahdi" (1844–85) revolted against the Turco-Egyptian regime, threw it out of Sudan, conquered Khartoum and killed General George Gordon. After his death his followers maintained a Mahdist-inspired regime for thirteen years (1885–98). The British who occupied Sudan in 1898 tried to suppress Mahdism, but it reincarnated itself into a major modern political movement. The paradox of that evolution is that in the process Mahdism, which was an anti-*tariqa* (*q.v.*) movement, became itself a *tariqa*. In 1945 Sayid Abd-er-Rahman al-Mahdi, posthumous son of the historic Mahdi, founded the Umma (*q.v.*) political party which has played a fundamental role in Sudanese politics ever since.

mandub (pl. *manadib*)   a position created by Sultan Ali Dinar in Darfur to replace the old *maqadim* (*q.v.*) who had turned into petty hereditary lords.

maqdum (pl. *maqadim*)   the old title of sub-district chiefs in Darfur

marahil   The migratory pathways left open between settled peasant lands in Darfur. It is the closing or obstruction of these channels after the 1984 famine which was one of the key reasons for the growing clashes between nomads and sedentary peasants. See *zeriba*.

muhajir (pl. *muhajirun*)   immigrants. Mostly used to talk about the *Fellata* (*q.v.*).

muk habarat   military security

Murahleen   lit. "the travellers", "those who are on the move". The term was traditionally used to describe to young Baqqara men travelling on horseback to escort their migrating herds of cows. The term was later extended to refer to the mostly Baqqara (but including some Zaghawa) militiamen organised by Brigadier Fadlallah Burma Nasir from 1985 on to go and fight the SPLA in Bahr-el-Ghazal. Their tactics of indiscriminate destruction closely resemble those of the *Janjaweed* (*q.v.*), some of whom were later recruited from that group.

nazir   a tribal chief, mostly in the Condominium system

quwaat ad-difaa ash-shabiyya   Popular Defence Forces. Name given to the various informal tribal militias initially created under the Premiership of Sadiq al-Mahdi and later given official status following the Islamists' coup. They were enlarged, strengthened and diversified after 1989, notably by adding Arab units to the forces.

qoz   sand. Used to designate the medium belt of Darfurian landscape.

ratib   the special prayer book compiled by the Mahdi. Long banned under the Condominium as a subversive document, it was a political symbol more than a religious one.

rottana   lit. "garbled dialect". A derogatory term used by Arabic-speaking people in the Sudan to talk about any "inferior" (i.e. African) language. English or French, even Chinese, are definitely not called *rottana*.

shari'a   the official system of Islamic laws. In Sudan the term is often used to talk about the body of legislation enacted by president Nimeiry in September 1983, which pretended to be based on the *shari'a*. In fact many of the laws voted then limited such things as freedom of association and freedom of the press and had obviously no Islamic canonical base. "The *shari'a*" has remained a political war cry in the Sudan, passionately defended by supporters of the Islamic regime and passionately attacked by its detractors.

shartay (pl. *sharati*)   district chief in the old Darfur Sultanate and during the Condominium. The word is still used in today's Darfur as a kind of honorific title.

tahaaluf   tactical accommodation, with a certain connotation of sophistry. The constant practice of *tahaaluf* has been a distinctive feature of the Sudanese Islamist movement.

tahjir (hist.)   the policy of forced migration carried out during the Mahdiyya to bring Western tribes to Omdurman.

tajammu   "Union" in the organizational sense (not in the sense of *ittihad* which refers to the binding of two entities). Of relevance here is the *tajammu al-arabi*, the Darfurian "Union of the Arabs", a militant racist group which appeared on the local political scene in 1972.

tariqa (pl. *turuq*)   Religious Brotherhood. With its Sufist form of Islam the Sudan is the land of the Brotherhoods, against which the historic Mahdi militated. In contrast with the rest of the country Darfur has been historically adverse to the *turuq* unless one considers, perhaps rightly, that the Mahdist movement has itself become a *tariqa*.

tawaali   lit. "in line with" or "following the footsteps of". This broadly polysemous expression was used to describe the political principle of Hassan al-Turabi's attempted political reform at the end of the 1990s. A perfect example of *tahaaluf* (*q.v.*), it lent itself to conveniently different interpretations

'umma   the community of believers in Islam. This grandiose name has been given by the Mahdists to their political party.

'umda   village chief.

zeriba (pl. *zaraib*)   an enclosure made of intertwined thorny branches to create a lightweight fortress. Historically in the nineteenth century the network of *zaraib* was coextensive with the *jellaba* system of land control for the purposes of elephant and slave hunting. In the 1980s the expression *zaraib al-hawa* (lit. "enclosures of air") was used by nomads in Darfur to reproach the Fur and other agriculturalists for fencing off unused land in order to avoid the free pasture of the nomads' cattle.

zawiya (hist.)   a cross between a fortress, a convent and a hostel for caravans. In its heyday it often played the role of *ribat* (fortified place of retrenchment) for militant Muslim groups.

zurug   from *azraq* which means dark blue. In Western Sudan it is used (particularly in its collective plural form of *zurga* which means "darkness" in classical Arabic) to mean "Black Africans" in a pejorative sense.

ABBREVIATIONS

ANR   Alliance Nationale de Résistance. Libya-based Chadian rebel movement.

AU   African Union, formerly the Organization of African Unity (OAU). Based in Addis Ababa.

CDR   Conseil Démocratique Révolutionnaire. Chadian rebel movement born in 1979 out a schism in the original Frolinat. It recruited mostly among the Chadian "Arab" tribes.

DDF   Darfur Development Front. A regionalist movement created in 1964 to legally defend the interests of Darfur Province.

DIA   Defense Intelligence Agency (United States).

DUP   Democratic Unionist Party. Sudanese political party created in February 1968 to merge the PDP (*q.v.*) and the NUP (*q.v.*). The PDP had initially been part of the NUP but had separated in order to preserve the interests of the *Khatmiyya* religious brotherhood. Both groups shared the same "Unionist" pro-Egyptian background but were distinct in their approach to the relationship between religion and politics.

EU   European Union

FAN   Forces Armées du Nord. Chadian guerrilla movement created jointly by Gukuni Wedeye and Hissen Habre in 1972 when they seceded from the FROLINAT "mother organization".

FANT   Forces Armées Nationales Tchadiennes. Name of the Chadian national army during the regime of Hissen Habre.

FAO   Food and Agriculture Organization of the UN.

FROLINAT   Front de Libération National du Tchad. Created in 1966 in Darfur, this was the original guerrilla movement fighting the Southern-led and "Christian" regime of President Ngarta Tombalbaye. Its members were all Northern Muslims.

GoS   Government of Sudan.

GUNT   Gouvernement d'Union Nationale de Transition. This was the government created in April 1979 in an effort to end the Chadian civil wars. It later became just another faction.

ICC   International Criminal Court

IDP   Internally Displaced Person. Mostly used in the plural form "IDPs".

ICRC   International Committee of the Red Cross.

IGAD   Intergovernmental Authority on Development. A kind of international diplomatic co-ordination between the various countries of East Africa. Created in 1988, it has had a leading role in negotiating the Sudan peace process.

IRIN   Integrated Regional Information Networks, a humanitarian news agency.

JEM   Justice and Equality Movement. A mostly Zaghawa Darfur guerrilla group of largely fundamentalist persuasion.

MSF   Médecins Sans Frontières. French emergency medical NGO, the original "French Doctors".

NDA   National Democratic Alliance. Umbrella organization of the Sudanese opposition forces after the Muslim Brothers' coup of 30 June 1989.

NIF   National Islamic Front. Created after the fall of Nimeiry in 1985, it was the label under which the radical Islamists ran for the April 1986 elections. It organized the 30 June 1989 coup and then led the new regime, first under the name of the National Salvation Council and then of the National (or Patriotic) Congress Party.

NUP   National Unionist Party. Created before independence, it regrouped the pro-Egyptian wing of the nationalist movement around the Khatmiyya Islamic brotherhood. It split in June 1956 between its secularist wing, which retained the

	original NUP name, and its religious wing which became the PDP (*q.v.*). Both parties were to merge again in 1968 to create the DUP (*q.v.*).
OCHA	Office for the Coordination of Humanitarian Affairs (United Nations)
OLS	Operation Lifeline Sudan. An inter-agency UN and NGO umbrella organization created after the big 1988 famine to try to prevent its recurrence. OLS is based in Kenya and delivers humanitarian help through out Southern Sudan.
PDP	Popular Democratic Party. The party created by a split from the NUP in June 1956 to defend the interests of the members of the Khatmiyya religious brotherhood and of the other smaller *turuq* which were allied with it.
SFDA	Sudan Federal Democratic Alliance. Darfuri political party created after the Muslim Brothers' coup of 1989 by former Governor Ahmed Ibrahim Diraige and the political activist Sharif Harir. The party split in 2003 over the question of whether to support the armed insurrection in Darfur.
SLA	Sudan Liberation Army. Initially called the Darfur Liberation Front, this is a multi-ethnic (but mostly Fur) Darfuri guerrilla movement, created in 2003. Its outlook is resolutely secularist.
SPLA	Sudan People's Liberation Army. The Southern Sudanese guerrilla movement created in 1983 by its present leader, Colonel John Garang.
UNHCR	United Nations High Commission for Refugees.
WFP	World Food Program of the UN.
WHO	World Health Organization of the UN.

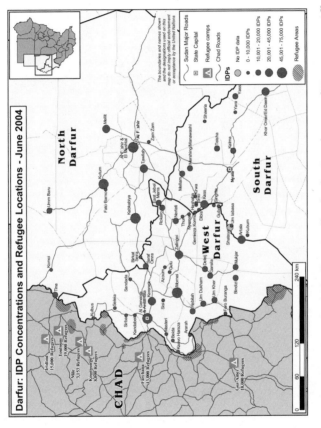

Darfur: IDP Concentrations and Refugee Locations - June 2004

Reproduced courtesy of ReliefWeb, UN Office for the Coordination of Humanitarian Affairs

xxiii

INDEPENDENT DARFUR
LAND, PEOPLE, HISTORY

In a book which aims at describing and understanding the massive political, security and humanitarian crisis which has enveloped Darfur since February 2003, this introductory chapter aims at giving not a detailed description of the region's geography, history and ethnography[1] but an overview to enable the non-specialist reader to grasp the context in which the crisis developed. Those structural traits are singled out which were "a portent of things to come", which announced and explained what would later develop. This second point needs to be accompanied by a word of warning: *everything* does not *make sense*. The global coherence of facts helps, but teleology is a pitfall to be avoided.

The economy and the lie of the land

Darfur is a region located in the westernmost part of present-day Sudan. But the name "Sudan" is itself an ambiguous appellation derived from the Arab geographers' name *Bilad as-Sudan* (Land of the Blacks). Evolved by Arabs to define Black Africa, it is so broad that there were two Sudans during the colonial era: the French *Soudan*, which was present-day Mali, and the Anglo-Egyptian Sudan. They stood at the two opposite ends of a cultural continuum stretching from Northern Nigeria to Kordofan or even Sennar.[2]

Darfur, located near the middle of this continuum, is perhaps more closely related to the Central Sahel and Northern Nigeria than it is to the Nile Valley. It displays a strong geographical and historical coherence which stands in marked contrast to its varied and contradictory ethnic makeup. It is big, with a surface of nearly half a million square kilometres (150,000 square miles) and it is generally dry without being desert. It was long an independent sultanate (from approximately the fourteenth century till 1916), later becoming a province of the Anglo-Egyptian Condominium (1898–1956) and then a state of the Republic of the Sudan on its independence.[3]

Darfur is separated from the Nile Valley by the large province of Kordofan, but this (relative) isolation is only one of the traits which make it one of the most landlocked parts of the African continent. Darfur is equidistant from both the Atlantic Ocean and the Red Sea. It is a little closer to the Mediterranean but the vast expanses of the Sahara desert largely cut it off from that world. To the south malaria and the tsetse fly discouraged casual travelling. Of course none of these geographical traits was absolute: through the Sahelian caravan routes Darfur traded with the sultanates of Kanem, Bornu and Sokoto in the West. The South was a reservoir of ivory and slaves, penetrated by periodic *ghazzua* (raids), and Darfur traded with the Nile Valley through Kordofan. It also maintained an active if perilous commerce with Egypt by way of the *darb al-'arbain*, the "Forty Days Road" which crossed the desert from Kubayh to Asyut in Egypt by way of the Salima oasis, the Shabb wells and Kharja.[4] Thus Darfur was both isolated (in everyday life) and "connected" (commercially and ideologically), but it was and has remained up to our time an extraordinarily isolated place, even if considered in the context of difficult African communications.

Darfur is basically a vast plain about 900 metres above sea level, marking the geographical divide between the basins of the Nile and

Lake Chad. Its centre is occupied by the massif of Jebel Marra, a mountainous area of volcanic origin. This small[5] but compact mountain zone has played a fundamental role in the life and history of the Darfur people. A mountain of refuge,[6] it has for centuries been, figuratively and practically, at the heart of the Darfur region. Its altitude (culminating at around 3,000 metres) gives it a micro-climate definitely cooler than the surrounding plain, and night frosts are not uncommon on the slopes of this island in the middle of the dry savannah. Rainfall and soils roughly divide the province into three distinct areas. First, there is the northern dry belt on the edge of the desert which gets only about 300 mm. of rain a year. This is the world of the camel nomads, and whatever agriculture exists is usually practised along the *wadi*[7] beds which have silt bands and retain some humidity at the end of the rainy season. Second is the central *Qoz* (semi-fertile sands) area, which receives around 500 mm. of rain a year, more on the slopes of Jebel Marra. Hoe agriculture is commonly practised but with very low yields. Millet, maize, sesame, okra, tomatoes and onions are the staple crops. This is an area of settled peasants. Third is the southern and south-western semi-humid belt, which can have up to 800 or 900 mm. of rain a year. Agriculture is more developed than in the *Qoz* area and yields are somewhat better. Groundnuts are grown as a cash crop, and mango and citrus trees are common. Since the 1930s bananas have been introduced, but there are only a few places where they grow, on the foothills of the mountain and usually in association with the big *haraz* trees[8] which provide them with protection against the night frosts. Cotton is grown but is of poor quality and used only for local consumption. This is an area populated by both sedentary peasants and the "Baggara" tribes.[9]

In Darfur geography and climate have defined population settlements and the economy up to this day. It could be argued that the region is poorer today than it was in pre-colonial times[10] because pre-colonial trade is dead, the population is much larger[11] and years of drought and over-grazing have made what used to be an abundant land supply into a problematic one.

The trade of the independent Darfur Sultanate depended on a number of items which are today outside the scope of possible economic exchange, namely slaves, ivory tusks and ostrich feathers. Gum arabic, which later became a staple trade item, was then only in limited use. Darfur was an autarkic economy as far as the life of ordinary people was concerned, even if its long-distance trade supported a fairly large merchant community which in turn stimulated the general economy of the region. In many ways the basic texture of today's economy still rests on an agro-pastoral autarky[12] but within a context of rising expectations which has turned traditional scarcity into perceived poverty.

Population: a complex ethnic mosaic

The present crisis has been presented in the media as consisting of a form of ethnic cleansing verging on the genocidal, as carried out at Khartoum's behest by "Arab" tribes against "African" ones. This is both true and false, and much of this book will be devoted to trying to disentangle the true from the false, the reality from the ideologically structured appearances.

The population of Darfur is a complex and interwoven ensemble of tribes, both "Arab" and "African".[13] The situation is further complicated by the fact that some of the "Africans" have lost their language and adopted Arabic, while others practise forms of entrenched diglossia and others still have retained their original tongue. Racially, to use this politically obsolete term, the mix is as complicated as linguistically. In terms of skin colour everybody is black. But the various forms of Sudanese cultural racism distinguish "*zurug*"[14] from "Arab", even if the skin has the same colour. Usually the difference has to do with facial features (shape of nose, thickness of lips), although this perception is influenced by what the observer knows of the ethnic background of the person he is confronting. Thus a very negroid Rizzeyqat will remain an "Arab" while a pale and thin-featured Zaghawa will be an "African". Intertribal marriages and slave concubines from the South have played havoc with visible racial distinctions. On this the old colonial geographer K. M. Barbour remarked philosophically: "The term "Arab" is used in the Sudan in a variety of ways and on different occasions its meaning may be based on race, speech, an emotional idea or a way of life. Not all who claim to be "Arabs" would be universally accepted as such and there are those who at one moment claim 'we are Arabs' and at another will dismiss a ragged stranger contemptuously as "he is only one of the Arabs"."[15] The ambivalence noted here had to do with the way of life. Nomads were deemed to be "Arabs" and nomads were poor. Therefore "Arab" was both a mark of "civilization" (as opposed to "African" savagery) but also a term of spite if applied in the context of nomad versus sedentary. In nineteenth-century travellers' descriptions of Southern Sudan one at times comes across the mention of "Dinka Arabs", a paradoxical expression if one recalls that the Dinka tribe was never arabized in any way, is racially Nilotic and was never islamized. But in that context the expression merely meant "nomadic". It is therefore vital to keep in mind that both the ambivalence and the dichotomy referred to an earlier time, that they have very little biological or even cultural relevance and that the present crisis operates within the context of a completely re-ordered system of perceptions. As we will see, the "Arab" versus "African" distinction took on its present meaning through ideological constructions which occurred much later, starting around the middle period of the twentieth century.

But if we try to go back to the "ethnic raw material" on which the present largely ideological distinctions are based, we see that

Darfur was populated by migratory movements mostly from the West and the East, due to the easy terrain to be crossed. The North, with its forbidding desert expanses, was not a way for population movements, and the South, with its large land resources and abundant rains, also did not,motivate migratory movements. On the contrary, it was a refuge for the vanquished in some of the early ethno-political power struggles in Darfur.[16]

Inasmuch as anybody can be described as "indigenous" anywhere in the world, the "Fur" were the key population of the region,[17] which justifies its name up to this day. It is difficult to go back in time before the fourteenth century, since before the advent of Islam in the region we are dealing with people without writing. But oral traditions and linguistic evidence point to three early sources of population migrations between the fourteenth and the sixteenth century: from the northwest came groups of Nilo-Saharans which can still be recognized today in the Berti, Zaghawa and Bidayat ethnic groups; from the northeastern section of the Nile Valley, on the borders of Egypt, came Nubian speakers such as today's Birged or Meidob; and from further northeastern reaches (and perhaps directly from the East) came Arab groups such as the Ziyadiyya, Ta'aisha, Beni Halba, Habbaniya and Rizzeyqat. These long-time settlers are at times described as "native Arabs" to differentiate them from the more recent arabized migrants who came from the Nile Valley in the eighteenth and nineteenth centuries. A second wave of large population arrivals had already come during the seventeenth century from the Sudanic belt itself, i.e. regions well to the west of Darfur reaching all the way to what is today the north of Nigeria. These were the ancestors of the populations described today as Hausa, Fulbe, Kanuri, Kotoko or Maba. They were culturally and at times linguistically arabized during their long migration and are mostly nomads.[18] But this was not the care with all of them, and some still speak Fulbe to this day. Sections of these migrants aggregated with earlier Arab migrants to form the Fellata nomads of Southern Darfur, who are today considered to be a "Baggara" sub-group.[19]

Finally the last sizable group of populations to come into Darfur were the "*awlad al-Bahar*" (literally "sons of the river", i.e. riverine Arabs) from such tribes as the Ja'aliyin or the Danagla who nested at the heart of the Sudanese power structure in colonial times and still occupy it today. These late-comers, who started to arrive during the period of Darfur's economic prosperity in the eighteenth century, were almost exclusively *fuqara* (religious predicators) or *jallaba* (traders) and settled in the towns. Although "Arabs", they had almost nothing in common with the old nomadic "native Arabs". They, and not the "native Arabs", constituted the nucleus of a quasi-colonial "foreign élite". In a way their installation in Darfur was not without parallel with their movements in the South some time later. But in the South these "Khartoumers", as they were called in the 1840s, were a completely "colonial" element, with nothing in common with the local population in either religion, culture or political interests; they came solely for the slaves and the ivory and remained un-acculturated. In Darfur the brothers of those "*awlad al-Bahar*", who had settled in the territory and who instead infiltrated further south, were termed "*Bahhara*" ("those of the river"). They seeped into Bahr-el-Ghazal and progressively cut the Darfurians off from their old slave- and elephant-hunting grounds, monopolizing the proceeds for themselves. Finally, in 1874, they completed this encirclement by coming up north and conquering Darfur itself, as we see in the next section. Thus their later identification with the "native Arabs" on grounds of language, culture and political destiny was largely spurious because, unlike the old nomads, they were conquerors rather than settlers. This spurious aggregation was nevertheless relatively easy because the Darfur-based *awlad al-Bahar* found themselves in the midst of a

Muslim population who welcomed them. Although they were an élite of largely exterior extraction, they operated—in contrast to what happened in the South—in a favourably disposed milieu which respected them because of their wealth and their Islamic learning, real or supposed.[20] In the South they stood out as alien invaders, but in Darfur they blended with the population as a nativized external élite. We see later what this élite did with its prestige and power.

The independent Darfur Sultanate[21]

The Sultanate of Darfur dates from the late fourteenth or early fifteenth century. It was initially associated with the Daju and Tunjur "African" tribes, which are today small ethnic units of no political significance. Little is known of the early period of this sultanate up to the mid-seventeenth century when Sultan Suleiman "Solung-dungo" ("the pale man") came down from Jebel Marra and founded what later became known as the Keyra Fur Sultanate.[22] "Solung-dungo" was reputed to be the son of a Fur father and an ethnic Arab mother, and his reign, from the early part of the century till around the 1640s, is the first chronicled in written texts. This sudden upsurge of the "Fur" Sultanate needs some explanation. There was a "Fur" tribe living in the mountainous area of Jebel Marra before its ascent to political pre-eminence, but its population seems to have been much smaller than it is today. In the late sixteenth and early seventeenth centuries the collapse of Tunjur authority left a kind of vacuum in the plains, leading to what R. S. O'Fahey describes as a quintuple process.

First came the conquest: the proto-Fur came down the Jebel Marra slopes and overran the plain below. But seemingly the new contenders for the Sultanate used a new tool, that of Islamization. This had several advantages: it brought to the newly Islamized kingdom a number of Muslim clerics who could strengthen its administrative capacity because of their command of the written word; it put Darfur on the map of "civilized" Muslim Africa, thus ensuring a better and more developed trade network with the already Islamized sultanates of the Sahelian belt and with Egypt to the north; and finally it gave the Fur Sultans a new legitimacy springing from their partaking in the regional and even worldwide culture of the *umma*, the community of Islamic believers which spanned three continents. In many ways this can be compared in Europe to the conversion of the Germanic tribes to Christianity after the eighth century or to the later adoption of the Byzantine rite by the Grand Dukes of Muscovy. The kingdom of Darfur stopped being a *de facto* entity to become a *de jure* one within a broader cultural context.

Forced displacement was another feature of the rise of the Keyra Sultanate. The conquering tribe coming down from the mountain was militarily strong and culturally intolerant. The conquered people in the plains had to convert to Islam or leave, which many did by moving southwards and "becoming Fertit". They are the ancestors of the Bahr-el-Ghazal tribes known today as Banda, Binga, Feroge, Shatt, Gula or Kara. Since they moved partly because of their refusal to become Muslims,[23] the word "Fertit" retains in Sudan a pejorative connotation to this day.

Assimilation was another step in the growth of the "Fur" Sultanate. If some refused to submit to the conquerors and become Islamized, others stayed behind and converted. They quickly "became Fur", whatever their previous tribal status may have been. As O'Fahey remarks, "Communities changed less frequently than their labels. The appointment of a Fur *shartay* [district chief] and the activities of this steward on behalf of the court could make a district "Fur" without any real ethnic change. Linguistic and religious acculturation followed the political and economic integration".[24]

Slave raiding completed the picture. Once the new kingdom became defined in terms of authority, religion and administration, once there was an "inside" and an "outside", the traditional dichotomy between *dar al-Islam* and *dar al-harb* became operative.[25] The existence of this "open field" for slave hunting (*ghazzua*) should not be mistaken for either the later development of "marches" (in the European medieval sense) such as Dar Zaghawa or Dar Meidob to the north where the inhabitants were Muslim and therefore not liable to enslavement even if they did not fully partake of the Keyra polity. It was also quite distinct from the existence of tributary states such as Dar Tama, the little kingdom the Daju had managed to maintain after their fall from greater power, which was unhappily sandwiched between Darfur and Dar Masalit and ended up paying tribute to both in order to survive. Marches and tributaries were not Darfur proper, but nor were they open ground for slaving, in contrast to the Dar Fertit.[26]

This process of conquest, Islamization, incorporation and border delimitation stabilized the Sultanate over a territory comprising 80% of today's three Darfur States. Within that world and for the next two centuries a complex society developed whose lineaments constitute a key counterpoint to the present crisis either because they survived or because what changed was started from the baseline it set.

The Sultan, who sat at the apex of the whole structure, was above all "*aba kuuri*" (the father of obeisance).[27] Sultan Muhammad Tayrab (1752–85) is described in one of the court letters as "*sultan al-'arab wa'l 'ajam*", i.e. "ruler of the Arabs and the Barbarians". The word "barbarian" has to be understood here in the ancient Greek sense as those backward people who speak a "*rottana*" (primitive dialect). It does not connote any religious unbelief (in which case the word would have been "*kuffar*"), and this points to an existing distinction between "cultural Arabs" and the rest, the uncivilised ones. A paradoxical situation was created: both communities were supposed to bow to the Negro Sultan's authority, but the Sultan, though "African", is seen here as the glorified carrier of the values of "Arabism". In fact, this paradox was at the heart of what has to be called the "Keyra Sultanate" rather than the "Fur Sultanate". The Fur had produced the Sultanate (and the other way around) but it soon stopped being exclusively or even mainly theirs. Since the kingdom's population was largely multi-ethnic (even after the "Fur assimilation" of the first years), it was held together by a complex system of Arabo-Islamic legitimacy and Sudanic sacred ritual. Everything was dual. Thus the 'ajam Barbarians could be second-class citizens in letters written to the outside world, but they were very much part of the Keyra polity in real life. Obeying the Sultan (and as a result benefiting from his benevolent protection) was the key to peace and happiness. Being without a lord and master was the ultimate catastrophe because it laid you open to raiding by anybody, whether you were "African" or "Arab". In their study of the diplomatic correspondence between Wadaï and Darfur[28] L. Kapteijns and J. Spaulding quote a letter where the Daju Sultan Ishaq Abu Risha admonishes three *shartay* of the by then very sick Darfur sultanate to submit to him, saying: "Formerly you had your Sultan and you were the concern of Darfur. But now the world has fallen into chaos.[29] ....You are like sheep without a shepherd, everybody is raiding you, the Masalit, the nomads and even our people, the Daju".

Darfur was a loosely feudal society where *protection* was the key word. And since that protection had to be extended to the members of various tribes, both "Arab" and non-Arab, Islam and its univer-salistic values provided a much-needed cement. The set of Arab cultural values, where language was prominent, was therefore fundamental. But this did not mean that the Sultan neglected the formerly pagan rituals which could complement and reinforce his

Islamic credentials. For example, the pomp and circumstance which presided over his accession to the throne were such that they distinctly put Darfur within the broad category of African sacred monarchies, with "*aadinga*" (succession rites) an absolutely key element in the king's legitimacy.[30] And as late as the nineteenth century a foreign traveller could still write that "the great Sultan appears almost as a divinity to his subjects".[31] The Sultan's *fashir* (palace) was carefully laid out to embody a cosmological symbolism which had nothing to do with Islam and audiences with the monarch obeyed a number of taboos and observances that were of distinctly "pagan" origin. This was also evident in the social place of women who played a very important role in the courtly system. The "*habooba*" ("grandmother", actually the ruling sultan's mother) was often the power behind the throne, her authority being only challenged by that of the "*iiya baasi*" ("favourite sister") the Sultan's favourite among his numerous sisters.[32] One *iiya baasi*, Zamzam Umm an-Nasr, has remained famous in Darfur history for ruling in place of her weak brother, Sultan Muhammad al-Hussein. When he went blind in 1856 she practically took over the Sultanate, deciding the state *firman* and riding at the head of the army. Nevertheless, on the death of her brother, who was the symbolic source of her power, she starved herself to death. Women could be freer than in the Islamic social order, but they still had to obey the pagan cosmological order which underpinned their freedom.

The court ladies at the *fashir* openly kept the old religion alive and served its cults from within the palace, something which shocked visiting Muslim clerics. But the Sultan, even if he professed a strict Islamic orthodoxy, was careful not to interfere with these rituals which he found convenient both to deny and to use.

In perfect feudal style the Sultan was the sole grantor of *hawakir* (sing. *hakura*, estate). Traditional Darfur land charters distinguish between ordinary *hawakir* which gave access to landholdings and the better *hawakir al-jah* or "estate with honour" where the grant dispensed the grantee from paying taxes. The grantees became "*cima kura*" or "big lords" and could in turn sub-lease parts of their *hakura* to "*cima gana*" (junior lords) who owed them taxes and military service in case of war. The armies were also "feudal", with a heavy cavalry of *fursan*[33] garbed in protective cotton quilt covered with heavy chain-mail armour, brandishing their double-edged Solingen blades,[34] accompanied by largely untrained peasant levees. But as firearms spread in the late eighteenth century these knights slowly degenerated into elegant military irrelevance, like their European and Japanese counterparts two centuries earlier. The last use of the Darfur noble cavalry sounded its death-knell when Sultan Ibrahim Qarad fell while charging at the head of his troops at the battle of Manawashi on 23 October 1874. He was shot dead by a "*bazinger*" (slave infantryman) of Zubeyr Rahman Mansur's army using an imported rifle.

But the use of horses for combat has remained a Darfur tradition which makes the present-day violence of the *janjaweed* particularly distasteful. The *fursan* of old Darfur were certainly not the Knights of the Round Table; they fought brutally and took part in the slave-hunting *ghazzua* in the South (although not with their full equipment). But they had panache and a certain warrior's ethic. Today's *Janjaweed* who rape women and slaughter children appear as a mocking echo of that great tradition of the *fursan* of old.

Civil administration was highly centralized, at least in theory. In practice there were numerous special situations where local native administration was maintained after the conquest and covered with the mantle of Keyra legitimisation. But the Sultans managed successfully to avoid that great danger of all feudal systems, the hereditary legitimisation of the nobility, which monopolizes the regional state administration. The *sharati* (pl. of *shartay*) did not inherit their positions and nor did the *maqadim* (sing. *maqdum* or sub-district chiefs). When those became hereditary during "the time of the troubles" which started with the conquest of Zubeyr Rahman Mansur and lasted till the end of the Mahdiyya, the restored Sultan Ali Dinar simply replaced them with a new corps of *manadib* who remained under his direct authority and left the *maqadim* to wither away. The "*eling wukala*" (village headmen) stood at the bottom of that three-tiered administrative hierarchy, ensuring continuity between the three or four small settlements for which they were responsible and the *maqadim* and *shartay*. One of the key duties of these state representatives was to oversee the administration of justice—which, like almost everything else in the Sultanate, displayed an Afro-Arab duality. People involved in a court case could choose either to take it to the *shari'a* tribunal or to remain within the precincts of the customary law of their tribe. This customary law was curiously called *siyasa* ("politics" in Arabic), perhaps because it could be more open to complex interpretations than the more strictly codified written *shari'a*.

For many years during the seventeenth and early eighteenth century Darfur spent most of its energies uselessly feuding with Wadaï. The two states were of comparable strength, and this recurrent warfare yielded no great result on either side. Then, during the late 1780s, Sultan Muhammad Tayrab turned his attention to the vast ungoverned territory of Kordofan to the east of Darfur, between Jebel Marra and the Nile. There were several reasons for this: a desire to defeat chiefs who continually raided Darfur from the east, the prospect of easy victory over armies that were no match for the Sultanate's, and probably also the urging of the growing *jellaba* community which knew that money could be made, both for them and for the state, through direct commerce with Egypt which would bypass the long and arduous *darb al-'arbain*. Victory in Kordofan was quick and immediate, and yielded all the hoped-for results. These were the best years of the Sultanate, which had almost doubled its territory and could rule and benefit from its new dominion without incurring any enmity from the conquered people. The protection of Darfur was worth the new taxes they were paying, which probably came cheaper anyway than the capricious rackets of the local chieftains they had lived under for many years.[35] El-Fashir (the palace), which is still today the regional capital, was founded in 1791 with the object of having a central location for governing the whole Darfur-Kordofan ensemble. Before that the Sultan had had a number of capitals[36] but all were located west or south of Jebel Marra. For the first time the capital stood to the east of the great mountain. It was an imperial capital, founded as the empire culminated. A few years later, with Kordofan lost, it was to become strangely off-centre.

Umm Kwakiyya, the time of the bandits[37]

In 1821 Muhammad Ali, Viceroy of Egypt, launched his armies upon the conquest of the vast territories south of his kingdom. At that time what we now call "Sudan" had no political existence whatever. The very term "Sudan" was borrowed from the medieval Arab geographers who called the whole land extending directly south of the Sahara "*beled as-Sudan*", "land of the Blacks". This "land of the Blacks" extended from what is today Senegal to the borders of Abyssinia, which was recognized as a distinct entity. To understand the arbitrariness of the name "Sudan", we should remember that during colonial times the French called what is today, Mali *le Soudan*. "Sudan", as we know it today, is a product of Turco-Egyptian occupation,[38] and at the time when Muhammad Ali's armies moved south is was mostly stateless. The two exceptions were the Sultanates of Darfur in the West and of Sennar in the East. In 1821 their destinies, once comparable, had diverged considerably. Sennar, ruined by civil strife and economic problems, was a shambles and it fell to the "Turks" without a fight. Darfur, by contrast, was at the height of its power and tried to resist. The invading forces which had quickly secured the Nile Valley down to the present site of Khartoum[39] advanced in Kordofan, but by 1821 the Darfurian army was no match for the Egyptian troops armed with cannon and trained by former officers of Napoleon's army. It was crushed at the battle of Bara in August 1821, and Muhammad Ali decided not to push his luck and to be content with what he had won. The Darfurians prudently retreated to their homeland and Darfur reverted to its original territory and re-switched its long-distance trade to the *darb al'arbain*.

But this was only to be a respite. Once the Turco-Egyptians had secured their control of what is today northern Sudan, they started to send expeditions into the South to hunt slaves and elephants. This was no different from what the Darfurians themselves had done for centuries, but it was on a completely different scale. The "Khartoumers", as the northern Sudanese merchant adventurers were soon called, had at their disposal vast resources of money and weapons. During the 1840s and 1850s they extended a far-flung network of *zarai'b* (sing. *zariba*, large thorn enclosures used as fortresses for the slaving expeditions) and pushed a commercial "front" into the South. The process was extremely brutal, and the memory of it remains today at the heart of Southern Sudanese resentment towards the North. Slowly the *zarai'b* crept southward and westward to reach the Mbomu and Uelle valleys in today's Central African Republic, where smaller bands of Darfurian slavers had preceded them. With their greater means the new traders took over from the old ones. One of these enterprising fellows, Zubeyr Rahman Mansur, went all the way down to the Zande country in what is today the north of the Congo, settled there and married a Zande princess. Soon he built a huge slaving and ivory-hunting network reaching from the Congo to Bahr-el-Ghazal. In frequent contact with Darfur-based merchants he finally conceived the project of conquering the old Sultanate.[40] With his well-equipped army of *bazinger* (slave soldiers) backed by a large levée of Zande mercenaries he moved against the Sultanate in late 1873. The conquest was easy, and after he killed Sultan Ibrahim Qarad at the battle of Manawashi in October 1874 he found himself in control of the Keyra Sultanate. Given the multi-ethnic nature of the old kingdom, there was no particular loyalty to the Fur nobility, and the tribes simply waited to see how their new master would treat them. But they did not have time to get used to the conqueror because he almost immediately found himself in a delicate position of competition with the Turco-Egyptians. The Khedive of Egypt was aware of the weakening of the Keyra Sultanate, and in parallel with Zubeyr's expedition Ismail Ayub, Governor General of the Sudan, had been ordered by Cairo to move against the western kingdom, arriving in El-Fashir four days after Zubeyr himself and claiming control of the situation. In order not to clash head-on with the Turco-Egyptian power Zubeyr tried to pretend that he too had been acting on behalf of the Khedive, and when this did not work he went to Cairo to try to argue his case at the highest level. This was a wrong move: in Cairo Khedive Isma'il received him very politely, but placed him under—luxurious—house arrest. Zubeyr never returned to the Sudan for as long he could be a challenge to Egyptian power.[41]

This double conquest, by a Sudanese merchant adventurer and the Turco-Egyptian colonial authorities, spelled the beginning of years of trouble for Darfur. As we saw in the letter of the Daju Sultan quoted above, many people became "like sheep without a shepherd". In fact they were largely prey to the wolves, hence the name *Umm Kwakiyya* given to these difficult times.

The conquest of Darfur by the Turco-Egyptians did not last long. By 1881 their whole dominion over the Sudan was challenged by a native uprising to be known later as the "Mahdiyya", the time of the Mahdi. In popular Muslim eschatology the term "*mahdi*", "the guided one", refers to a person "who has a particular measure of divine guidance and is the repository of esoteric secrets".[42] The appearance of a *Mahdi* is associated with the end of the world and combines in popular beliefs with Christian eschatology. Thus *al-nabi Isa*, the Prophet Jesus, is supposed to come after the death of the Mahdi and fight Dajjal, the Antichrist. The end of the world and the Last Judgement will then follow. In 1881 a thirty-seven-year-old *sheikh* from Dongola in the Nile Valley proclaimed himself to be the expected Mahdi. He was a respected member of the Samma-niyya, a minor Islamic brotherhood from northern Sudan, and capi-talized on popular resentment throughout the Sudan against the Turco-Egyptian domination. His movement cleverly combined an appeal to religious reformism (the "Turks" were seen as very lax in their practice of Islam) with a growing proto-nationalism. His re-volt spread like wildfire and within four years he had laid siege to Khartoum, taken it from the Turco-Egyptians[43] and founded a new political regime in the Sudan.

This new political regime did not cover the totality of what had been the territory controlled by Cairo. The Mahdists had a very spotty control over the South and with time they lost it altogether. Their control of Darfur was equally thin. Rudolf Slatin Pasha, the Austrian adventurer who had served under Gordon and been made by him Governor of Darfur, was caught between the growing Rizzeyqat sympathies for the Mahdiyya and an insurrection of the Fur who rallied to the uprising of Abdallah Dud Banja, a pretender to the throne of the Keyra Sultanate who was using the troubles to try to restore the old kingdom. Slatin was finally forced to sur-render in January 1884, a year before the fall of Khartoum. Darfur passed under the nominal control of Muhammad Khalid, who was both a former subordinate of Slatin and a cousin of the Mahdi. But in

June 1885, five months after his victory, the Mahdi died, to be followed as head of his new state by a much less prestigious leader the Khalifa Abdullahi, himself a Westerner from the tribe of Ta'aisha. But this did not mean that Darfur was ready to bow to the new authority. The Ta'aisha are a very minor tribe and Abdullahi was a man of humble birth. Muhammad Khalid, the Mahdist Governor of Darfur, found it exceedingly difficult to be obeyed, and the new government in Omdurman[44] was soon to initiate a policy of forced migration called *tahjir* which did not make it more popular. According to *tahjir* (which in fact could be almost translated as "deportation") the fighting members of the Western tribes were to move to Omdurman to strengthen the regime.[45] This vast move of the rough Western tribesmen to Omdurman has at times been perceived as a kind of looting spree, an invasion by uncouth tribal levées coming to the Nile Valley and living off the fat of the land. In a way it was; but they did not come willingly (the Khalifa Abdullahi had to coax and threaten them before they came), and once they were in the capital their obnoxious behaviour cost the new regime more popularity than it brought it in support. Worse, their presence at the centre of power did not prevent revolts regularly taking place in Darfur itself. The Rizzeyqat and the Kababish revolted, partly out of sheer refusal of any authority and partly because they did not like the policy of *tahjir*. They were crushed, largely through the agency of the new Mahdist Governor of Darfur, Yusuf Ibrahim. But Yusuf was an ethnic Fur, and after his victory on the Arab tribes he used his position to try to gain independence from the Mahdist state. The Khalifa had to send an expedition to subdue him, and Yusuf was duly beaten and decapitated, his head being brought back to Omdurman. But almost as soon as he was dead a new revolt started, led by an illuminated *faki* (holy man) who claimed magical powers. Nobody even knew his name and he was called Abu Jummayza, "the one who came down from the wild fig tree". Abu Jummayza, who was probably not even Darfurian,[46] gained a large but motley assemblage of followers people discontented with Mahdist rule, from West African pilgrims to Mecca who were blocked by the new regime[47] to former Turco-Egyptian officials and from nostalgic supporters of the Fur Sultanate to the Masalit who resented Mahdist encroachments on their still semi-independent *dar* (kingdom). The Abu Jummayza revolt slowly petered out when its charismatic leader died in early 1889.

Thus we can see that although in popular Sudanese perception the Mahdiyya is often still that of a largely "Western" movement, particularly after the death of the riverine-born Mahdi and Abdullahi's ascent to power, this perception is in fact largely misleading. As for the Darfurians, both Arab and non-Arab, they have almost the opposite one; for them the Mahdist state, like its Turco-Egyptian counterpart before him, was essentially "foreign", i.e. emanating from the Nile Valley, and they never stopped trying in one form or another to reassert their independence. They finally succeeded in 1898 when the Mahdist state collapsed at the centre under the blows of the conquering British army.

Ali Dinar and Darfur's last independent years (1898–1916)

Ali Dinar was a distant relative of the last Keyra Sultan who in 1892 had been forced by Khalifa Abdullahi's policy of *tahjir* to go to Omdurman. There he waited for an opportunity, and as soon as he saw the Mahdist state collapsing under the British onslaught he made his way back to Darfur and proceeded to restore the old Keyra Sultanate. Sir Reginald Wingate, first Governor General of the Sudan, wanted to reoccupy the whole of the former Turco-Egyptian territories, but Lord Cromer, his direct hierarchical superior in Egypt, was opposed to the reoccupation of Darfur which he considered of little or no economic value to the newly-established

Anglo-Egyptian Condominium. In addition he thought that, given its the great distance from Khartoum, administering it would be exceedingly difficult and that definition of the Dar Masalit border might develop diplomatic friction with the French, then engaged in the conquest of Chad. Thus after a short-lived attempt at backing a pro-British candidate to the Sultanate, Cairo and London were happy to let things be and, having secured a promise of loyalty from Ali Dinar, let him rule as a *de facto* independent Sultan. Cromer insisted that Ali Dinar be held "with the lightest of threads",[48] his only obligation being limited to a largely symbolic yearly payment. Ali Dinar, who like many Darfurians had hated the Mahdiyya, was very keen on re-establishing a tight administrative control on the Sultanate and, as we saw earlier, created the position of *mandub* to replace the old *maqadim* who had become a kind of hereditary petty local feudality. He was also extremely wary of any prophetic Islamic developments, and although it would be anachronistic to call his government "secular", it was not far from it. He systematically discouraged any extension of the powerful Senusiyya Islamic brotherhood, refusing it to let it build *zawiya*[49] in Darfur. And when he allowed representatives of the West African Tijjaniyya to set themselves up in his kingdom he did so only under a strong supervision by the state.

His hostility towards neo-Mahdism was relentless and drove him to summarily execute several preachers claiming to be heirs to the Mahdist movement. Later, in the mid-1900s, he worked a kind of rapprochement with the Khatmiyya, but only because this brotherhood, as a protégé of the Cairo regime, was expected to get him better relations with the Condominium authorities. His main problem came from the French who were nibbling away at Darfur's western borders from Chad; by 1909 they had conquered Wadai and installed figurehead Sultans in the small border states of Dar Sila, Dar Tama, Dar Gimr and Dar Masalit. But in January 1910 they were defeated by the Masalit at the battle of El-Geneina and Ali Dinar immediately saw this as an opportunity to stop their eastward encroachments. He sought to reassert his authority over Dar Sila and the other petty border Sultanates, but he was beaten by the French in April 1910 and these skirmishes caused protests from Paris which were an embarrassment for the British. Paris was pushing London to occupy Darfur, a move which was not greeted with much enthusiasm by the Condominium authorities. But then the First World War broke out and London became extremely nervous about the possibility of Turkish propaganda swaying Darfur,[50] bringing about an immediate change of views about Ali Dinar. All in all his authority had been traditional and moderate and had marked a period of calm for the Sultanate after the violent and painful years of the *Umm Kwakiyya*. But with the war and the sudden fear that Darfur could become an bridgehead in Africa for the Central Powers,[51] he was suddenly denounced in British official documents as a tyrant and even as a criminal. Through a kind of self-intoxication the Condominium authorities declared themselves persuaded that "Ali Dinar has absorbed the Turco-German poison"[52] and made preparations to take military action against him. An ultimatum was sent to him but he declined to submit and in May 1916 his troops were swiftly defeated by the British army near El-Fashir. Ali Dinar refused to surrender and took refuge on the lower slopes of Jebel Marra, the traditional Fur bastion in times of trouble and he and his two sons were ambushed there by a British force on 6 November 1916 and shot dead as they tried to flee on horseback. Darfur's independence had passed to history and from then on the old Sultanate would have to live within the confines of "Sudanese" authority, whatever this would mean.

What conclusions can be drawn from this summary of the geography, people and independent history of the Darfur Sultanate? First, that the country, though extraordinarily diverse, was in many ways one. Arabs and non-Arabs did not live in peace, but nor did they feud systematically with each other; most conflicts pitted communities or sections of communities against each other, without any reason to attach to them the "Arab" and "African" labels used in the 21st-century crisis. Darfur was an ethnic mosaic, not a land divided along binary lines of fracture. Second, there was, beyond the mosaic picture, a strong historical/geographical coherence. Darfur was definitely not a nation-state, but it was also not simply a ragged assemblage of tribes without any form or internal logic. Darfur did exist, even when at war with itself; it was an entity immediately recognizable to its neighbours, and the inhabitants of Dar Sila or Dar Masalit never had any doubts about what Darfur was. Its borders were clear in the east and west, either with Kordofan or with the petty sultanates of what later became Eastern Chad. They were vague both in the north and the south. It did not matter in the north where Darfur directly opened on to the emptiness of the desert. In the south it was more complicated since the various Baggara tribes (particularly the Rizzeyqat) cut Darfur off from its profitable Fertit hinterland. But these borders were in a rough sense clear. Third, Darfur was prosperous, even if not rich, in terms of its traditional economy, but it did not have either the natural resources or the geographical position to allow it successfully to enter the new world that colonization was slowly ushering in. Fourth, if Darfur had to be seen within a "Sudanese" context, it immediately became a periphery. It could not be at the centre of anything; it could be the easternmost link in the chain of Sahelian African sultanates on the southernmost extension of the Trans-Saharan trade routes. It could be the distant western province of a Nile-based state (which is what finally happened).

Once it lost its independence Darfur became cursed with never being seen as itself but always as the appendage, real or supposed, of some other bigger ensemble. Darfur had long been left to its own devices. In 1874 a first intrusion resulted into more than twenty years of trouble, and then the sultanate briefly staggered back to its separate life. But the world around was slowly tightening up and drawing Darfur into its embrace. This did not mean a passionate imperialistic interest—far from it—but merely that Darfur would become an annex to problems (and to "solutions", at times worst than the problems) not of its own making. Darfur was going to trot, stagger and attempt to run to the crack of distant whips, and this would finally lead to its complete collapse into organised chaos.

DARFUR AND KHARTOUM (1916–1985)
AN UNHAPPY RELATIONSHIP

Colonial benign neglect: romanticism and underdevelopment

The extension of the Anglo-Egyptian Condominium authority over Darfur was so smooth as to be almost unnoticeable. Most of the native civil servants who had served the Sultanate went on to work with the new authority, which in any case was not very keen to do anything that would represent any form of change or break with the past. The Anglo-Egyptian Condominium[1] was a very conservative institution, run by a most extraordinary administrative body called the Sudan Political Service.[2] The Sudan Political Service was as much, or perhaps more, a club than an administration. It recruited mostly upper-middle-class graduates of Oxford and Cambridge Universities and had a definite taste for athletic young men, who while educated were not "intellectuals". The gentleman and sports-man was the ideal. In 1906 an applicant who, though British, had been born and raised in Belgium and who had listed "French" as his mother tongue, was rejected because of this. Another was rejected because "there was something Levantine about him".[3] The ideal type was a man like Wilfrid Thesiger, the son of the British ambassa-dor to Addis Ababa, born in Ethiopia, Oxford-educated, a soldier and a gentleman who dressed in native garb and became famous for his hunting and explorations. He served in Darfur in 1935 and what he wrote in his autobiography about his life there typifies the flavour of the times:

In the evenings, as we sat around a large fire over drinks, the others talked shop ... ...Listening, I realized how completely they had identified with the people in their charge and I sensed their misgivings about the changes that had inevitably to occur ....We fed on *assida* and *mullah* ... .or just a handful of dates .... I sat or slept on a rug on the ground ....I enjoyed the easy informal comradeship that this life and our surroundings engendered.[4]

This spartan, adventurous life was an extension of the life of the English public school. For the men selected to be its leaders it was a dream come true: serving King and Country, bearing the White Man's Burden, taking care of the lesser breeds, and enjoying great personal freedom in an unspoilt country. They were like small noblemen in their own fiefs which were often enormous. In the period 1899–1939 only 315 men joined the Sudan Political Service, and they ran a territory of 2.5 million square kilometres. When Martin Daly and Francis Deng called their famous study of British administration in the Sudan *Bonds of Silk*[5] they could have used a metaphor signifying the lightness of a feather; or, to be less polite, to say that Sudan was terribly under-administered. And since within that huge ensemble Khartoum and the Blue Nile Province attracted the bulk of investment and administrative resources, little was left for the "outlying areas"—such as Darfur.[6] As Thesiger noticed, his romantic comrades sitting around the campfire at night had "completely identified with the people in their charge", but this implied strong value judgements. The interests of the administered people were seen as embodied by their traditional ways of life, according to the British administrators' perceptions. Modernization was shunned, and since there was no money to carry it out this was just as well. What the British administrators in the Sudan hated above everything were "the Effendi types", the pro-Egyptian and partly educated civil servants (more rarely traders) who "put ideas into the heads of the natives". The natives were basically happy as they were and should not be interfered with, particularly by the "Effendi types" who could only lead them to rebellion, immorality and even Bolshevism. The best style of government was therefore the lightest.

But "traditionalism" should be understood as a deep cultural/tribal preference. And Mahdism, which was "native" as could be, was seen as a revolutionary abomination which had to be rooted out. During its first years neo-Mahdism was the Condominium administration's main danger and archenemy. Sayid Abd-er-Rahman al-Mahdi, the posthumous son of the Mahdi born in 1885, who had survived rather well his first early and difficult years, slowly began climbing back into a position of religious and political influence during the First World War. Before that the British administration had treated him with the utmost suspicion, all the more so because there were periodic outbursts of "Mahdist" insurrection all over the Muslim parts of the Condominium during its first years of existence. They never seriously endangered the solidity of British rule but they were worrisome and harked back to the tragic 1880s. Although these outbursts were typical millenary movements—i.e. popular, spontaneous and unorganised—the British administration always tended to see the hidden hand of Sayid Abd-er-Rahman behind them. The Sayid, who had nearly been murdered by the British a couple of times as a boy, was extremely careful never to enter into any harebrained insurrectionary scheme. But he remained suspect until the war against the Turks suddenly made him useful. Mahdism had a long history of hostility to the Ottomans and after 1914 Sayid Abd-er-Rahman became a valued propaganda asset. He played his role impeccably. He also lost no time in building on the modicum of respectability he had gained by establishing a parallel administration in the provinces, even if this was even lighter than that of the Condominium. But it had the advantage of being able to count on the goodwill of numerous people throughout the country. By 1917 he had twenty-four "agents" throughout Northern Sudan, all duly declared and registered with the government, of whom three were in Darfur which for the Mahdists was missionary territory. The Mahdiyya, as we saw, had not left very good memories and Darfur did not like the Mahdists. But the men who had lived through the 1880s were now dead or very old and Sayid Abd-er-Rahman was very good at capitalizing on the neglect of the Condominium administration. Slowly his influence in Darfur grew.

The September 1921 "Mahdist" uprising in Nyala was a major setback for this cautious policy. In September 1921 a Masalit *Faki*, Abdallah al-Sihayni, rose against the government. The insurrection, which lasted about two months and resulted in some 800 deaths, was multi-ethnic, with both "Arab" and "African" tribes taking part. But was it really "neo-Mahdist" as the government claimed? There are great doubts about this (although it remains the accepted historical wisdom to this day) since al-Sihayni did not claim to be the expected Mahdi, the *ratib*[7] was nowhere in evidence, and the movement appears to have been due much more to a massive increase in taxes in a year when the crops were poor than to any sort of "religious fanaticism". In addition slave emancipation had upset a lot of people (slaves were often the only capital of the poor) and there were not enough administrators to implement the measures decided by Khartoum. Nevertheless Mahdist agents were banned from Darfur for a while which caused an immediate rise in the Sayid's popularity in the province. By casting him as an enemy the Condominium administration in fact rendered him a service and Westerners soon flocked to his domain on Aba Island[8] to work, as the saying went, "*li'l dura wa'l baraka*" (for a bowl of millet and a blessing). Many of these Westerners were not even in fact Sudanese; they were Fellata *muhajirun* (immigrants), who were mostly from

Nigeria where Mahdism had extended its influence and considered going to Aba almost as good as going to Mecca, or perhaps even better. The Sayid was a shrewd farmer and businessman who used the latest techniques and made a lot of money out of that nearly free labour.

Channelling Darfur's discontent was not difficult since the Khartoum administration did almost nothing, good or bad, in its late-acquired province. This benign neglect parading as cultural respect was embodied in the system of "Indirect Rule", for which Frederick Lugard had provided the theoretical basis at the beginning of the twentieth century.[9] "Indirect rule" could be considered either as a prime example of racism or alternatively as the most culturally respectful of possible colonial policies. In summary, the British should exercise their power only through the agency of local traditional authorities which would respect native culture, avoid affronting local sensibilities, and introduce changes gently and in harmony with the local order. Opponents of this philosophy called it a recipe for stagnation and for building a two-tiered society in which the natives, on the pretext of cultural integrity, were marginalized from the benefits of the modern world which the colonialists could monopolize for their own advantage. Darfur under the Condominium was a prime example of Indirect Rule. Since the Sudan Political Service was so thinly spread, the immense territory was divided into "Dar" (tribal homelands), which were roughly delimited and handed over to a variety of *nazir, sheikh, maqdum, mandub* and *'umda*, depending on the tribe and on the administrative level, to exercise rule.[10] In theory it could have been a good idea, but those appointed to these charges were often incompetent, illiterate and corrupt. Since they knew that they benefited both from a "traditional" legitimacy (real or manipulated) and from the support of the Condominium administration, they tended to behave like petty tyrants. When they were honest their main positive quality was the capacity to render justice, but there was little they could do beyond that and they were usually incapable of implementing any form of technical or administrative progress or of dealing with problems of education. This suited the local British administrators, who believed that education and technical change would only "spoil" their charges. By 1935 there were only four government primary schools in the whole of Darfur, with a combined annual budget of £1,200. A request by the Darfur Director of Education for an extra budget of £55 "to introduce some kind of education" in North Darfur was rejected by Khartoum "on financial grounds".[11] The administration relied mainly on the native system of *khalwa* schools, which were almost a joke. When H. C. Jackson, the Governor of Dongola Province, made a tour of the local *khalwa* in 1928, his found to his dismay that most of the teachers could not locate Mecca on a map, that they did not know the name of the Governor General of Sudan (one of them mentioned Wad Nejumi, a long-dead Mahdist *amir*), could not list the provinces of the Sudan, and thought that "Gordon was the man who built Gordon College"; and Dongola Province was in the "favoured" Nile Valley[12]. Most of the *khalwa* teachers in Darfur were reputed not to be able to write their name. Among the 510 students in 1929 at Gordon College, the only establishment of higher learning in the Condominium, there was not a single student from Darfur while 311 were from Khartoum or the Blue Nile Province. This did not seem in the least to disturb the local British administrators, who actually boasted of the situation. Philip Ingleson, Governor of Darfur in 1935–44, could write without embarrassment:

We have been able to limit education to the sons of Chiefs and native administration personnel and we can confidently look forward to keeping the ruling classes at the top of the educational tree for many years to come.[13]

As late as the 1950s there was no government agriculturalist in Darfur, and the Civil Secretary Sir James Robertson refused to appoint one "because the province never had one before".[14] Out of eighteen maternity clinics in the Sudan eight were in Khartoum and there was not a single one in Darfur. In the domain of justice the administration was hostile towards the *shari'a* courts, not so much because they were a Muslim institution but because it was feared that in the "outlying areas" they would "lead to detribalisation", which in the eyes of the Sudan Political Service was the ultimate sin. It is interesting that today, as Darfur sinks further and further into "tribal" anarchy, there is a kind of nostalgia for the old system of the "Dar" and for the tribal authorities of the colonial period. This is evident in the evaluation of the tribal administration presented some forty years later in a well-informed essay by a British technical expert, James Morton, who worked in Darfur in the 1980s, as the clouds of war were gathering over the Province. He wrote:

Between 1921 and 1931, various ordinances were issued, both extending the areas covered and the powers of the tribal leaders. It is clear that, as far the British were concerned, tribal administration based on these ordinances was a considerable success. The series of extensions granted during that decade reflected their wish to exploit that success rather than any preconceived plan. They felt that Native Administration had proved infinitely adaptable and not merely an interesting survival mechanism convenient for dealing with backward areas.[15]

The notion that the extension of tribal administration was purely pragmatic and not the result of "any preconceived plan" is definitely open to question since Lugard had developed—and applied—this theory during his experience in Uganda, and it was later carried out in many British colonies from Somaliland to Nigeria. But much depends on what one expects from an administrative system. And one soon realizes, in reading Morton's essay, that his main concern is conflict management and the dispensation of justice, the area where *al-idara al-ahliyya*[16] was most efficient. Morton himself honestly admits this much: "Although described as an administration, the basis for the system was in fact judicial." The problem is that, although rendering justice and avoiding conflicts is a big part of life, especially in nomadic societies, to argue that this is the entire role of an administration is difficult. One could argue almost the opposite: there will be more and more conflicts to arbitrate if the administrative system is not able to do anything else effectively besides rendering justice and completely neglects any development in education, health, transport and the economic system generally. Tribal administration, while efficient at rendering justice, did hardly anything else apart from levying taxes. This was a poor model for the future of an independent Sudan; indeed this benign neglect and glorification of tribal ways and days was exactly the kind of romantic "nativism" which led to the problems of Southern Sudan and Northern Nigeria. Economic and social underdevelopment contained the seeds of future conflicts which would eventually be much worse than the simple criminal cases or problems of pasture and well management that the tribal administration sponsored by the Condominium authorities had had to deal with. Admittedly the later removal of the tribal administration, which did nothing about the legacy of underdevelopment, could only make matters worse.

Towards the end of the Condominium period Darfur was still hopelessly underdeveloped. Since it was also almost completely insulated from the outside world and the pressure of demographic growth had yet to be felt, it did not matter much. The Condominium had brought global peace, and people lived in relative harmony with problems that the native administration could deal with adequately. But this peaceful surface was deceptive in view of the challenges that the progressive incorporation into a broader world would unavoidably bring. Transport costs between El-Fashir and Khartoum were higher than between Khartoum and Juba, the capital of the "deprived" South. Out of twenty-three intermediate schools operating in the Sudan in 1952 only one was in Darfur. Absolutely no industrialization had taken place even in the sectors where it would have been feasible such as food processing, skin and hide treatment, and simple textiles. By the end of the Condominium period 56% of all investment was concentrated in Khartoum, Kassala and the Northern Province as against 17% in both Darfur and Kordofan. Since Kordofan was the more developed of the two, one can estimate that only 5–6% of the investment for the whole of Sudan had reached Darfur.[17] This has to be seen in the light of the fact that the "high benefit" part of the country had 2.3 million people while the West had 3 million. A 1955 economic report on the Province (the first one in thirty-nine years) wrote that Darfur must "strive for self-sufficiency", and export-substitution industries were recommended. Coffee and sugarcane were vaguely mentioned[18], local spinning and weaving industries "should be encouraged". The last point had been mentioned in administrators' reports as far back as 1930, but nothing had ever been done. The purity of tribal life had been preserved at the expense of its future.

Writing at the beginning of the 1980s, a young Southern Sudanese author described the same attitudes among the British administrators of the South, adding that they considered the huge Southern region as a kind of "human zoo".[19] In case one would take this formula as an expression of nationalistic exasperation, one can look directly at what the administrators themselves could write at the time: «*What is needed is for the Southerners to remain quiet, contented and peaceful, with few desires and few worries, happily singing in the sun to their cattle.*»[20] The same could not have been written about Darfur. In the North the romantic feelings about the country took a slightly different turn. There the "noble savage" was more noble and less savage. Gentlemen could play among them without lowering themselves,[21] and Darfur was not a human zoo but a gentleman's playground. History was not going to be very forgiving of this kind of nostalgia.

On the margins of history: Darfur and Sudanese nationalism

On 15 May 1944 the first Advisory Council of the Northern Sudan opened in Khartoum.[22] Ibrahim Musa Madibo, Sheykh of the Rizzeyqat, and the Sultan of Dar Masalit were among the three representatives from Darfur. The new body was purely advisory and the Governor General determined its convening schedule, rules and regulations. Twelve of its twenty-eight members were tribal Nazirs, Sultans and Sheikhs. The Graduates' Congress immediately decided that it should be boycotted, and the head of the powerful pro-Egyptian Khatmiyya *tariqa* (brotherhood) looked upon it with misgivings because of the Mahdist influence in the new body.[23] But the race for independence was on. In October 1944 the Khatmiyya and its allies founded the Hizb al-Ittiyaddiyin (Unionist Party) whose main political agenda focused on the future "unity of the Nile Valley", i.e. the union with Egypt. In February 1945 Sayid Abd-er-Rahman countered the move by creating his own modern party, the Umma, whose all-embracing name was symbolic of the Mahdists' hegemonic hopes in a future independent Sudan. The British had by then become pro-Mahdist, a far cry from their former hostility. But since the Mahdists were anti-Egyptian, an alliance could be struck with them in exchange for delaying independence:

The job of the British in this country is to delay the day of self-government as long as possible. [...] The absence of the *Khatmia* in the Assembly is therefore a useful weapon in our hands.[24] [...] We might strike a bargain with the *Umma* on the lines of "we will not press amendments to bring the *Khatmia* in during the next three years if you will not press us now for self-government". This may sound a bit Machiavellian but I think these days we must use any weapon we have.[25]

The British were fighting rearguard actions which had little to do with Sudan itself. Their main fear (realized in 1956) was that Egypt would ask them to take their armed forces away from the Suez

Canal Zone. Haggling over Sudan (and perhaps finally giving in to the "Unity of the Nile Valley" concept) was seen as a bargaining counter in the game with Cairo, but the times were moving fast. By 1946 a Communist Party and a Hizb al-Ikhwaan al-Muslimin (Muslim Brotherhood Party), both local "sections" of much wider movements, had appeared in Sudan. For Darfur both the complex diplomatic game with Egypt and the flurry of modernistic political activity in Khartoum were only distant rumours. Sir James Robertson had become Civil Secretary on the death of Sir Douglas Newbold in March 1945, and he considered all these "modern" developments fraught with danger. An "old hand" of the Sudan Political Service with rather limited and traditional views, he was going to try, in Martin Daly's words, "to save the Sudan from itself". For Robertson provinces like Darfur were "safe" because they simply were not part of the modernizing equation. Suez and Cairo were very far indeed from El-Fashir, and inasmuch as the Darfuri participated in the debate they were quite opposed to the "unity of the Nile Valley", and this for several reasons. The first was cultural and geographic. Darfur's centre of gravity was in the Sahel and its natural hinterland consisted of Chad, Libya and the Ubangi-Shari rather than the Nile Valley. The second one was linked to Sudanese politics. After being briefly banned from Darfur in the 1920s Sayid Abd-er-Rahman, as we have seen slowly regained and enlarged his political audience in the West. By the mid-1940s "neo-Mahdism" had triumphed in both Darfur and Kordofan—so obviously that the British administration did not even try to fight the trend but rather tried to adapt to it and tame it. This had succeeded rather well since the Khatmiyya and its Ittihadiyin political arm were now a common enemy. Thus in Darfur opposition to the "Unity of the Nile Valley" concept was both popular and encouraged by the administration, a combination that made for political quietism and continued neglect. Being so tame, Darfur was automatically taken for granted. In

December 1953 the first elections for a Sudanese Parliament were held, and surprisingly the Unionists won 50 seats out of 97, with 22 only going to the Umma. The rest were shared by independents (12 seats), Southerners (9 seats) and the SRP, a short-lived pro-British party (3 seats).[26]

Did this mean then that the majority of the Sudanese wanted union with Egypt? Not really. The victory of the Unionists was largely due to the forceful and efficient political work of Ismail al-Azhari, the future "Father of Independence". Al-Azhari had long been leader of the pro-Khatmiyya faction of the Graduates' Congress and he was reaping the fruits of his uncompromising stance on independence from the British. However, he tended to be vague about any future commitment to the "Unity of the Nile Valley", something which did not escape the notice of the Egyptians who did not trust him.[27] But in Darfur such subtleties were lost on the voting public. People voted for the Mahdists because they had a network of local agents, having been for years the most resolute adversaries of the British because they were strongly opposed to Egypt. If we look at the sociology of the vote, there is absolutely no trace of an "Arab-African" split in the electoral choices. The Mahdists were everyone's favourite candidates and those independents who got elected were traditional leaders chosen because of their social and ceremonial role. Darfur's vote was strong, unequivocal and crude. For Sayid Abd-er-Rahman it was a safe bet.

Reaching for the Centre: the frustrations of democratic politics in Darfur

Independence was achieved on 1 January 1956 and for Darfur it did not mark any sort of watershed. What interested most people was the extension of the railway from El-Obeid to Nyala, on which work had started a few months before[28] and life went on much as it had before. The first post-independence elections, held in 1956, were won by the Umma. Darfur, which by then had twenty-two constituencies,[29] saw nineteen of them go to the Mahdist party and only three to the Unionists. Still, playing such a key role in the national victory of "their" party nevertheless gave the Darfurians no political clout in the capital. Sayid Abd-er-Rahman and his close kin, who ran the Umma like a family business, were so sure of the province's fidelity that they did not feel they had to bother about rewarding it in any particular way, but even if Darfur was remote and unsophisticated, this attitude on the part of what some people jokingly called "the royal family" started to rankle. But what could be done? The Unionists were disliked, and voting for the Communists or the Muslim Brothers seemed wild and unthinkable, except for a very small fringe of educated people in El-Fashir, El-Geneina, Nyala or Kutum. Darfur was stuck with the Mahdists and was getting nothing in return.

Meanwhile the young democracy was not in the best of health:

By November 1958 there was a strong sense of national crisis: economic setbacks coupled with a sharp decline in foreign exchange reserves, a series of costly strikes in the nascent industries, constant floor-crossing by opportunistic parliamentarians in the weak coalition government, the same government's inability to make any progress in controlling or extinguishing the continued rebellion in the Southern region and ever present rumours regarding subversion or possible invasion from Egypt.[30]

The feeling of crisis was so pervasive that the parties practically abdicated in the hands of the Army. In November 1958 Brigadier-General Ibrahim Abboud took power with the tacit approval of many in a kind of flight from political responsibility. The new ruler appointed prominent military figures to head all the ministries and put politicians from the two major parties under their authority. Abboud himself was of the Shaiqiyya and he embodied all the military prejudices of that tribe, which had traditionally been a key element in the armed forces since the Turco-Egyptian regime. His regime was characterized by two things: a high degree of stability verging on stagnation[31] and a foreign policy closely following the lead of the Nasserite regime in Cairo. Over time this heavy regime ossified still further, slowly losing any view of its civilian partners, and the political agitation which brought back civilian rule in October 1964 was due to a feeling that the military had finally painted itself into a corner both economically and in its handling of the Southern insurgency. The regime's naked practice of pork-barrel politics was extremely discouraging to the Sudanese public, which had had high expectations from independence. But in Darfur the feeling was that the regime made no difference: civilian or military, the men in power in Khartoum paid no attention to their distant colony, and the Nile Valley remained their only preoccupation. The return to civilian rule did not change that basic perception. Sayid Abd-er-Rahman had died during the period of the military dictatorship, and the Umma party went to his grandson Sadiq al-Mahdi after a brief period of internecine struggle. Sadiq was a complex character. Though British-educated (and very proud of his middling academic achievements at Oxford), he was deep down an oriental autocrat who felt that his ancestry had given him the right to rule. There was a constant contradiction between his very real organisational capacities and his nepotistic and manipulative political style. Given the central role of the Umma in the country's destiny, Darfur—and indeed the whole Sudan—were going to be disastrously affected by his public personality for the next forty years.

The first post-dictatorship elections, held in May 1965, were won by the Umma with 76 seats out of a total of 173. The surprise of those elections was the strong showing of the Communist Party which won eleven seats and indirectly controlled two others which went to extreme-left members of the Unionists. But all these seats were won in the Graduates' College,[32] a fact which showed the irritation felt by the younger members of the élite towards the sectarian parties. In Darfur the Mahdist party predictably won, with 16 seats out of 24; the only new and unexpected result was the election of an Islamic Charter Front[33] candidate in the northeastern constituency of Kutum. This is worth noting because almost forty years later northeastern Darfur will be the base from which the pro-fundamentalist Justice and Equality Movement (JEM) guerrilla movement will organize itself among the Zaghawa, thereby reflecting a durable anchoring of the radical Muslim electorate in the sub-region. Although timid and limited, this break in the duopoly previously enjoyed by the big sectarian parties in Darfur reflected a growing disappointment with the way the hegemonic Umma treated its regional electorate. In direct line with the old British Native Administration policies, the Umma had established its political base among the regional elite, rewarded it by giving it positions at the Centre and abandoned the popular electorate of the Periphery to its own devices. This was all the more shocking since the Mahdists had repeatedly used their mobilisation capacities in the West as a way to scare and impress their political competitors, as during the anti-Egyptian demonstrations which had marked the independence period.[34] The Darfur Mahdist devotees were good enough to carry spears and knives in the Mahdist militia, to vote for the Umma party and to work for a pittance in the domains of the family-run sect, but this did not earn them the right to claim a fair share of the budget from the government to whose election they had made a decisive contribution.

The 1960s were the period during which such distortions started to be questioned and one of the first signs was the debate around the constitution. The Constitutional Committee created after the 1965 elections discussed the type of constitution which would be appropriate for the Sudan. There were three projects: an Islamic constitution supported by the ICF, a secular one supported by the

Southerners, and some secular-minded Northerners and a constitution with an "Islamic orientation" supported by the Unionists.
Hassan al-Turabi, the young and dynamic leader of the Muslim
Brothers, was a member of the Constitutional Committee and he
logically defended the Islamic Constitution project. Surprisingly
the main opposition came not only from the Southerners but also
from the delegates representing Darfur, the Nuba Mountains and
the Red Sea Hills, because

....although Muslims they regarded an Islamic constitution as a ploy for
consolidating the hegemony of Northern and Central Sudan under the
umbrella of an Islamic and Arabic culture which would perpetuate the
marginalization of Sudan's Southern, Western and Eastern populations.[35]

This perception of a kind of "Islamic false consciousness" was one
the first political manifestations of a broader split in the ranks of the
Muslim majority in Northern Sudan along ethnic and regional lines.
It was limited, but it showed that the Islam-based universalist claims
of the main sectarian parties, which were localised in the Centre
and North while courting the vote of the otherwise neglected
"outlying areas", had begun to wear thin. The Islamic glue was
beginning to melt. It was of course not Islam as such which was concerned, but the political use of Islam made by the groups which
since the Turco-Egyptian regime had quarrelled, been reconciled,
intermarried[36] and shared among themselves the legitimacy, the
government, the administration and the wealth. The term "Arab"
was used to denounce them but only in passing—and by people
who in some cases were "Arabs" themselves. What they meant by
this was *awlad al-beled* as opposed to what in the preceding chapter
we called "native Arabs"; the term "Arabs" was used to mean the
"true élite" Arabs as opposed to the *awlad al-gharb* (children of the
West) "tribal Arabs" or the Eastern Beja tribes. It was the beginning
of some acrobatic ethnic semantics which were later to contribute
to the creation of a deadly ideological machinery.

This split had not yet opened before the 1968 elections when the Darfur Development Front (DDF) started to play a role. Created in December 1963 by Ahmed Ibrahim Diraige, son of a local Fur *shartay*, the DDF was a regionalist organization. Although Fur flocked to it because of its leader's tribal origin, it was open to all tribes whether "African" or "Arab". Its name was given in English, and by incorporating the word "development" in its appellation it strongly implied that this was indeed the main problem of the region. Both Arabs and non-Arabs shared the same sense of alienation from Khartoum.

Meanwhile the Umma had gone into a major crisis when Sadiq and his uncle, the Imam al-Hadi, had started to fight for control of the party.[37] By the time new elections were held in February 1968, the party had finally split into two separate organisations, one supporting the uncle and the other the nephew. Darfur, being an Umma stronghold, became the scene of some of the strongest pre-electoral infighting, all the more so because in their frantic quest for votes the two rivals appealed to different branches of the electorate. Calculating that the demography would favour the Fur and the other "African" tribes, Sadiq struck an alliance with Ahmed Ibrahim Diraige, leaving the Imam al-Hadi with no choice but to court the "Arab" tribes.[38] Since the two electorates were in fact quite interwoven (and partly intermarried), electoral tactics forced them to exaggerate the kind of racial-cultural rhetoric which had begun to grow. Demagoguery is part of politics, and the "African" electorate was told that if Darfur had been neglected it was the fault of "the Arabs"—something which the Fur, the Masalit or the Zaghawa were only too ready to believe given that their tribes were largely absent from the Khartoum power structure. But the counter-rhetoric of the "Arabs" introduced a dangerous ambiguity. It was true that the riverine Arabs did not care much for the distant "Black" tribes, but they did not care either for the equally distant

"Arab" ones. The social and economic marginalization of Darfur was regional, not racial or cultural.[39] But the discourse about "Arabism" offered the hope for the Arabized tribes to be co-opted, however symbolically it could be, into the Arab ruling group at the Centre. At the same time it also laid them open to the criticism of being closer to their "Arab brothers" in the Nile Valley than to their "African" neighbours in Darfur. The "African" tribes, speaking their *rottana*, did not even have the hope of a possible "Arab" identification at the Centre to look forward to. With DDF support Sadiq's Umma came ahead with 13 seats out of 24, while the branch of the party led by his uncle al-Hadi got only 7. The Mahdists were still the dominant force in Darfur politics. But blinded by their factional quarrels they had stepped on the dangerous and divisive ground of ethnic politics. They were soon to be reconciled when the parliamentary regime was toppled by a military coup led by Colonel Jaafar al-Nimeiry in May 1969. Sadiq al-Mahdi and Ahmed Ibrahim Diraige were both arrested and jailed, and Imam al-Hadi was killed while trying to flee to Ethiopia. Like the other sectarian parties, the Umma had been ruthlessly marginalized by the new military regime, which relied on the backing of the Communists. But the legacy of its ethnicisation of Darfurian provincial politics was to grow during the following years when the province would become a key element of the fight between Nimeiry and the Mahdists. The overspill of the Chadian civil war and the proxy intervention of Libya, which used the province as a staging post to fight the Nimeiry regime, would only make matters worse.

The Chadian-Libyan factor: a fundamental element of destabilization

Since 1965 a mixture of bad administration, intellectual revolutionary ferment and ethnic-religious tensions between North and

South had pushed Chad into what was to be one of the longest civil wars of the continent, and from its beginning Darfur played a key role in that conflict. Symbolically Frolinat (Front de Libération Nationale du Tchad), a guerrilla movement which was to be at the heart of the civil war for many years, had been founded on Sudanese territory, at Nyala, in June 1966.[40] The causes of this are hard to establish precisely, but some were both practical and ideological ones: with the same Muslim tribes on both sides of the border Darfur, much more than the Central African Republic, Cameroun or Nigeria, could be a natural hinterland for a Chadian rebellion. Then at the level of governmental geopolitics Chad's dual division between Northern Muslims and Southern Christians was undoubt-edly a factor motivating Khartoum's support for Frolinat, a northern and Muslim organization fighting the Southern-led gov-ernment of President Tombalbaye.[41] Frolinat was also "anti-imperialist" at a time when all the various components of the Sudanese political landscape, even the tamest ones like the Umma, were fond of playing with that Nasserite rhetoric. Sadiq al-Mahdi's accession to the Premiership in July 1966 proved a turning-point. By September Frolinat had established rear bases in Darfur from where it could wage war against Tombalbaye's troops.[42] Given the fractiousness of the Chadian revolutionary movement, this almost immediately proved to be a problem for the host-country, and in November 1971 violent fighting between competing Chadian factions left dozens dead on the Darfur side.[43] This led the Sudanese government of President Nimeiry to kick out his brutal guests, a pattern which would be repeated several times in the future.

The picture became further complicated when Colonel Muam-mar Gaddafi developed a growing interest in the Chadian conflict. In the words of Burr and Collins, the young revolutionary leader who had taken power in September 1969 "was consumed by geo-politics". His first major political moves had been to expel the

Italian settlers still living in Libya and to close down the British and American military bases which had been in the country since the Second World War. Soon after he was boasting of helping the Republicans' struggle in Northern Ireland and the Muslim rebels of the Moro Liberation Front in the southern Philippines. By his own account he had become "a world-wide opponent" and Chad, an immediate neighbour of Libya, was bound to be a target of his global revolutionary enthusiasm. As early as November 1969 Frolinat was given rear bases in Libya, and Tripoli's media were denouncing "Tombalbaye, the tyrant of Chad". Soon after Gaddafi revived an old border quarrel between Libya and Chad by claiming the Aozou strip of land between the two countries.[44] But another dimension, little noted at the time, was Gaddafi's racism. Part of his hostility to Tombalbaye's regime was due to the fact that the Chadian president was a black African and a Christian and that in his early "revolutionary" days Gaddafi was not only a strident Pan-Arabist but an Arab cultural supremacist as well:[45]

His Bedouin background was replete with the folklore of the treacherous *Zurqa*, a pejorative term used by Arab Bedouins to describe the non-Arab Gourane of Libya, Chad and the Sudan whose Toubou culture made them implacably independent. [...] They were not to be trusted and Gaddafi systematically reduced the Toubou influence in Libya. [...] Thousands of Toubou were driven off from Fezzan in 1970.[46]

The protestations of the Chadian ambassador in Tripoli, Beshir Sow (himself a Muslim), that there was no persecution of Muslims in his country were of no avail. So from the beginning, Gaddafi's support for the Chadian rebellion acquired a very particular racial tinge where the *zurqa* were suspected of siding with the "imperialists", while the "Arabs" (a concept even more elusive in Chad than in the Sudan) became the very incarnation of "revolutionary" purity. Gaddafi had initially supported the Nimeiry regime in Khartoum because he saw it as an "Arab Nationalist Revolutionary Movement" and at a meeting in late 1971 had even offered him a merger of their two countries. He was particularly embittered when Nimeiry turned down his offer and instead negotiated a peace settlement with the black Christian Southerners in 1972. Disappointed in his plans for a peaceful "Arab Union"[47] the Libyan leader then began to arrange for more radical means of achieving the same aims, and Darfur loomed large in his subversive plans for the Sudan. In 1972 he created the Failaka al-Islamiya (Islamic Legion), which in his mind was to be a tool for the revolutionary unification and arabization of the region. In Darfur proper he supported the creation of the Tajammu al-Arabi (Arab Union), a militantly racist and pan-Arabist organization which stressed the "Arab" character of the province. The first target of the Failaka al-Islamiya was to be Chad and the second the Sudan. And when Sadiq al-Mahdi got out of gaol and sought a base from which he could fight Nimeiry, Gaddafi welcomed him in Tripoli.

The racial conundrum was made worse by the drought and famine which affected the Sahel during the early 1970s. France, which supported the Tombalbaye regime against all efforts at destabilization, shipped 50,000 tons of food aid to Chad in 1973, but the Southerners who stood behind the Tombalbaye regime got first pick at that relief effort, and little food reached the North. Thousands of northern Toubou and Zaghawa tribesmen fled to Darfur seeking help. These people, who were seen as *zurqa* on the Libyan-Chadian confines, were perceived as "Arabs" by the "real" African tribes of Darfur. And these "Arabs" were angry, hungry and armed.

Meanwhile Tombalbaye had been assassinated in April 1975 by one of his own Sara officers. This weakened the cohesion of the southern-dominated regime, which put the next president, General Félix Malloum, also a Sara, into a more fragile situation than his predecessor. Nimeiry, worried about Sadiq al-Mahdi's militant presence in Tripoli,[48] adopted a very conciliatory attitude towards the new Chadian president. For Gaddafi this was an added sign of

Nimeiry's "betrayal" of the revolutionary Arab cause. In July 1976 a Sudanese militia force of about 1,200 men trained and equipped by Tripoli left the Ma'tan as-Sarra military base in south-eastern Libya and struck across the desert directly at Khartoum.[49] The attackers at first occupied the capital but Nimeiry counter-attacked with tank units led by Brigadier Abd-el-Qassim Mohamed Ibrahim, a resolutely secular officer who saw the attack as "a fanatics' coup". In three days of fierce street fighting the loyalists regained control of the city. The attackers were called *murtazigha* (mercenaries) in the official media and the repression was pitiless. Brigadier Abd-el-Qassim executed hundreds of prisoners, and Darfuri civilians accused of sympathy with the insurgents were hunted down. A large numbers who had taken refuge in the Wad Nubawi mosque in Omdurman were slaughtered, some even being buried alive. The whole operation caused over 3,000 deaths and Darfur was left in a state of shock.[50]

The battle for Khartoum left a legacy of mutual hatred between Nimeiry and Gaddafi. As a result the Sudanese president decided to support the most anti-Libyan of all the potential Chadian leaders, Hissen Habre, a North Chad Goran of the Anakaza tribe who was both anti-Malloum and anti-Libyan, thus representing in Nimeiry's view a perfect mix. Soon Habre's Forces Armées du Nord (FAN) were solidly settled in Darfur from where they started to harass the Chadian army. They too were perceived as "Arabs" and their presence was not welcomed locally.

This rough handling of Darfur by the Libyans, the Chadians and the Khartoum forces decisively worsened the regional ethnopolitical landscape. Tribes which had seen themselves primarily in local terms were suddenly catapulted into a broader artificial world where they were summoned to declare themselves as either "Arab" or *zurqa*. The "Arabs" were "progressive" or "revolutionary", while the "Africans" were "anti-Arab" and "reactionary".[51] These labels were largely attributed to them by the outside world, but two other factors combined with this outside intervention. First, at the domestic level, the province's administration began to be manipulated to support or combat Khartoum's regional policies. Thus to the administrative neglect, which remained as bad as it had been since the Condominium, a factor of political manipulation was now superimposed. Darfur did not seem to matter enough to be taken seriously at the level of good governance, but it certainly mattered enough to become an increasingly racialized battleground between Khartoum, Tripoli and Ndjamena. Then a second factor, which was an act of God and not of man, started to give the "Arab-African" dichotomy another more immediate dimension: the 1970s had been years of recurring drought leading to increased desertification. Thus the rapidly degrading ecological situation further polarized politically manipulated ethnic identities. Alex deWaal has made the provocative assertion that "there are no true nomads in Darfur. Most of the people described in that way are in fact semi-nomadic or transhumant and most of the animals are owned by people who are principally farmers."[52] If we accept this even in part, the semi-nomadic way of life and the fully settled way of life largely recouped the "Arab-African" dichotomy. And drought leading to an advance in desertification was playing havoc with the "Arab" tribes' means of survival at the very moment when they were encouraged to see themselves as basically different from their "African" neighbours. Khartoum could have played an essential role in defusing an increasingly explosive situation, but as usual, found great difficulty in paying attention to Darfur *itself* rather than seeing it as a pawn in a wider political and military game.

From maladministration to famine: the 1984 catastrophe

In late 1979 the Regional Government Act was enacted in an effort at making provincial governments closer to the needs of the local populations. To symbolize this new regionalizing approach, all the provincial governors had to be local people—all except in Darfur where Governor al-Tayeb al-Mardi was a Nile Valley *walad al-beled*. He was a military man whom Nimeiry had put in this position mostly to oversee the support Sudan was giving to Hissen Habre, under CIA supervision. The CIA had opened a station in El-Fashir and had its own plane doing monthly trips between Cairo (its rear base for the Darfur operation), Khartoum and El-Fashir.[53] For the local people it simply meant that once more their own fate was a secondary consideration in Khartoum's geopolitical calculations. Darfuri all across Sudan demonstrated against their neglect, and three students were killed. Nimeiry was worried, less by that popular unrest than by the prospect that he would lose control of his anti-Libyan base of operation. In January 1980 he dismissed al-Tayeb al-Mardi and called in Ahmed Ibrahim Diraige whose DDF credentials immediately cooled down the situation. Diraige, who had accepted no salary for his position, set out to overhaul completely the provincial government structure. His main approach was to cut down on the political patronage which had proved so disastrous, with Mahdist notables running their own shows in an atmosphere of utter corruption and neglect, and to name a provincial cabinet of largely apolitical capable technicians. Another (unspoken) criterion was defusing the tribal "Arabs versus Africans" time-bomb, and in order to achieve this he selected an ethnically very broad government. As his deputy he chose Mahmood Beshir Jama, a Zaghawa. The Speaker of the Provincial Parliament was a Fur, the Deputy Speaker a Beni Halba, the Minister of Internal Affairs a Ziyadiyya, the Chief Whip a Rizzeyqat, and the Minister of Education and Health was Ali al-Hajj, a Takruri and the only openly political man.[54] The Minister of Public Works and Water was a *jallaba*, the Minister of Regional Affairs was a so-called *walad ar-Riff* of Egyptian origin, the sub-governor of South Darfur was Ibrahim Madibo, a well-known local Rizzeyqat, and the sub-governor of North Darfur, Hussein Abbakar, was a Masalit. Irrespective of their tribal origins all these men had one thing in common: since 1964 they had been known members or sympathizers of the DDF and had advocated more attention being paid by the central authorities to the neglected province. Now they were confronted with the results of many years of administrative neglect, at a dramatic moment when "racial" antagonisms were rising, when the Chadian conflict was once more spilling over into the province, and when, perhaps worst of all, drought and desertification threatened to turn the looming food scarcity into a real famine. The few so-called "development projects", much vaunted by the government, were symbolic totem poles to which everybody paid respect but which had no impact on the local agriculture.[55] And the situation was serious, with sharply diminishing rain levels over the preceding few years.

This list is roughly arranged in a north-south order and shows how much worse the drought was becoming in the north. As the rainfall diminished, the northern areas slowly became impossible to cultivate, forcing the semi-nomadic tribes and their dwindling

EVOLUTION OF MEAN ANNUAL RAINFALL (mm.)

	1976	*1986*
Kutum	295	197
El-Fashir	270	162
El-Geneina	510	373
Nyertete*	791	575
Zalingei*	612	460
Garsila*	666	558
Nyala	464	351
Ed-Da'ein	486	422
Buram	643	568

* Localities influenced by Jebel Mara relief rainfall.
Source: Alex de Waal, *op. cit.*, p. 83.

herds to become fully nomadic, encroaching more and more upon the remaining pasturelands belonging to the sedentary peasants.

The Diraige administration was soon engaged in a desperate battle for water resources. More boreholes were needed and few had been dug over the previous twenty years. The thousands of *hafir* scattered across the countryside were in a sorry state of neglect and many had not been dredged since the British times.[56] Even the water system in the provincial capital of El-Fashir was so degraded that the town dwellers were increasingly getting sick from drinking water polluted by sewage. Funds earmarked for water projects had been stolen, miles of piping imported for Darfur had been lying for years in Port Sudan with nobody bothering to collect it, the rural water teams did not receive their salaries on time, and the relevant ministries in Khartoum simply issued glorified statistics bearing no relationship to reality. Diraige and his men did their best but they could not make the rain fall and they could not stop the desert from encroaching further and further south. They needed more help from the government and this help was not forthcoming. Khartoum could find money to help Hissen Habre's guerrillas, who by now had started yet another war of westward reconquest from Darfur, but it could not find money to start overhauling the province's economy and infrastructures.[57] During 1983 the situation became ever more threatening and in November Diraige wrote Nimeiry a letter, later to become known as the "famine letter", warning the President that unless serious food aid was requested from abroad, a famine in Darfur was unavoidable in 1984. Nimeiry was furious. Since 1977 he had started a process known as *al-Mussallaha al-Wataniya* or "patriotic reconciliation" in which he had called back home all his old Arab opponents and their parties: Sadiq al-Mahdi and the Umma, Mohamed Osman al-Mirghani and the Unionists, and Hassan al-Turabi and the Islamists. In a touching display of "Arab" unanimity he had then became reconciled with the oil monarchies which had long retained doubts about him because of his early association with the Communist Party. By the early 1980s, cuddled by the United States and benefiting from massive investment from the Gulf states, Sudan had been dubbed "the future breadbasket of the Arab World". Diraige's "famine letter" and his plea for foreign food aid threatened the whole artificial propaganda edifice, and it was the last thing Nimeiry wanted. He refused to answer and Diraige went to Khartoum on 23 December 1983 to confront the President. Nimeiry flew into a rage and refused to issue a call for emergency aid for Darfur, forcing Diraige to walk out of the meeting. Forty-eight hours later he was in a plane bound for Saudi Arabia, escaping arrest by a few hours. Since news of the row had spread, Nimeiry's Minister of Finance Ibrahim Moneim Mansur publicly answered the famine warning, which he dismissed as "exaggerated". By early 1984 the FAO estimated Darfur's minimum food deficit to be 39,000 tons. The Khartoum government again disparaged the warning, countered with a figure of 7,000 tons and slowly released about 5,400 tons, too little to have any serious impact. By August 1984 the famine could no longer be denied and Nimeiry finally proclaimed Darfur a "disaster zone", asking the world for 160,000 tons of food aid.[58] Large IDP camps appeared in Darfur itself while 60–80,000 starving people walked clear across the country to sprawling camps on the outskirts of Khartoum. The government's first reaction was to declare that they were all Chadian refugees[59] and to deport masses of them by truck to Kordofan.[60] By February 1985 the ironically named "Operation Glorious Return" had brought their numbers down to 13,000, but they were soon back, again on foot, because no relief food was available in Kordofan. Given Nimeiry's solid pro-US engagement Washington was beginning to panic. Sudan's debt stood at $11 billion and the IMF had threatened to suspend Khartoum in January 1985.[61] Even if the famine was less severe than in Darfur, it was rapidly spreading to other regions of the country. In March 1985 Vice-President George Bush rushed to Khartoum to announce the imminent disbursement of $192m of US aid hitherto blocked by Congress and the delivery of an extra 250,000 tons of food. Washington was ready to do a lot for a regime it saw as a bulwark against both Ethiopia's Communists and Gaddafi's rogue dictatorship, and by April it had committed itself to 975,000 tons of relief aid.[62] This was too late. Bread prices had shot up by 33% and there was a general strike.

A combination of students, trade unionists and professionals quickly organized an insurrectional committee and on 5 April 1985 the Nimeiry regime was overthrown after a few days of street riots,[63] when a segment of the Army decided at the last minute to join the dissidents in order to preserve the officer corps' interests in the future. General Swar ed-Dhahab, the neutral head of the military wing of the coalition, promised to hold elections within a year. Basically this meant that the clock had been turned back to 1964. Another civilian intifada (insurrection) had overthrown another military dictatorship but many of the old-guard politicians had learned nothing and forgotten nothing. The competition among them was going to be as it had been before the 1969 Nimeiry takeover—relentless, sectarian, confused and without a hint of concern for the national interest.[64] And once more Darfur was going to loom large in the electoral landscape, not because of its desperate misery but simply because it represented the largest single lodestone of coherent political votes available anywhere on the political map of the Sudan. For Sadiq al-Mahdi and the Umma winning Darfur was the necessary path to political success. But Sadiq needed money for the coming electoral campaign, and in his mind Darfur was also going to provide that, albeit indirectly. The reason was that Gaddafi was still looking towards Darfur as a stepping-stone leading to Chad and a Greater Sahelian Arab Empire and that since the mid-1970s he had considered the Umma leader to be the mixture of ally and puppet he had so often used in the region. This enabled Sadiq to tempt him with a promise of delivering Darfur to Libya in exchange for several million dollars of election funds,[65] all the while a firmly intending never to keep his side of the bargain. But this political trick was going to prove hard to pull off since the Libyan Shylock was firmly resolved to claim his pound of flesh, and Darfur's post-famine ethnic wounds laid it wide open to his manipulations. The worst period in Darfur's history since the days of the Mahdiyya was about to begin, and in early 2005 one can say that it has not yet ended.

FROM MARGINALIZATION TO REVOLT
MANIPULATED "ARABISM" AND "RACIAL" ANARCHY
(1985–2003)

Consequences of the 1984 famine

In July 1985 the junta's strongman, the Minister of Defence Brigadier Osman Abdallah Mohamed, rushed to Tripoli to sign a defence agreement with Gaddafi, and Washington voiced its "grave concern". General Swar ed-Dhahab, head of the government, declared: "Our western friends have no reason to worry."[1] The new regime's desire to make a clean break with the pro-US Nimeiry policies was both evident and clumsy because the famine had not ended with the fall of the dictatorship, and USAID was providing 80% of the food aid. The transitional government dealt with the situation in haphazard fashion, succeeding both in irritating Washington politically and yielding to its every whim at the level of humanitarian aid. The Americans had decided to give a quasi-monopoly for transporting the food to a strange joint venture between a businessman from Baton Rouge, Louisiana, and a Lebanese wholesale grocer in Khartoum. The resulting company, Arkell-Talab, had proved remarkably inefficient and out of the 68,000 tons of food aid allocated monthly to Kordofan and Darfur only 123,000 tons had been transported between December 1984 and June 1985 i.e. an average of little more than 20,000 tons a month, barely a third of

the planned figure.[2] Most of the 20,000 trucks which were supposed to be used for the food convoys were in fact out of commission,
and people continued to starve in the midst of plenty. The situation
was chaotic, and the statistics given by the international community
and by the Sudanese government were increasingly diverging and
equally unreliable.[3] Libya was taking advantage of the confusion in
effect to occupy Darfur. On 23 August 1985 the first of many large
Libyan humanitarian/military convoys arrived there with grain,
powdered milk and guns. It had covered the 2,200 km. through the
desert between Benghazi and El-Fashir in twelve days while the
Arkell-Talab drivers, running on admittedly poor roads, would take
fourteen days to come from Khartoum, 1,000 km away. It had thus
been proved that Tripoli was in a position to intervene directly in
Western Sudan and on 5 March 1986 a giant 350-truck convoy
arrived in El-Fashir. This time Gaddafi had negotiated its coming
directly with Sadiq al-Mahdi whom he already considered as the
next head of state in the Sudan[4]. With the convoy came an 800-strong
Libyan military force which settled in El-Fashir and began arming
the Baggara Arab tribes whom Gaddafi considered as his local allies[5].

The promised elections were held between 1 and 12 April 1986,
and Sadiq's Umma predictably won with 101 seats out of 264. Out
of Darfur's thirty-nine seats thirty-four had gone to the Umma[6] and
of those thirty were controlled by the DDF, a fact which was to have
far-reaching consequences since the resolutely secular DDF parliamentarians opposed Sadiq's plan of an "Arab and Islamic Union"
cabinet.[7]

On 14–15 April US planes bombed Tripoli and Benghazi, and
Brigadier Osman Abdallah immediately rushed to Libya to show his
support for Colonel Gaddafi whose adoptive daughter was killed in
the raid. The Libyans were by then an essential part of the Sudanese
war effort in the South, and Rumbek, which had fallen to the SPLA
in early March, was re-taken by the Khartoum forces in May with

significant Libyan logistical and air support. In such circumstances it was increasingly difficult for the Sudanese government to deny Colonel Gaddafi a creeping involvement in Darfur, and secret negotiations began between Khartoum and Tripoli to decide on the modalities of that presence. Apart from the potential problems this posed in terms of sovereignty and border delimitation, a major question was the blatant partiality of the Libyans in Darfur towards the Arab tribes and their open support for the Tajammu al-Arabi forces at a time when inter-ethnic relations were becoming increasingly difficult in the wake of the now receding famine.

In Darfur the *maja'a al-gutala*[8] had lasted from August 1984 to November 1985, killing an estimated 95,000 people out of a total population of 3.1 million. Everybody knew that it had been entirely preventable, but in addition to the grossly uncaring treatment the province had received once again at the hands of Khartoum its consequences were unevenly distributed.

The drought, the wandering in search of food, the massive population displacements had created durable mental and cultural damage to what Alex deWaal calls the "moral geography" of Darfur. This "moral geography" was dual. On the one hand, for the settled populations such as the Fur the world was seen as a coherent block centred on their own *Dar*, particularly on their historic homeland Jebel Marra. To the north were the deserted expanses of the Sahara followed by the *khalla* (wild bush) zone, home of the Zagahwa and the Arab camel-herders. To the south was another *khalla* zone populated by the Baggara groups and, still further away, the wild Dar Fertit lands. For the nomads the pattern was quite different. It resembled a kind of chessboard where settled farming communities occupied the black squares and they themselves weaved among them, from one white square to another, while on their way from the northern dried-up pastures to the southern ones.[9] The drought not only shrunk their grazing resources but upset their mental picture of the world. Farmers trying to hang on to all potential agricultural land now often blocked the traditional *marahil* which had once led to the southern pastures. The nomads called these fenced-off unused agricultural land *zaraib al-hawa* (literally "enclosures of air"), and for them it was a catastrophe. Their world was suddenly closing up, with traditional pathways and temporary forage suddenly out of reach while the northern isohyets marking their former grazing possibilities kept sliding southward. In their eagerness to push towards the still wet south, they started to fight they way through the blocked off *marahil*. Farmers carrying out their age-old practices of burning unwanted wild grass were attacked because what for them were bad weeds had become the last fodder for the desperate nomads' depleted flocks.

Everybody knew that Ahmed Diraige, a son of Darfur and an "indigenous African" whose administration had been the first to care for the ordinary man since independence, had been forced to resign because the government had chosen not to prevent a preventable famine in order to safeguard the interests of Nile Valley élite. Nile Valley interests were "Arab" interests, even if they were definitely not those of the Darfur "native Arabs". That same government had played an anti-Libyan game with the Chadian insurgents, causing a trail of destruction in the province and infusing it with wave after wave of cheap weapons even as the famine was increasingly threatening. Now Libya was back in Darfur, supporting new groups of anti-Ndjamena Chadians, partly through support for the very "Arab" nomad groups who had paid and were still paying the highest price for the famine. Battle-lines began to be drawn, setting the common victims of these disastrous policies at each other's throats in a desperate effort to put the blame on the "enemy" community. The Libyan presence, tolerated by the provisional government and later actively supported by the Sadiq al-Mahdi cabinet, acted like acid on open social and economic wounds which were being re-interpreted in increasingly ethnic and "racial" terms.

The "Arabs" did not care about the famine which the "African" governor had tried to prevent. Now that it was over, the "Africans" were trying to make the "Arab" victims pay and to cut them off from available pastureland. The "Arabs" were thieves who were trying to steal the livestock which remained in "African" hands. The selfish "Africans" shot at the "Arabs" who were then just recuperating from the famine. The "Arabs" were killers who got weapons from the Libyan troops and the Chadian insurgents to steal what they could from the "Africans".

All of these clichés contained elements of truth and all were ultimately false if the causative criteria were taken to be ethnic or cultural. But in a world deeply shaken both materially and culturally by the famine, these myths began to gain credence, especially as outsiders were now peddling an aggressive ideology of international "Arab" superiority. In fact the reality had always been both political and domestic. Successive governments in Khartoum, going as far back as the British, had never cared about Darfur. Independence had not improved matters and now that catastrophe had finally hit, the Nile Valley rulers were trying to set up two largely imagined and constructed communities against each other in order not to be seen as responsible for the neglect shown to both. Obsessed with its own class interests and with the problem of the war in the South, the new "democratic" government in Khartoum was going to subject Darfur to even worse treatment than the Nimeiry dictatorship had done because it added passive incitement to racial hatred and active support for community confrontation to the neglect shown by the former regime.

Khartoum's "democratic" politics and the Chadian conflict

If Darfur had been forgotten at the time of the famine, it was not forgotten where its required contribution to the war effort in the

South was concerned. Although precise statistics on the subject are lacking for obvious reasons, Darfuri made up an inordinately high proportion of the troops going to fight in the South. In April 1986 there were riots at the Nyala railway station when Fur conscripts refused to board a train bound for Wau. Leaflets were distributed saying: "Why should we fight our brothers in the South? Are we not the same?". On 13 September there were new riots in Nyala during which the government's office were ransacked. Two demonstrators were killed and forty wounded. Sadiq al-Mahdi rushed over to Darfur, but Gaddafi, who also wanted to come, was discouraged from doing so.[10] Three weeks later Darfur's new governor Abd el-Nabi Ali Ahmed was in Khartoum to negotiate with the Libyan ambassador to Sudan the "integration" of the province with Kufra.[11] On the same day Sadiq al-Mahdi's nephew Mubarak al-Fadl, who combined the positions of Minister of Industry and "Special Envoy" to Libya, flatly denied that his uncle's government had accepted Libyan help for the war in the South or that there were any Libyan soldiers in Darfur.[12] The Libyans were arming the new *Murahleen* militias which the government was busy organizing, supposedly to fight the SPLA in Bahr-el-Ghazal but actually to attack Dinka civilians, killing many and enslaving the survivors.[13] On 20 February 1987 the Prime Minister appointed Brigadier (ret.) Fadlallah Burma Nasir, founder and acknowledged leader of the *Murahleen*, as his new State Minister for Defence.

But in spite of the growing involvement of the Libyans in Darfur-based militia activities aimed at the South, Tripoli's main concern remained Chad. In southern Libya Gaddafi had assembled a force estimated at between 13,000 and 20,000 men to invade his southern neighbour. In addition 2,000 were now in Darfur, with the task of opening a second front as soon as the offensive moved forward. The United States had delivered $15 million worth of new weapons to Hissen Habre's government[14] and Sadiq was beginning to get worried, that he might become drawn into a major international confrontation. He sent Ali Hassan Taj ed-Din, a member of Khartoum's "Council of State"[15] and son of the Masalit Sultan of El-Geneina, to Tripoli to ask Gaddafi to slow down the "Libyanization" of Darfur.[16] Then when he realized that he could not calm down the "Guide" he flew to Cairo and signed a "Brotherhood Charter" with the Egyptians, which earned him $52 million worth of new weapons for the war in the South.[17] To assuage Gaddafi's hurt feelings he again denied that there were any Libyan soldiers in Darfur.[18] Then on 7 March, in one of the about-turns so typical of his erratic policies, he ordered the Libyan troops out of Darfur "not to bring any support to the various parties now engaged in the war in Chad".[19] Idris al-Banna, Deputy Chairman of the Council of State, went to Tripoli but only to get a serious drubbing. How dared Sadiq, he was asked, order the "Libyan troops" out of Darfur when half of them were in fact Sudanese citizens as members of Failaka al-Islamiyya and most of the rest were Chadians? These were the "International Brigades" of the "Arab revolution", and in any case Sadiq's envoy was reminded that Sudan, or rather Sadiq's party, had been paid for the facility.[20] Omar al-Hamidi, Secretary of Libya's Arab People's Congress and in charge of the Unity Charter with Sudan, declared that "Sudan's southern war will never end till Sudan becomes a progressive country and unites with Libya". He demanded a denunciation of Khartoum's recent treaty with Cairo and forcibly sent Idris al-Banna back to Khartoum.[21] To add a little carrot to the stick Gaddafi then donated four MiG-23 fighter-bombers to the Sudan Air Force,[22] and Sadiq declared that "the whole problem of the Libyan troops in Darfur is now solved as Tripoli has accepted the Sudanese peace plan"—whatever that meant. In a daring raid carried out between 17 and 24 April the Chadian army entered Darfur and attacked the Libyan and Failaka al-Islamiyya forces, destroying most of their strike capability.[23]

While international politics were once more being played on their backs, the Darfuri were increasingly contaminated with the atmosphere of violence and ethnic hatred that the outside forces were deploying in support of their aims. A group of Rizzeyqat *Murahleen* had been infuriated by the loss of seventy of their men in an ambush in Safaha. They tried to attack Dinka IDPs in retaliation for their defeat and the Southerners fled from them by train with the help of the local authorities. The militiamen then caught up with the train in the small town of Ed-Da'ien, and slaughtered between 1,000 and 1,700 civilians.[24] The Tajammu al-Arabi was financing the training of more militia recruits, not caring whether they would fight in the South or at home in Darfur. In late September 1987 the police tried to dismantle an "Arab" militia camp near Nyala. Fifty men were killed on both sides and thirty were arrested for unlawful armed association, only to be released discreetly later at the government's behest. Zaghawa and Salamat militiamen of the Chadian "neo-GUNT" forces now routinely attacked fur villages.[25] DDF activists started to look desperately for weapons in Chad, and Umma Agriculture Minister Omar Nur ed-Daiem, one of the government's "heavyweights", declared in October: "We have to answer violence with violence and arm all the tribes."[26]

The Darfuri "Arab" tribes were now increasingly involved in the cross-border war. In November the Chadian Army crossed once more into Darfur, attacking Libyan/Chadian and militia camps in Kabkabiya, As-Sireif and Gama, killing over 200 combatants and an unknown number of civilians.[27] When the Failaka al-Islamiyya tried to counterattack, it was stopped southeast of Abéché, losing forty-four of its number.[28] By then civil war in Darfur and the Chadian "foreign" conflict were both in full swing and completely enmeshed. The Western politicians in Khartoum were divided: the "Arab" ones[29] tended to be wilfully blind and support Sadiq al-Mahdi's waveringly pro-Libyan policies, even in their worst tribal militia excesses; Fadlallah Burma Nasir was the main offender, responsible for the worst exactions of the *Murahleen* and for the government's complicity in the Tajammu al-Arabi recruitment. But the "Black" ministers such as Mahmood Beshir Jamaa, the Minister for Irrigation (Zaghawa), and Ali Hassan Taj ed-Din, the Masalit member of the Council of State, were divided. They felt that control of the situation was slipping out of their hands and their loyalty to the Prime Minister and to the Umma party was severely tested. The DDF-linked parliamentarians were threatening to resign if security did not improve in Darfur, and many Fur conscripts fighting in the South were now deserting, some of them even joining the SPLA. The DUP kept harassing its Umma coalition partner, Interior Minister Sid Ahmed al-Hussein and Minister of Foreign Affairs Sharif Zeyn Abdin al-Hindi, neglecting no occasion to berate Sadiq for his sell-out to the Libyans. Burma Nasir and the Sudanese Army Chief of Staff, Brigadier Fawzi Ahmed el-Fadl, travelled to London, asking Ahmed Ibrahim Diraige to come back and support the government because they feared a disintegration of the Fur fighting units through increased desertions.[30] Fighting across the Chadian border had become constant and the Failaka al-Islamiyya forces were repeatedly in operation, usually losing a lot of men and laying Darfur open to revenge counter-attacks from the Chadian forces.[31]

By January 1988 an independent journalist familiar with Darfur estimated the number of deaths through fighting in the province during the past year at 3,000.[32] The Libyans, using the voice of Acheikh ibn Oumar, were openly saying that annexation to Tripoli was the only way to restore the peace in Darfur[33]. The provincial Governor, Abd-el-Nabi Ali Ahmed, was half African Berti and half *jallaba* Arab and therefore trusted by neither side. The Libyans had extended the runway at their Saaj en-Naham military base, 15 km. out of El-Fashir, and were flying twice-weekly delivery flights with their transport planes from Tripoli or Kufra.[34] They were pouring weapons into the hands of their Salamat allies, with a mandate to terrorize the *zurqa* into accepting annexation to Libya, while young DDF activists were starting to create financial solidarity networks among the Fur expatriate workers, inside Sudan and in the Gulf States. The purpose was to acquire weapons, something which was not easy since Hissen Habre, the most likely source given the political configuration, did not seem to trust them.[35] But a Fur militia was slowly taking shape, and in early March 1988 there was a pitched battle near Kabkabiya when it tried to stop Chadian CDR forces supported by local "Arab" tribes from establishing a training camp in northern Jebel Marra. Nine villages were burnt and over eighty people were killed, leading the DDF to organize a 40,000 strong demonstration in Khartoum against the Libyan presence in Darfur.[36] Since August 1987, when the DUP had left the coalition cabinet, Sudan had had no legal government and the NIF, which had been kept out of power largely through the agency of the DDF-influenced Umma MPs, was agitating in the streets to be included in any new cabinet. Criticizing the Prime Minister's "sell-out" of Sudanese national interests in Darfur to Libya was one of the key themes of this NIF agitation. But when Hassan al-Turabi finally achieved his purpose on 18 May 1988 and Sadiq al-Mahdi offered the NIF five key cabinet posts,[37] the whole theme of denouncing the Libyan presence in Darfur was immediately dropped. In reciprocity Sadiq forced the Darfuri Ali Hassan Taj ed-Din from the collective presidency and replaced him with a NIF nominee. But by then the situation in Darfur was almost completely out of Khartoum's control:

In El-Fasher a Kalashnikov assault rifle sells for a mere $40 and rocket-propelled grenades are found in the market. [...] Local militias are aligned with participants in the Chadian conflict, such as the pro-Hissen Habre Bidayat or the Libyan-sponsored Beni Halba. [...] Although Khartoum denies it, Darfur has become a staging post for Gaddafi's Islamic legion, a

motley group including Africans of many nationalities as well as Lebanese
Druze. [...] 400 Libyan troops are camped in the desert outside El-Fashir
... actively recruiting among nomadic Arabs. Libya finds other allies
among the remnants of the National Front which tried to overthrow then
President Jaafar Nimeiry in 1976. [...] Pitched battles are taking place
between the CDR, supported by local Arabs, and the local Fur tribe. [...]
The people of Darfur realize that they can get no help from Khartoum.
[...] The local economy has collapsed and the government is faced with a
virtual political rebellion.[38]

Angry crowds stoned the new Minister of Defence Abd el-Majid
Khalil when he went to visit Nyala. He ordered the police to shoot
the demonstrators, which they could not do because they had no
ammunition.[39] He came back to Khartoum in a frantic state, fired
the pro-Umma Chief of Staff Brigadier Fawzi Ahmed el-Fadl, and
replaced him with a capable apolitical officer, Major-General Fathi
Ahmed Ali. The Minister and the new Chief of Staff then tried to
mount a "Darfur Special Force" to re-establish order in the western
province. Gaddafi immediately tried to pressure Sadiq al-Mahdi
into firing both Abd el-Majid and the new Chief of Staff who
enjoyed the support of the Egyptians. In his usual confused way
Sadiq neither backed the Darfur Special Force initiative nor fired its
sponsors. The Fur militia was now 12,000-strong, and Ahmed
Diraige, in exile in London, was desperately trying to acquire
weapons for them from Chad.[40] In August the murderous mess
reached a new peak when two factors were added: first, Acheikh
ibn Oumar fell out with Gaddafi and was arrested in Tripoli, leading
2,000 of his CDR fighters to flee to Darfur, and secondly, to add to
the confusion, a huge Nile flood drowned Khartoum, durably dis-
rupting communications with Darfur and destroying food storage
and transport capacities, just as an infestation of crickets and a
renewed drought again created a state of food scarcity.[41] Meanwhile, in the South the SPLA launched renewed attacks which the
army was ill equipped to resist. In such dire straits Prime Minister

Sadiq al-Mahdi became desperate for any sort of help. But the only help which could take the shape of quick disbursements of cash, whether for purposes of peace or war, could come from Libya, and Libya kept insisting on its promised prize, Darfur. Sadiq then sent a government delegation to Tripoli on 23 October, and when no results were forthcoming went there himself on 13 November begging. By then everybody admitted that Darfur was another war, about which there were wildly diverging estimates of casualties: Governor al-Tijjani Sissi admitted to 500 deaths, the Fur said 30,000 and the reality was roughly 9,000 casualties in 1985–8. What made the violence different from that of the 2000s was that there was no specific counterinsurgency and that the killings were piecemeal, closer to the theory later developed by the Khartoum government of a "tribal conflict". This type of explanation had been somewhat closer to the truth in 1988 than in 2003, even if it was ultimately wrong in both cases. But in 1988 the instrumentalization of ethnicity was more limited, more amateurish. Nevertheless it was then that the word *janjaweed* was first coined, even if those early "evil horsemen" were less murderous than their later counterparts.

Meanwhile the "democratic" politics at the centre were showing increasing signs of strain. On 16 November 1988 Mohamed Osman al-Mirghani met John Garang in Addis Ababa and signed with him a preliminary memorandum for peace. Sadiq, alarmed at the popular support for this move, refused to accept it, arguing that it was "a party decision" which did not commit the government. The NIF supported Sadiq's refusal of any peace opening, and the DUP officially went into opposition in December. This created a new political space for the Darfuri trying to resist the Prime Minister's criminal neglect in the West, and the NIF parliamentarians elected in the province in 1986 publicly broke with their party to protest at Hassan al-Turabi's new silent acquiescence in the violence in their constituencies. Following their break they immediately joined the DUP.

Meanwhile Acheikh ibn Oumar had reconciled with Hissen Habre, and his 2,000 men, trapped in Darfur, wished to surrender to the regular Chadian forces. To stop that from happening the Libyans manipulated a group of Hadjarai tribesmen into attacking them in December 1988 and the FANT crossed the border into Darfur to help the beleaguered CDR; 122 fighters and an unknown number of civilians were killed in the ensuing battle.[42] Clashes multiplied in an increasingly confused atmosphere; ninety-six people were killed on 15 February 1989 and another forty on the 17th, nobody knowing precisely any more who was fighting whom. The only certainty was that the army was not part of the conflict because it could hardly hold its own in the South and it had no desire to skirmish with Libyan or Libyan-supported forces in Darfur. Washington had given forty-five Hummer light armoured vehicles to the Sudanese Army "to secure the Darfur border against Libyan incursions", a strange idea since the Libyans were inside. But the army was so desperate for equipment that the Hummers soon found their way to the south to fight the SPLA instead.[43] The situation was quickly reaching a point of global unmanageability. On 22 February Chief of Staff Major-General Fathi Ahmed Ali gave Sadiq al-Mahdi an ultimatum to accept the recent Peace Memorandum signed in Ethiopia by the DUP; otherwise the army "would feel authorized to take the measures necessary to safeguard national unity". The countdown to some kind of a coup had begun[44] and since one of the coup-plotting groups was the NIF itself, Sadiq kicked it out of government on 25 March, calling back the moderate DUP. The situation had reached a point of utter confusion where turmoil at the centre was increased by the violence on the peripheries and vice versa.

Meanwhile Darfur was getting even further embroiled in the Chadian-Libyan-Sudanese triangular conundrum. During the night of 1–2 April 1989 two Zaghawa officers, Idris Deby and Hassan Djamouss, tried to kill Hissen Habre[45] but failed and fled to Adare.

Djamouss was captured by the FANT and later tortured to death but Deby was only wounded and managed to escape to Darfur.[46] There he could count on Libyan support because by then Darfur had fallen almost completely under Tripoli's control. Thus the specialized *Indian Ocean Newsletter* could write at the time:

The annexation of Darfur to Libya implies submitting the Negro-African tribes (particularly the Fur) and a takeover by the "Arab" tribes. This process of annexation is well on the way: Libyan currency is in use in Darfur, columns of Libyan trucks travel directly between Kufra and El-Fashir, governors in Darfur deal directly with Tripoli without referring to Khartoum and the province is awash with Libyan guns which are handed out to the nomads ... ... Young Fur think that peaceful protest is now useless and they are trying to get support from the SPLA.[47]

On 29 April Deby flew to Tripoli with Mubarak al-Fadl al-Mahdi to get help from Libya for what he saw as his next campaign against Habre.[48] Deby took with him information that was very valuable for the Libyan government because while with the FANT he had been in charge of liasing with Colonel Khalifa Haftar Abdul Gassim's National Front for the Salvation of Libya, the CIA-sponsored anti-Gaddafi outfit based in Chad.[49] Gaddafi was delighted and gave an all-out support to his new ally. In Darfur this translated itself into more war. Three thousand Missiriya tribesmen from Kordofan, attracted by Libyan money, crossed into Darfur to help their Rizzey-qat cousins, and fighting flared to such a point that the government had to admit to 453 deaths.[50] In fact there had been over 1,000, and sixty Libyan trucks then arrived in Kutum in early June to replenish the military supplies stored at Saaj en-Naam. But meanwhile the race between the DUP and the NIF over the peace process had come to a head in Khartoum. During the night of 30 June–1 July a small group of pro-NIF officers led by the lacklustre Colonel Omar Hassan al-Beshir overthrew the government before it could send another delegation to meet the SPLA in Ethiopia.[51]

Libya's "victory" in Chad, a new Darfur famine and the
Daud Bolad insurrection

In its early days the new Islamist regime had more serious concerns than Darfur. At the time it did not think that it could last more than a few weeks if it came out in the open as an avowedly radical Muslim regime, and it did all in its power to deceive the world regarding its true nature.[52] Some of the measures were comical such as when the coup-makers arrested their own leader Hassan al-Turabi and took him to the Kober jail: between July 1989 and January 1990 he was officially under arrest but he came out at night to attend political meetings and plan the new regime's strategy. Other measures were more sophisticated, such as when the NIF parliamentary fraction leader Ali Osman Mohamed Taha managed to co-opt superior officers who were nostalgic for the Nimeiry regime and to convince them that they would be key elements in the new government. To reinforce this deception Nimeiry's wife was asked to come to Khartoum, and she and her family were issued with new Sudanese passports. She was also allowed to repossess seized property, and several stalwarts of the "May regime" then in jail were freed. In Cairo the old dictator was fretting, ready to come back at any time, but he was not asked to do so even if the Egyptian Ambassador, who was in the pay of the NIF, kept deceiving his government about the true nature of the coup by writing reports where the Islamist officers were described as being merely "pious Muslims". The expression later became a byword for this whole period of Islamist deception, causing bitter laughter in Cairo political circles.

The "masked junta" was lucky over the Darfur issue. Quite independently of the Khartoum political class, the local tribal leaders had started their own process of traditional negotiations for peace making. This *mu'tamat at-tasaluh* (conference of reconciliation), which started in late May 1989, had several motivations. First, everyone was exhausted and there was a growing awareness that the clashes were largely being manufactured by Libya for its own (Chadian) interests. Then Hissen Habre had finally crossed the threshold of involvement and started delivering weapons to the Fur militia instead of simply carrying out hit-and-run raids across the border. The result had been the ultimate failure of the combined Missiriya-Rizzeyqat offensive of early May. The Fur had learned to dig trenches around the villages under attack and cavalry charges were broken up by automatic gunfire from protected positions. This contributed to a new willingness to negotiate on the part of the Arab tribes. The conference finally came to a result in early July, shortly after the Muslim Brothers' coup, and the new regime became the involuntary beneficiary of a process it had not initiated. Darfur slowly regained a modicum of precarious peace during the second half of 1989, leading the Khartoum junta quickly to forget about its very existence.

But the new regime was still in the same position concerning the South as Sadiq al-Mahdi had been, and nothing was solved. Thus Brigadier Tijani Adam at-Taher again found his way to Tripoli to beg for means of carrying on the war. Gaddafi did not refuse but his price was the same as before: the control of Darfur from where he intended to support a renewed Deby-led onslaught on Chad. The Islamist regime did not have much of a choice and by September clashes re-started in Darfur as the Libyans resumed their policy of arming Arab tribal militias. On 16 October Hissen Habre's FANT carried out another of its daring cross-border raids, hitting Deby's bases in Kabkabiya, Kutum and Zalingei.[53] Shortly after this Hissen Habre himself summed up the situation clearly: "Khartoum is quite incapable of controlling Darfur and it is unwilling to curb Tripoli's activities there since Libya supplies the regime with oil, weapons and money."[54] As if to emphasise the truth of this statement President Omar el-Beshir went to Tripoli and announced on 5 March 1990 "a total union with Libya which will be carried out within the next four years as a first step towards the full unity of the Arab world". Deby started again harassing the Chadian forces by carrying out raids on Tinay, Bahay and Iriba, and the FANT retaliated again by crossing the border and hitting him. There were over 600 casualties during late March and once more the Chadian-Libyan war merged into a Darfuri civil war as Libyan-supported "Arab" militias raided "African" villages. Villages were burnt and wells poisoned, using locally available stores of Aldrex-T pesticides. Government authorities showed a clear partiality against the "Africans", and many young Fur were detained in Shalla prison, a maximum-security hellhole.[55] Since Gaddafi felt that the new Islamist regime in Khartoum was somewhat dragging its feet over the promised "total union" Tripoli suddenly refused to deliver the 600,000 tons of fuel it still owed as per the July 1989 "Union Treaty". A docile Khartoum accepted to sign a new "final treaty of integration" which was supposed to lead to a merger between the two countries. Gaddafi delivered 100,000 tons of fuel as a kind of wedding gift, but the marriage remained unconsummated.

But even if the global "union" between the two countries continued to be a paper reality only, the Libyans kept behaving on the ground as if Darfur were definitively Libyan territory. There were constant cargo flights between Kufra and El-Fashir to re-supply Deby's forces and the cross-border fighting intensified. Deby was preparing for a final attack on Chad, and in September Hissen Habre mounted a large offensive to try to stave him off. Chadian forces invaded Darfur, occupying El-Geneina, Kutum and Zalingei. The Sudanese army ran away and more than 900 people were killed in ten days of fighting. This was to be the FANT's last hurrah. In early November Deby launched his final offensive and reached Biltine.[56] Hissen Habre made one last attempt to stop him on 24 November in the Djagaraba plain; this was a massive battle, with over 300 armed Toyota "technicals"[57] on each side. The FANT were crushed, losing 2,700 men killed, 220 Toyotas destroyed, and 1,025 men and over 5,000 individual weapons captured.[58] The next day Deby's forces reached Qoz Beida and On 1 December entered Ndjamena after a wild 1,500-km. dash across the whole of Chad. Hissen Habre, abandoned by his men, had crossed the river into Cameroon, and what Burr and Collins have called "Africa's thirty years war" finally came to an end. Deby fulfilled his promises and the CIA hastily evacuated Colonel Khalifa Haftar's 600 anti-Gaddafi commandos to Nigeria.[59] Meanwhile Darfur, Deby's now forgotten springboard, had been left in a state of total chaos.

Due to a combination of renewed drought, war destruction and poorly coordinated government policies,[60] Darfur was once more on the brink of starvation.[61] The government started by foolishly denying that there was any food emergency,[62] only to panic a few days later when the Finance Minister, Abd-er-Rahim Hamdi, admitted that the 1990 harvest had fallen to between 500,000 and one million tons short of expectations.[63] In fact the overall shortage was of 1.2 million tons, and barely 50% of the necessary relief was to be distributed during the crisis because of the political tensions between the Islamist regime and the West following Khartoum's support for Saddam Hussein during the Kuwait invasion crisis. The losses in the human lives were never properly chronicled.

But Colonel Garang had become aware of the possibilities that the Libyan loss of interest in Darfur and the province's state of polarized ethnicity opened for the SPLA. Even before Deby's final triumph, he had started to work with Hissen Habre to streamline and improve Chadian help for the Fur militia and to explore the avenues of an eventual collaboration with the Baggara tribes—an audacious exercise in bridge-building across the increasing cultural divide. In July 1991 Khartoum put the NIF activist al-Tayib "Sikha" in charge of Darfur and he tried, using a characteristically strong-arm approach, to regain control of the province. He launched a series of military operations on the Darfur-Kordofan border against "bandits" (in fact rebellious Missiriya groups)[64] and other operations against the Zaghawa and the Fur.[65] With the Libyan-Chadian disengagement, this was now becoming again a purely Sudanese problem. By mid-November Garang publicly claimed that the SPLA had occupied southern Darfur.[66]

Before going further into the nature of that exaggerated claim, we have to take a brief look as to why the SPLA leader had suddenly become so keen on Darfur. From the very beginning of the Southern rebellion in 1983 he had always fought for the concept of a united "New Sudan" in which a secular state would give all regions and ethnic groups equal social status, a share of the national wealth and political access. This was in strong opposition to the feelings of his rank-and-file troops who were much more interested in secession, plain and simple. But Garang felt that the secessionist objective had been one of the key reasons why the 1956–72 Anya-Nya war had failed to achieve a major geopolitical redistribution of cards in the global Sudanese national environment. Nevertheless it was difficult for him to keep implementing this unitary policy in the face of a continuous feeling in favour of secession. When Garang lost his major source of outside support with the collapse of the Mengistu regime[67] this difficulty in controlling his movement combined with ethnic tensions and disenchantment with his extremely autocratic style of leadership to give birth to a neo-secessionist group which rose against his authority in August 1991.[68] This, the so-called "Nasir group",[69] posed a major challenge to Garang who felt that he had to insist on his "unitary" credentials, first, to reassure the Muslim non-Arab population of Sudan; second, to try to appease the Arab League; third, to consolidate his standing with the UN, the OAU and other international elements; and, fourth, to please Washington. What better way than to intervene in Darfur in order to show that his "New Sudan" concept included the "liberation" of all the "marginalized areas" of the Sudan and not only in the South?

Garang soon announced that a certain Daud Bolad, a native of Darfur who had received military training in South Kordofan after joining the SPLA in 1990, led the SPLA force. Both President Beshir and al-Tayeb "Sikha" bluntly denied that there was anything like an attack in Southern Darfur.[70] Which they had good reason to do since Daud Bolad was quite well-known to them and his name was an embarrassment for the junta. Daud Bolad was an ethnic Fur who had been a long-standing member of the Islamist movement, a personal friend of al-Tayeb "Sikha" and a former Chairman of the Khartoum University Student Union. He had been arrested by Nimeiry's police in 1971 and severely tortured. When, later, he was freed from gaol he had maintained high-profile militant activity and after graduating from University had moved back to Darfur and become a small businessman there. But he had started to have second thoughts about his militant engagement in 1988 when Hassan al-Turabi's entry into the "Islamic Trend cabinet" suddenly silenced all the NIF criticism of the Libyan-sponsored mayhem in Darfur. Another element of his disenchantment was the repeated element of anti-African racism that he found in Northern society, including the ranks of the Islamist movement. He had deeply believed that, as the Koran says, all men are equal in the eyes of God once they have fully taken part in the Muslim *umma*. But his daily practice of life in the Islamist movement had showed him that reality was different and that "even when I go to the mosque to pray, even there, in the presence of God, for them I am still a slave [*abd*] and they will assign me a place related to my race"[71]. Deeply disappointed, he had gone to Chad in 1989 hoping to get support from Hissen Habre to start a guerrilla movement in Darfur. When he failed to get that support, he went to Ethiopia to meet John Garang and he joined the SPLA.

But the whole of his "invasion" of Southern Darfur in late 1991 was ill-planned and ill-executed.[72] Very little had been done in the way of advance preparations, and Abd-el-Aziz al-Hilew, whom Garang had made responsible for helping Bolad, did not receive enough equipment. Bolad's fighters were Dinka, who were perceived in Darfur as foreigners. The provincial Mahdist networks, the only well-organized opposition in Darfur, did not look kindly upon this new political competition, and Governor al-Tayeb "Sikha" was a ruthless and efficient opponent. Daud Bolad ended up being betrayed by the Mahdists to the police, and his small military force was easily overwhelmed. One element which contributed to make the Bolad episode even more bitter for Darfuri was the fact that the government, being short of troops, used Arab *Murahleen* militiamen to hunt him down, thereby practically confirming the pertinence of his racial analysis. He was captured and taken to Khartoum, where he was tortured to death in January 1992.

The failure of Daud Bolad's insurrection, coupled with the end of the Chadian war and the subsequent decline of the Libyan presence in Darfur, ushered in a period of apparent calm in the province. This was deceptive because nothing had been solved in depth, but on the surface things had slowed down. It was not exactly peace, but it was no longer open war—just a state of diffuse insecurity where villages would be attacked once in a while, where trucks travelling to and from the markets were liable to get ambushed but where long periods of calm would give the impression that things were basically all right and that all this was simply an expression of some kind of "traditional" or "tribal" violence. For the government it was all due to "bandits", an explanation obviously insufficient but not without some element of truth given the number of guns floating around and the massive poverty.[73]

There remained only one part of the province which was not "pacified", Dar Masalit in the Northwest. The problem there had started with the February 1994 reform modifying federalism.[74] Sudan had been a federal state since February 1991, at least in theory, but the central government had kept juggling gubernatorial nominees and state boundaries as it saw fit. In February 1994 the new Minister for Federal Affairs Ali al-Hajj decided to change the administrative divisions completely, dividing all nine existing states (except Khartoum) into three to give birth to twenty-six new states. He also re-established the old tribal administration (*al-Idara al-Ahliyya*) which Nimeiry had abolished in 1971. The idea was for the NIF to rely on the traditional tribal chiefs in order to undercut the local influence of the Umma and the DUP. The result was extreme confusion. The government kept nominating the local Governors but asked them to bring their states to a situation of financial autonomy[75]. As a result the Governors who did not have a sufficient tax-base to achieve financial autonomy had no authority, while those who could mobilize the necessary funds from the centre due to their political connections turned into *de facto* local tyrants. In early 1995 the West Darfur Governor Mohamed Ahmed Fadl had restructured the local "tribal administration", in fact filling most of the new positions with *awlad al-beled* friends and relatives brought from Khartoum or with local Arabs, particularly members of the Jallul tribe. The Masalit protested against the marginalization of their community in the name of tribal administration, and Mohamed Ahmed Fadl was replaced by General Hassan Hamadein who put the area under *de facto* military rule, arresting all those who protested. As a result the period 1996–8 saw the development of a low-intensity guerrilla movement against the government. This culminated in January 1999 when clashes between Masalit and Arab herders were taken by the government as "constituting a fifth column in Western Sudan in league with the anti-government rebels [SPLA]". Khartoum sent troops and combat helicopters to Dar Masalit, killing 2,000 in a few days, internally displacing almost 100,000 and forcing 40,000 to flee into Chad[76]. Northwest Darfur was temporarily subdued, but nothing was solved.

Centre versus Periphery: Darfur in a global Sudanese perspective

It is a cliché that Sudan is a complex country, and the problem with clichés is the element of truth which gave rise to them in the first place. During the colonial period the British considered the Sudan to be basically a Middle-Eastern country with an "African" append-age which was of little consequence. The "Arabs" in Sudan fully shared that view and looked at the South as a backward place where Christian missionaries had unfortunately been allowed to operate. This had pitted against the natural northern élite savages who would have been better off if they had been integrated (at an appropriate level) within the Arabo-Islamic cultural and religious sphere.[77] As for the non-Arab Muslim people, they were almost never con-sidered to be any kind of a "unit". One of the reasons was their extreme diversity. From the eastern Beja to the western Fur and Masalit, by way of the various partly or completely Islamized tribes who had much, little or no "Arab" blood, there was a bewildering array of people who were neither "Northerners" nor "South-erners". They could be the objects of anthropological literature but they were extremely unlikely ever to be considered the subject of political analysis. Another reason was that Islam acted as a kind of "false consciousness" (*falsches Bewustsein*, if one wants to use the Freudian-Marxist vocabulary of the 1960s), which for many years systematically prevented the Muslim (or Islamized) populations from achieving any kind of separate self-consciousness. Being a Muslim meant being "Arabized", at least to some extent, and the almost sacred place of the Arabic language as *lughat Allah*, the language of God, played an enormous role. Therefore the "Arabs", whatever that meant,[78] remained at the Centre of the imaginary landscape of the Sudanese Muslims. There was of course a core material reason for this continued pre-eminence of the *awlad al-beled*:[79] 80% of all that mattered, from doctors to banks and from university graduates to pharmacies, has been concentrated in the

Central Province and in the Northern part of Blue Nile—a trend only reinforced by the growing importance of oil money in the country since 1999. With its 7 million population and obvious prosperity in the face of an otherwise stagnating land, Khartoum has evolved into a kind of separate country. When Darfur militants came out with the *kitab al-aswad* ("Black Book") in 2000,[80] it said nothing to the average Northern Sudanese that they did not know already. What created a shock were not the contents of the book but simply the fact that an unspoken taboo had been broken and that somebody (obviously not a *walad al-beled*) had dared to put into print what everybody knew but did not want to talk about.

Many authors have seen the North-South dichotomy in the Sudan as the core problem of the country. In a way it is, but not essentially so. In other words the North and the South are most opposed because they lie at the furthest ends of a continuum which is already massively variegated before you reach its extremities. There are several consequences in viewing the Sudanese "war of visions"[81] in such a light. First, it implies a refusal of essentialism. "Arabs" and "Black Africans" are not at each other's throats because they are like cats and dogs but rather because, for the "Arabs" at least, they are not completely sure of what and who they are. In the Sudan they are "Arabs", but in the Arab world they are seen as mongrels who hardly deserve that name. They desperately strive for recognition of their "Arab" status by other Arabs, who tend to look down upon them—even using for them the dreaded name of *abd* (slave) that they use for those more black than they are. In many ways "Arab" society in the Sudan resembles the Creole societies of the Caribbean. There is a lot of good humour and light banter across the fantasized colour line, there is sex but seldom marriage, and there is a cast-iron social and economic hierarchy which can easily be denied by using the examples of those who have "passed" and enjoy a social status superior to that to which their birth should have limited them. And above all there is a massive amount of hypocrisy which enables everyone to deny the obvious and pretend that "We are all brothers". The fact that this brotherhood is a sham is laid bare by the matrimonial practices which not only completely seal off North from South and Christian or animist from Muslim but also submit the non-"Arab" Muslims of the various peripheries to severe tests concerning their ancestry in order to avoid sullying one's family line with "slave blood".[82]

None of the so-called "parts" of the Sudan is homogeneous. Almost all observers are aware of this as far as the South is concerned because the great variety of tribes there reproduces a common "African" pattern. But for a long time the "North" was assumed to be relatively homogenous, probably because its Islamic character tended to obscure its considerable ethnic and cultural diversity. Anthropologists did recognize that the Beja tribes in the East were indeed a rather distinct entity, even if their specificity tended to be played down. But the rest of "the North" was more or less assumed to be one. If superficially considered, the country's history since the 1821 Turco-Egyptian occupation tended to reinforce that feeling. "The North" had experienced the same *Turkiyya* regime, the same Mahdiyya dissidence, the same stance facing the British re-conquest. That Darfur had not been included in "the North" before 1916 tended to be overlooked because of its previous involvement in the history of the *Turkiyya* and the Mahdiyya. This made Darfur a perfect example of the danger of considering "the North" as a coherent entity; economically it was a periphery at least as marginalized as "the South". And by any criterion chosen, Islam and belonging to "the North" failed to bring any kind of concrete advantage to Sudan's westernmost province. But its "Islamic false consciousness" did not prevent Darfur from paying the highest price in terms of supplying soldiers for the various wars of "the North" in the South, during both 1955–72 and 1983–2002. The mechanics,

both social and cultural, which drove Darfur to play a dispropor-
tional role in fighting Southerners to protect northern *awlad al-beled*
interests are typical of the province's marginality. First of all was
the false claim by the riverine Arabs that "we are one" and that
therefore the Darfuri had to stand up for the "common" interests of
the imagined community. Then there was the reality of the riverine
Arabs perceiving the *awlad al-gharb* as inferior. Muslims yes, but
second-rate ones. This situation is not special to Sudan, and dom-
inated social groups often pay a disproportionate price when used
in a "national" war by their socially dominant co-nationals.[83] The
Darfuri played along with this Muslim false consciousness *vis-à-vis*
the South for over forty years. As we see in the next chapter, it was
largely the changes in the diplomatic North-South relationship
which finally worked as an eye-opener for the young people of the
West and drove them to take up arms.

The final and tragic dimension which would lead to the particular form of violence experienced in Darfur since 2003 was the
ethnic consciousness split. In terms of brutal economic reality
Darfur's discrimination was regional and global, not ethnic, racial
and cultural. But as the preceding pages show, this reality was dif-
fracted by the prism of political manipulation. There were two
levels of political manipulation: one was the political stance taken
by the various ethnic groups during Sudan's wider conflicts (i.e. for
or against the Mahdists, for or against the Nimeiry regime); and the
other was the position into which each wider group, "Arab" or
"African", found itself forced by the Libyan intervention in the Chad
conflict. Both levels were arbitrarily determined by non-Darfuri,
but given the extreme economic poverty of the province, outside
actors, whether from Khartoum or from Tripoli, could quite easily
manipulate an economically deprived population into supporting
them for real or hoped-for economic benefits. The Darfuri thus
ended up in a situation of double alienation: first they were per-

suaded by their *awlad el-balad* masters that as good Muslims they had to fight the *kufar*, and then they were persuaded by the same people and by the rich Libyans that they had to fight each other in the name of "progressive" Arabism versus "reactionary" Africanism. When these Cold War labels wore out in the late 1980s, they were readily replaced by "Arabist" cultural stereotypes fitting the same delimitations. This led to the paradox of Darfur's "African" tribes being asked to fight in the South for the defence of an ideology in whose name they were killed at home.

Thus reaction to the alienation imposed by the political, economic and ideological Centre of the country to its periphery was bound to have a double aspect: against that Centre itself and, unfortunately, against the ethnic groups locally perceived as supporting that Centre's oppression. In turn it was not going to be difficult for the Centre to mobilize what we earlier called the "native Arab" tribes for the defence of the Centre's interests, even though the "native Arabs" were themselves in an economic and political situation not much better than the people they were going to be encouraged to kill.

4

FEAR AT THE CENTRE

FROM COUNTER-INSURGENCY TO QUASI-GENOCIDE
(2003–2005)

Darfur in the late 1990s was an increasingly marginalized, violent and frustrated place. But its woes remained far from the national consciousness at the Centre and far from government preoccupation, even if complex political agendas kept lingering in the shadows. Northern Sudanese public opinion and its government, for once in agreement, saw as their main international problem the achievement of a peace deal with the South. And the regime's main internal concern was not the distant and troubled West but rather the power struggle developing within its own ranks. Little did it realize that the two would soon violently merge.

Centre versus Centre: the Islamists' internal quarrels and their spillover into Darfur

On 12 December 1999 the proclamation by President Omar el-Beshir of a national state of emergency forced Hassan al-Turabi, the Sudanese Islamist Revolution's "Guide", to resign from his position as president of the Parliament. In fact this was a "soft coup" and tanks were out in the streets in case the "Guide" would have tried to resist.[1] Parliament was dissolved and on 1 January 2000 the whole

GoS cabinet "resigned". A new law called "Law for Political Parties and Organizations" soon replaced the Turabi-inspired "Political Associations Act"[2] and Turabi was reduced (apparently) to crotchety impotence. What had happened?

In order to understand it we have to both look into Turabi's personality and go back into the history of the Islamist movement in the Sudan. Hassan al-Turabi, highly educated, intellectually brilliant and a master political tactician, is also an extremely authoritarian personality, deeply persuaded that he is always right and that he knows what is the right path for his movement. This in turn nurtures an inordinate taste and surprising capacity for tactical twists and turns, resulting in the most unprincipled forms of *tahaaluf* (temporary alliances). In the words of a specialist, "Turabi's interpretation of Islamist ideology has enabled him to stretch pragmatism to its utmost limits."[3] When he came back to the Sudan in 1964 after the overthrow of Abboud's dictatorship, he found an Islamist organization which had suffered greatly and prided itself on its unrelenting courage and ideological purity. This did not lend itself to his style of politics and he proceeded relentlessly to reorganize the Muslim Brotherhood and turn it into the obedient tool which would not question the practical *tahaaluf* strategy he favoured. All the "historical" leaders of the *ikhwaan al-Muslimin* (Rashid at-Taher, Sadiq Abd-el-Majid, Mahmood Burrat) were eliminated in a series of quick and clever bureaucratic moves which left Turabi the unchallenged leader in complete control of the organization. When Nimeiry carried out his coup in May 1969, Turabi at first went to jail but later accepted the dictator's offer of reconciliation in 1977. Since many in his party did not, he carried out another purge with the aid of his ally Interior Minister Ahmed Abder-Rahman; and when the purge was completed he got Nimeiry to eliminate Ahmed Abd-er-Rahman.

The beneficiaries of these organizational hecatombs were bright young men[4] who were going to have long and adventurous careers.

Having fought against democracy, Communism, the Nimeiry regime, their own colleagues and the sectarian *turuq*-based parties since the 1960s, they finally achieved power in June 1989 and set out to enjoy the fruits of their efforts. But the men who had come to power (and who are still at the core of the present GoS) were no longer the thirty-something ambitious radicals of the 1960s and 1970s. They had become a staid establishment, a new *tariqa* eager for power, money and comfort. For the ordinary people of Sudan they had become *tujjar ad-din*, "merchants of religion"; and they knew from experience their leader's capacity for deadly manipulation. But for Hassan al-Turabi they remained mere boys, even if they were in their fifties and sixties, boys who could be told what to do. Omar el-Beshir had been picked as President because of the limitations which made him an excellent figurehead, able to man an empty political centre where the various factions of the movement would cancel each other out. But the understanding was that the "Guide" would always retain the last word. By the late 1990s it had become obvious that this arrangement was coming under increasing strain and Turabi began to prepare for another political purge.[5] But the circumstances were not those of thirty years before, and the "young men" he was planning to unseat were now in positions of power with money, the control of organizational apparatuses and minds of their own, who realized that in many ways the old man was an international liability for them since his name was identified with the most radical and aggressive policies of the Islamist regime. His political demise might open the way for a new course of *détente* on which they were particularly keen since Sudan was now entering the select club of international oil producers[6] and would need a modicum of international respectability. So the generation of the former young men refused to put their heads meekly on the block, and the power struggle was on.

The December 1999 "soft coup" was the outcome of this power struggle and it looked as if Turabi had lost. In fact this was only the first battle and the old leader still had many trumps to play. First he and his faithful ones had the signatures on a number of well-garnered foreign bank accounts which would have made his physical elimination quite expensive.[7] Then he had influence among the *quwaat ad-difaa ash-shabiya* militias which, even if they could not really confront the regular army, meant that he still had a military nuisance value. And finally, given his prestige and charismatic personality, he retained the loyalty of a majority of the provincial branches of the Party. This enabled him to reach out into rural constituencies where the predominantly city-based regular Party cadres found exerting influence difficult. And among those regions where he retained a fair degree of influence, there was Darfur. The conflict then began to change shape.

In May President Beshir, now more than ever the consensual leader of the Party's centre, suspended the Mutammar al-Watani's National Secretariat and closed down the party's secretarial offices in the twenty-six states. Turabi, who saw that his bureaucratic tentacles were being cut, was furious and declared that "all the possibilities exist, including those of an armed confrontation"[8]. Six weeks later, having been formally dismissed from his position as Secretary General of the Congress Party, he launched his own political party, the Mutammar al-Watani ash-Shabiyi (Popular Patriotic Congress). The name was well chosen: it mirrored that of the Government's party, adding only "popular", which implied that this was what the government's party was not. The situation was getting paradoxical. Bona Malwal, veteran Southern politician once a minister under Nimeiry, journalist and long-time political opponent, could write that "for all practical purposes Turabi now plays the opposition role."[9] Turabi moved ever further along the road to denouncing what he had formerly supported, declaring at a political rally in Omdurman that the Southerners were right to have taken up arms against Khartoum because they had been wronged.

Some observers who lacked imagination and did not realize how far Turabi's *tahaaluf* could go, began to say that he was "on a politically suicidal course"[10]. Other observers simply began to notice that most of his close aides and the cadres of the new *shabiyi* party were from the West, mostly from Darfur. A mysterious *kitab al-aswad* ("Black Book") was published, without the name of the author, the place of publication or a copyright notice, detailing the monopoly of power enjoyed by the riverine Arab tribes at the expense of the rest of the country, particularly the west which did not enjoy a level of political representation anywhere near what its 32.6% of the population allowed it to expect. September and October 2000 were marked by a series of riots in which Turabi's partisans tested the ground to assess the feasibility of an *intifada* (popular insurrection) on the 1964 and 1985 model. The conclusions were negative and they withdrew into their protective organisational shells. Then the unbelievable happened: on 19 February 2001 representatives of the Mutammar al-Watani ash-Shabiyi signed in Geneva a "Memorandum of Understanding" with the SPLA, programming their coordination in fighting the GoS. The language was that of "peaceful political struggle", but the conclusions were obvious: the two opposite extremes of the Sudanese political spectrum were now going to unite their very different forces to overthrow the Khartoum government. The reaction was quick. On 21 February Hassan al-Turabi was accused of "conspiracy and subversion" and arrested, although his party was allowed to continue operating.[11] But the GoS did not have a serious case against its former leader and in addition felt that given its political minority position in the country, a violent and open fight might be foolish. In October the "legal case" against Turabi and his party was dropped but he was kept under "precautionary detention". The GoS was still hoping to regain control of its disjointed pieces and in a typical carrot-and-stick operation the PPC Acting Secretary General, Abdallah Hassan

Ahmad, was arrested in October while Turabi himself was released from jail into house arrest in November. But on 11 December the regime decided nevertheless to extend the state of emergency for another six months. It was right not to feel secure.

For Turabi this was a fight to the death and signing a document of political alliance with his old Southern guerrilla opponents was a clever bit of *tahaaluf*. But as long as the SPLA kept an army in the field and he did not have one, Turabi would remain the junior partner in the new anti-government alliance. He therefore needed his own armed branch and this was just what Darfur could provide for him. It would definitely be a mistake to think that Turabi caused the Darfur insurgency. As we have seen, the historical roots of Darfurian feelings of alienation and marginalization stretch back to the Mahdiyya and to the Condominium periods. Independence had brought no improvement to the status of the province, and democratic politics had played havoc with the supposed ballot-box influence of the Westerners. Chadian problems dovetailing into Libyan subversion and Sadiq al-Mahdi's irresponsible politics had completed a picture of social, political and finally military rejection by the centre. Since 1985 Darfur had been a time-bomb waiting for a fuse.

Turabi was fully aware of this state of affairs. In 1985 he had been at the forefront of those denouncing the presence of *failaka al-Islamiya* forces in Darfur as representing a dangerous factor of destabilization, even if his indignation had been largely tactical. NIF implantation in Darfur was then only slight. But after 1989 the Islamist regime had worked from a position of strength and had achieved a certain amount of recruitment since joining it could open the way for careers at various levels. This recruitment was tribally uneven. It achieved some success among the Zaghawa and the Ma'aliya, but the Mahdist tradition among the Baggara made them hard to penetrate for political newcomers. As for the Fur, they could not accept NIF blandishments: for them the Islamists remained wedded to Arab supremacy, which they deeply distrusted. But now the time had come for Turabi to try to capitalize on his previous political investment. Frustrations in Darfur were such that since he had started fighting with his former friends, many who would previously have doubted him were now ready at least to collaborate with him. As we see below, there was another quite different strand of Darfur oppositional politics, linked to a more secular approach. Both were going to rely on SPLA collaboration, attempting again what Daud Bolad had failed to achieve earlier.

Immediately following the signing of the Geneva Memorandum of Understanding, *shabiyi* operatives had arranged to acquire weapons and transport them to Darfur, with the help of the Eritrean government and the SPLA.[12] Given the complicated logistics involved, the pre-positioning of the equipment took a long time.[13] The SPLA then tried to move into Darfur in force, launching an offensive from Bahr-el-Ghazal in June 2001. Its hope was to bring troops from the South which could support the impending insurrection. It managed to occupy Deym Zubeyr and Raja, causing over 30,000 IDPs, mostly Fertit, to flee on foot towards Nyala. But it did not manage to reach Darfur itself and the offensive petered out at the border of the province. Memories of the failed Daud Bolad uprising were still burning. The GoS then recaptured all the lost ground during September–October and its vengeance was brutal. By early November Khartoum had unleashed the *Murahleen* on northern Bahr-el-Ghazal, causing a new movement of IDPs, this time southward, towards Wau and Tombura. With thousands of civilians fleeing a murderous combination of aerial attacks and militia raiding, and with the SPLA calling for a "no-fly zone", the situation was a model on a smaller scale model for what would develop two years later in Darfur.

The government had been scared and the repression which followed was accompanied by indiscriminate attacks on civilians.

The simmering Masalit insurgency was now seen in Khartoum as increasingly dangerous. In early April 2002, at Shoba in Northern Darfur, "Arab" raiders burnt 600 houses, killed seventeen people, wounded scores of others and stole 2,000 heads of cattle. In August there had been clashes in Golu as the Fur had attacked the local police station to recover the guns the police had confiscated from them. Khartoum accused the Masalit of being in league with the Fur over the guns,[14] and seventy Fur notables, mostly lawyers, teachers, sheikhs and *sharti*, were arrested. Among them was Abd-el-Wahab Mohamed Nur, a thirty-seven-year-old lawyer who would later become the first Secretary General of the Sudan Liberation Movement (SLM) and who was held for months in an insanitary cell with twenty-five other detainees, none of whom had been formally charged. It was in that heavy atmosphere that Turabi's weapons were slowly hauled into place.

Naivasha[15] *and the "feel good factor"*

In order to understand the international context in which the coming Darfur insurrection was to develop, we must first look back at the prevailing atmosphere then surrounding the Sudan, which at the beginning of the 2000s hopeful if cautious. Oil began to flow in August 1999, and the first Sudan peace talks had started in Nairobi in January 2000.[16] Common sense appeared at long last to be prevailing, an impression reinforced by Turabi's arrest in February 2001. The event was interpreted abroad not as an internal power struggle within a homogeneous political group but rather (and this view was strongly supported by the winning faction in the GoS) as a move to purge an extremist element. The Islamist core succeeded in "selling" the elimination of its old leader as a fundamental change of political course, while infact it was at best a tactical adaptation. The regime began to be regarded as, if not yet "moderate", at least on its way towards a more moderate dispensation.[17] The "young men" had learnt the art of *tahaaluf* from their old master and used it to whitewash many abuses, such as those that followed the failed SPLA offensive in Bahr-el-Ghazal.

Paradoxically the September 11 2001 al-Qaida suicide attack on New York further improved the international community's view of Sudan. In the months following September 11 President Bush was sorely in need of "good Arabs", and Khartoum was quick to understand that for a born-again Christian president a repented sinner would be more valuable than a routine ally. In addition US diplomacy was thrown into confusion when it became known that in 1996, before Osama Bin Laden left the country to go back to Afghanistan, Khartoum had offered to deport him to Washington. Suddenly, in a world growing increasingly manichean, the "young men" in Khartoum looked like "good guys" and the Clinton adminis-tration like bunglers.[18] President Bush and his aides quickly saw the benefits, both practical and ideological, to be derived from a change of policy towards the Sudan, and Washington began collaborating closely with Khartoum on the issue of terrorism. At the same time President Bush developed a policy of supporting a negotiated set-tlement of the North-South conflict in order not to alienate his Christian fundamentalist electorate which felt quite strongly about the civil war in the Sudan. Naivasha began to turn into a strange theatre where the actors appeared driven to compromise more by American pressure than by any inner conviction that peace should actually be negotiated.[19] Everybody progressively got into the act (Norway, Britain, President Kibaki of Kenya, USAID, and even the president of the French Parliament's Committee on Foreign Affairs, who seemed a bit lost). This caused the GoS and the SPLA to sign several agreements concerning particular topics: first, the Macha-kos Protocol (June 2002), defining the duration of an interim pe-riod for the future transitional government (six years, after a "pre-interim" period of six months) following which there would be a referendum on the question of Southern independence; second, an Agreement on the ending of hostilities (October 2002); and third, a "Memorandum of Understanding" (November 2002) which outlined in very broad terms the principles which would govern the relationship between GoS and SPLA civil servants during the interim period. Although none of these documents constituted the "global peace" everybody kept hoping for, they looked like prudent and constructive steps towards it. Some observers felt that the whole process was on the contrary a form of systematic procrastination by the GoS and that Khartoum was only trying to buy time.[20] But in the atmosphere of increasing optimism such views were generally discounted. This allowed the Darfur question to be at first considered a secondary matter, an unseemly blemish on an otherwise encouraging picture. Actually it was not till the spring of 2004, when the situation had degenerated into catastrophe, that the international community began to take serious notice. The term "ethnic cleansing" had appeared in the media only in late 2003,[21] and when Jan Egeland, then head of UN Emergency Relief Coordination, had declared (8 December 2003) that "the humanitarian situation in Darfur has quickly become one of the worst in the world", his anguished appeal had fallen mostly on deaf ears. The whole of 2003 and of early 2004, when the usual violence of the GoS progressively metamorphosed into a quasi-genocide, were lost months during which all eyes remained fixed on Naivasha. As casualties piled up and hundreds of thousands fled their incinerated villages in Darfur, the international media and the Western chanceries kept congratulating themselves on the "successful" development of the North-South talks, chronicling each new paper advance on the diplomatic front as if it were a great victory for peace. A Security Agreement had been signed in November 2003, broadly outlining the position of the GoS and SPLA forces during the interim period;[22] a Wealth-Sharing Agreement had followed in January 2004; and finally a Power-Sharing Agreement had been signed in May 2004. The best description of the prevailing mood at the time was probably given by professor Michael Kevane of the Economics Department of the University of California: "There is a giddiness in the air about the profits and careers to be made from a Peace Agreement in Sudan. This giddiness is leading to mass wilful blindness: never mind what the various Agreements actually say, just sign the damn things."[23] By then Darfur was in flames, up to 80,000 people had probably been killed, there were over 100,000 refugees in Chad and more than a million IDPs. The world then suddenly seemed to wake up to the fact that all was not well in the Sudan, even if the agreement-signing machine in Naivasha seemed ready to keep on churning new documents for many more months to come.[24] In May 2004 the Managing Committee of the Washington Holocaust Memorial had been the first to dare utter what some authors call "the big G-word", "genocide", and on 24 June members of the US House of Representatives had also used the term. But it was very late indeed if one considered the what had taken place on the ground in the mean time.

Khartoum wakes up to the danger

While the Naivasha show continued to attracting all the attention of the international community, the situation in Darfur was quietly sinking to its point of no return. The GoS could feel that this was happening, but its main preoccupation was with the South and the danger of US threats, not with domestic matters in the West. Nevertheless, Ali Osman Mohamed Taha, the regime's strongman, was getting worried and he visited Darfur in early November 2002. He gave a well-attended public speech in which he warned his audience "not to repeat in your area the colonial error which has paralysed

Southern Sudan."[25] In what appeared to be a *non sequitur* but which was in fact perfectly coherent, he added that the government would "build one hundred kilometres of good roads"[26] and "multiply by three the budget for water connection". But it had all been said before and nobody was much impressed. Seven weeks later "bandits" killed eleven policemen in South Darfur.[27] The fighting had picked up and was not going to stop.

At mid-January twenty-four people were killed and nineteen wounded in confused clashes at the Chadian border. Nobody understood clearly what had happened, but the trans-border character of the violence was enough to prompt a meeting between the Chadian Prime Minister and Mubarak al-Fadl al-Mahdi.[28] But on 26 February a group of about 300 men supported by thirty "technicals"[29] attacked the small town of Golu, killing nearly 200 soldiers and forcing the garrison to flee. "We heard the word 'insurrection' used for the first time and so the Sudanese people knew that what was now running in Darfur was not simply armed looting or an action of the road-cutters, as the government alleged."[30] The government understood very well what had happened, but it was taken by surprise—not because Darfur had been peaceful. On the contrary, a certain "acceptable" level of violence in the Western province had been routine, and nobody was very worried by "normal" killings. But 300 men and their technicals—this was a level of organization which was new. Almost immediately the Government sent a mission to Darfur "to negotiate with the new armed group from Jebel Marra",[31] implicitly disowning the version it would later try to sell to the international community, namely that the troubles out West were due either to "bandits" or to "ethnic fighting" or both. True, the mission was only headed by the President of Parliament's Transport Committee, Idris Yusuf, a choice which showed that the government still thought it could get away with promising a few more "hundred kilometres of good roads" to people it felt were backward peasants. In Nairobi Ahmed Dirdeiry, the usual GoS spokesman for Naivasha, immediately declared that "these people are not rebels but bandits", hurriedly adding: "It will not jeopardise the peace process".[32] The GoS declared that nobody had ever taken Golu and both Amnesty International and Sadiq al-Mahdi asked for a Commission of Inquiry. The government gave "the new armed group from Jebel Marra" an ultimatum to surrender within ten days or suffer the consequences while Adam Hamid Musa, Governor of South Darfur State, added: "If dialogue does not work in Darfur, the Army can solve the situation in twenty-four hours."[33] On 5 March Khalil Ibrahim, an Islamist militant who had been Minister of Education for Darfur Province in the 1990s, and self-proclaimed author of "the Black Book" (see above, page 85), claimed from London the credit for having initiated the revolt in the name of a hitherto unknown Justice and Equality Movement (JEM).[34] The SLA ridiculed his claim of military victory in Golu and the JEM later scaled down its position, only saying that it operated "in alliance with the SLA".

What were the facts behind these claims and counter-claims? As we have seen, the Turabi faction of the Mutammar had planned the insurrection since perhaps late 2000 or at least early 2001 and it had acted in cooperation with the SPLA. But since it had to rely on its limited recruitment in Darfur (essentially a section of the Zaghawa,[35] where the Islamist movement had been active since the 1960s) its forces were small. The SLA had different origins. It derived directly from the Fur self-defence militias created in 1988–9 to fight both the Failaka al-Islamiya and the Darfur "Arab" tribal militias. After the peace conference of June 1989 they had agreed to disband but in fact had only gone underground, almost literally so because they often buried their best guns and only handed over their old ones to the police. The police, who were mostly recruited among the "African" tribes, tended to look the other way. By late

2001, after the failure of the SPLA offensive from Bahr-el-Ghazal, it had become clear to a number of their leaders that sooner or later there would be a major confrontation between Darfur and the Khartoum government. They had then begun a dual process, both encouraging desertions from the many Fur soldiers and especially NCOs garrisoned in the South and sending young recruits to be trained by the SPLA at a camp in northern Bahr-el-Ghazal. Unlike the future members of JEM, their outlook was resolutely secular and they had no difficulty in recruiting, given their broad tribal base. One of the SPLA officers supervising the operation was none other than Commander Abd-el-Azziz al-Hilew, the veteran Masalit chief of the failed Daud Bolad uprising.

The "alliance" with the future JEM was mostly at the financial and logistical level where SLM was weakest. Young jobless high school graduates and high school dropouts were the main source of recruitment for both organizations. The extreme youth of the soldiers in the rebel movements had several consequences: first there was no need to recruit child soldiers;[36] second it was semi-educated, thus making abuses against civilians less likely; and finally it had little respect for the traditional tribal authorities that had administered Darfur for so long. This was noted in one of the best reports on the Darfur crisis:

The generational dimension of the rebellion's core has escaped the notice of analysts and the government's strategist alike. The government continues to manipulate traditional tribal leaders in its search for ways to weaken the rebellion but the young rebels do not appear to trust these leaders and at time have abducted, attacked or evicted them from areas under their control. They consider that the successive governments have used them to perpetuate the hegemony of the northern and central elites to keep Darfur and other peripheral regions marginalized.[37]

The other side of that situation was that the two movements sorely lacked fully educated cadres. Given its secular outlook the SLM attracted a number of anti-Khartoum dissidents like Sharif Harir,[38] but both movements remained "bottom-up" rather than "top-down", a characteristic which both made them genuinely representative of the people and gave rise to their often clumsy attitudes when it came to negotiating.

The government was thoroughly confused about what to do. In early March it sent Governor Ibrahim Mohamed Suleiman, head of an *ad hoc* Darfur Security Committee, to negotiate with Khalil Ibrahim in London. The Governor came back empty-handed.[39] In June there was a second attempt when Minister of Education Ahmed Babiker Nahar and Nile State Governor Abdallah Ali Masar approached the rebels with a view to negotiating a settlement. Babiker Nahar is a Zaghawa and Ali Masar a Rizzeyqat Arab, and both belonged to the "Reformed Umma" of Mubarak al-Fadl al-Mahdi. As Darfurians and old Mahdists both could see beyond the frantic rhetoric of the Mutammar and both realized that this time serious social and economic grievances had to be addressed.[40] The SLA told them it had twelve demands, the first of which was to stop being called "armed bandits" and to have their political status recognized.[41] Mubarak al-Fadl was furious at being by passed by two of his subordinates and he used his better access to Beshir to undercut them.[42] Then in August 2003 he fired the Darfuri who had acted independently. Many other Westerners in the Reformed Umma did not appreciate and resigned, something which considerably weakened the party and destroyed its capacity to act as an intermediary between the government and the rebels.

On the ground the rebels showed that they meant business. On 25 April they had attacked both Nyala and El-Fashir in a coordinated operation. Fashir was the biggest target:[43] they killed thirty government soldiers and two officers, occupied the airport, blew up two Antonov An-12 "transport bombers" and three Mil Mi-17 combat helicopters, and captured Brigadier Ibrahim Bushra Ismail, the air force base commander. According to US sources they also executed around 200 army prisoners after they had surrendered in what seems to have been one of the rare rebel atrocities of the war.[44] In late May they killed in combat almost 500 GOS soldiers near Kutum, in July they attacked Tinay again killing nearly 250 of the enemy, and on 1 August they managed to take Kutum and kill a large part of its garrison.

After the El-Fashir attack it had become plain to all who had some experience of the situation that things were getting serious. 150 notables from Darfur residing in Khartoum[45] wrote a petition to president Omar el-Beshir. This requested the opening of political dialogue with the rebellion; a ceasefire; the freeing of Darfur political prisoners; the organization of humanitarian aid before the beginning of the rainy season; and an end to the growing practice of using irregular militias for the repression. In response the GoS declared a State of Emergency in Darfur and multiplied the arrests of people suspected of sympathizing with the rebellion. In late April and early May President Omar el-Beshir dissolved the old Committee on Darfur Security, which was considered "too soft", and assembled a Special Task Force on Darfur which regrouped a number of people he particularly trusted either for their Darfur experience or for their loyalty, preferably both: el-Tayeb Mohamed Khair "Sikha", who had been Darfur Governor at the time of the Daud Bolad insurgency and now a member of the President's staff; the Minister of Defence, Bakri Hassan Saleh, an original member of the 1989 *Inqaz* and notorious Army hardliner; Abd-er-Rahim Mohamed Hussein, Minister of the Interior, another well-known hardliner; Salah Abdallah and Abdallah Gosh, heads of two different Security outfits; Abdallah es-Safi an-Nur, former Governor of Darfur and director of the Military Engineering Office; and the governors of the Zalingei and Wadi Saleh provinces. The Governors of North and West Darfur states were fired and replaced by "energetic" successors. This was a combat team rather than one designed for negotiation.

The GoS had clearly decided on a military solution to the crisis, counting on being able to crush the insurrection fast enough for it to be over before the delicate process of bringing the SPLA into Khartoum could take place. But to do that it had to have the means at its disposal, and the army, largely made up of recruits and NCOs from Darfur, was not considered to be fully trustworthy—at least, not before the various units had been screened. During May 2003 the new Task Force began seriously to explore the possibilities of formalizing the government's relationship with the already existing *Janjaweed* militias.[46] As we saw above, these rough armed bands had existed since the late 1980s in an undeterminate zone half-way between being bandits and government thugs. At times tolerated, at times repressed by the authorities, their reference to "Arabism" guaranteed them a modicum of support from the riverine Arab administration. Now the question was how to bolster their fighting capacity as well as how to increase their numbers.[47] Contrary to what has often been written, these militia groups are no more a "popular" and "organic" expression of all the Arab tribes of Darfur than the dreaded Rwandese Interahamwe militiamen were a "natural" and "popular" expression of the Hutu of Rwanda. In both cases what we have are organized, politicised and militarised groups which, though recruited among people of a certain ethnic origin, do not "naturally" represent them. Sociologically the *Janjaweed* seem to have been of six main origins: former bandits and highwaymen who had been "in the trade", since the 1980s; demobilized soldiers from the regular army; young members of Arab tribes having a running land conflict with a neighbouring "African" group—most appeared to be members of the smaller Arab tribes;[48] common criminals who were pardoned and released from gaol if they joined the militia; fanatical members of the Tajammu al-Arabi; and young unemployed

"Arab" men, quite similar to those who joined the rebels on the "African" side.

The recruits were paid what amounted to a good salary in the economic circumstances of the region: $79 a month for a man on foot and $117 if he had a horse or a camel. Officers—i.e. those who could read or who were tribal *amir*—could get as much as $233. The weapons were provided in the camps that started to open.[49] Many *Janjaweed* received regular army uniforms and carried insignias of rank; they sported on the breast pocket a badge showing an armed horseman. Some of these irregulars gave themselves colourful names such as "the border intelligence division", "the second reconnaissance brigade" or even "the quick and the horrible".[50] They later operated in full cooperation with the regular army, and in spite of later denials there were too many proofs of government involvement in the setting up of the formalized *Janjaweed* militias for any credible denial to be possible.[51] By early June the mechanism of repression was getting into place. President Omar el-Beshir then dissolved the Special Courts in a move he himself characterized as "designed to improve the human rights situation".[52] Some observers saw this as a belated admission that the Special Courts had indeed been part of the human rights problem in Darfur, but it is more probable that the hardline group that was preparing to unleash the *Janjaweed* on the territory did not want rough-and-ready courts with extensive powers of arrest and an almost unlimited judicial capacity to remain around. In a complex ethnic and regional situation this could lead to regrettable slip-ups. The *Janjaweed* needed a clear field of action.

All the more so because Khartoum was beginning to doubt the trustworthiness of its Chadian ally. At the beginning of the insurrection the GoS had benefited from almost total support from Idris Deby who even sent troops and a couple of helicopters to help chase the rebels.[53] But with time his position had evolved. Many of his closest aides were Zaghawa with relatives on both sides of the border, and voices in Ndjamena began to be raised in support of the rebellion. The opposition began to use the issue against the President, and Mahamat Saleh Annadif, Minister of Foreign Affairs and a member of the ruling PLD, announced his candidature for the presidency in 2006, openly criticizing the President's support for Khartoum in the Darfur conflict.[54] Saleh Annadif is known as a close friend of Libya and by then it was an open secret that Abdessalam Trikki, Tripoli's Minister for African Affairs, was organizing support for the rebels.[55] Even more disquieting, during the last battle for Tinay Chadian Zaghawa, some from the Chadian Army, had fought on the side of their Sudanese cousins (11–15 July 2003). Ndjamena was talking about mediation, but Khartoum was failing on that front too. When the mediation attempt of Ahmed Babiker Nahar and Abdallah Masar aborted, Abdallah Gosh, head of the *Mukhabarat*, openly declared that all diplomatic efforts had failed and that a solution had to be obtained by military means.[56] The government then unleashed the *Janjaweed* on a grand scale.

"Counterinsurgency on the cheap"[57]

There had been violence before, but by late July 2003 it had assumed a completely new scale and exploded. New patterns of repression emerged.[58] First aircraft would come over a village, as if smelling the target, and then return to release their bombs. The raids were carried out by Russian-built four-engine Antonov An-12s, which are not bombers but transports. They have no bomb bays or aiming mechanisms, and the "bombs" they dropped were old oil drums stuffed with a mixture of explosives and metallic debris. These were rolled on the floor of the transport and dropped out of the rear ramp which was kept open during the flight. The result was primitive free-falling cluster bombs, which were completely useless from a military point of view since they could not be aimed but had a deadly efficiency against fixed civilian targets. As any combatant with a minimum of training could easily duck them, they were terror weapons aimed solely at civilians. After the Antonovs had finished their grisly job, combat helicopters and/or MiG fighter-bombers would come,[59] machine-gunning and firing rockets at any large targets such as a school or a warehouse which might still be standing. Utter destruction was clearly programmed. When the air attacks were over, the *Janjaweed* would arrive, either by themselves or in the company of regular Army units. The militiamen would be mounted on horses and camels and often be accompanied by others riding in "technicals". They would surround the village and what followed would vary. In the "hard" pattern they would cordon off the place, loot personal belongings, rape the girls and women, steal the cattle and kill the donkeys.[60] Then they would burn the houses and shoot all those who could not run away. Small children, being light, were often tossed back in the burning houses.

In the "soft" pattern the militiamen would beat up people, loot, shoot a few recalcitrant men, rape the females, often scarring them or branding them with a hot iron so that they would become recognizable as "spoilt" women in the future. It is during these "soft" attacks that insults were hurled at the villagers and that references were made to their "African" origins which, said the *Janjaweed*, justified their fate as they were "*zurqa* [black]" and the land "now belonged to the Arabs". Some groups of boys and men were taken away and executed. Girls and women were also abducted but, contrary to what had happened before in the South, they do not seem to have been sold as slaves. They were simply used as sexual toys for a few days and then either let go or murdered.[61] The accounts given by the victims after they managed to find refuge in Chad, are painfully monotonous:[62]

"The Arabs arrived and asked me to leave the place. They beat the women and the small kids. They killed a little girl, Sarah Bishara. She was two years old. She was knifed in the back." (Aisha Ali, female, aged 23, from the village of Sasa near Kornoy)

"The day of the attack was 7 July, a Saturday. They came with more than 200 men and they had ten vehicles. There were soldiers from the army among the Janjaweed and we were surprised by the attack because it was 8 a.m. They had Kalashnikovs, bazookas and big weapons mounted on vehicles. They killed 27 people." (inhabitants of Amir, a village of 350 near Jafal)

"It is the Janjaweed who burnt our houses and stole our cattle and belongings. Cattle theft had been happening for a long time but the burning of houses is recent. They came with horses and a lot of weapons. They are composed of Arabs from the area and others from far away. They attacked women, men and children even though they did not have weapons. I would say that at least 240 people were killed in the attack. This is more than half the population of Garadai which counts 400 inhabitants. They killed mainly the young men although many old and disabled people were killed because they were not able to get out of their [burning] houses." (inhabitant from Garadai village, near Jafal, about an attack on 16 August 2003)

"The Arabs and the government forces arrived on both sides of the village with vehicles, on horseback and on camels. They were armed with big weapons. The Arabs cordoned off the village with more than 1,000 horses. There was also a helicopter and an Antonov plane. They shelled the town with more than 200 shells. We counted 119 people who were killed by the shelling. Then the Arabs burnt all our houses and took all the goods from the market. A bulldozer destroyed the other houses. Cars belonging to some merchants were burnt and generators were stolen. They said they wanted to conquer the whole territory and that the Blacks did not have a right to remain in the region." (Chief of Abu Gamra village, between Tinay and Kornoy)

"The Janjaweed were accompanied by soldiers. They attacked the people, saying: 'You are opponents to the regime, we must crush you. As you are Black, you are like slaves. Then the entire Darfur region will be in the hands of the Arabs. The government is on our side. The government plane is on our side, it gives us food and ammunition.'" (survivor of the August 2003 attack on Jafal, near Silaya)

A number of common features emerge from the many such accounts later collected among refugees in Chad. First of all, it was not an attempt to kill everybody; rather, it was a matter of large-scale attacks and massacres aimed at terrorizing and displacing the population. Genocidal elements were present in the oft-repeated remarks and insults of the attackers who derided their victims as "Blacks" and "like slaves", who in future would not be allowed to live in Darfur. Some of the attackers would even clearly spell out the economic and ecological motivations for the actions, as when one attacker said "You are in the fields, the rest is for our horses. You have nothing for yourselves." Then the fact that the government supported the attacks was repeated *ad nauseam*, as if the perpetrators needed to convince themselves of their good fortune. Survivors were allowed to flee (even if they could later be picked on at random along the roads and casually raped or murdered) and take refuge either in Chad or in the towns: Kornoy, Kutum, Zalingei, Kabkabiya, El-Geneina and of course El-Fashir saw thousands of internal refugees congregate around them. Within weeks of the *Janjaweed* offensive these towns had tripled or quadrupled in population. The army and the police "protected" the displaced people in a loose kind of way; the police were particularly nervous since its manpower was mostly "African" and it was scared of doing its job too well. Some policemen were killed, while others deserted and fled to Chad. The militiamen kept marauding around the huddled refugees, stealing what they could and raping girls and women when they came out of the "secured" perimeters to look for water and firewood. The whole thing amounted to a very crude version of the "strategic hamlet" policies so well known to counter-insurgency theorists.

Counter-insurgency is as old as guerrillas. The word "*guerrilla*", meaning "small war" in Spanish, appeared in 1808 in Spain when the people, refusing to submit to the French conquest, started to

fight Napoleon's army in small, highly mobile civilian groups of
fighters. At the time this new form of warfare greatly surprised
military theorists. It was later to gain considerable fame through its
use during the South African war of 1899–1902 and even more
during the anti-colonial and revolutionary wars of the mid-twent-
ieth century. The main problem of large conventional armies when
faced with the repeated pin-pricks of smaller but highly mobile
forces supported by the local civilian population was how to catch
the elusive enemy before it became strong enough to pull a Dien
Bien Phu on you. Mao Zedong, both a theoretician and a practi-
tioner of guerrilla warfare, wrote the oft-quoted principle that
"guerrillas should be among the people as fish are in water". The
logical conclusion of counter-insurgency theorists was that if you
could not catch the fish, you could always try to drain the pond
where it was swimming. The first to try were the British who
invented both the artefact and the name "concentration camp"
during their anti-Boer campaigns in South Africa. In one form or
another concentrating the civilian population, which represented
the guerrilla support group in circumscribed controlled areas, became an obsession of counter-insurgency theorists. This seems to
have been what the GoS was clumsily attempting to do in Darfur
during the second half of 2003. When Alex deWaal calls this phenomenon "counter-insurgency on the cheap" he is right as far as the
means employed and costs incurred are concerned. But this begs
two questions: first, do "refined" or "efficient" forms of counter-
insurgency exist? The predicament at the time of writing of the
Israeli army in Palestine and even more of the US army in Iraq are
cases in point. Even if the dominant army tries to restrain its forces
and kill only when necessary, and to keep repeating public relations
slogans to the point of dulling peoples' receptivity, the results tend
to be poor. Genuine guerrillas defend economic, social, political
and even cultural causes which make them the organic expression

of a large segment of the population.[63] "Careful" or "focalised" repression techniques aimed at separating an insurgency from its causes are largely a techno-military dream. The Darfur *Janjaweed* are crude and brutal, but with all due allowances being made, so were the French forces in Algeria, the US troops in Vietnam and the Red Army in Afghanistan. Contemporary US efforts to fight a "clean" anti-insurgency campaign in Iraq also do not seem very successful. The basic problem for the GoS in Darfur was not counterinsurgency as such (the very fact of being needed showed that it was already too late) but rather the degree of alienation of the ordinary population whom a distant political power had casually governed for the last twenty years through varying degrees of violence.

Second, what were the Khartoum authorities actually doing in Darfur? We see in the next chapter that the problem of defining whether it was a genocide or not was largely a foreign problem since the vocabulary used had much larger implications for the international community than it had for the Darfuri themselves. In Darfur the reality lived by the people was a sudden spectacular growth of what they had had to live through for the previous twenty years— from ethnic cleansing on the instalment plan to the full blast of the real thing. The present GoS is an expression of traditional Northern feelings of the legitimacy of Arab domination in the Sudan. Its racism is not exceptional and is definitely no worse than that of the traditional sectarian elites.[64] Since beginning of the 1990s it has killed many more civilians in Southern Sudan than it has killed in Darfur since February 2003. The Islamist regime has come to power with the explicit aim of stopping the 1988 *Ittihadiyin*/SPLA peace initiative which it had judged "treasonable"[65] and it has later kept its hold on power largely because it showed itself much more capable of maintaining Arab supremacy in the Sudan than its sectarian predecessors. Within such a context of permanent war (or through "negotiations", which were the pursuit of war by other means) counter-insurgency had been a permanent policy feature. Darfur was no exception. It is rather that *the whole of GoS policy and political philosophy since it came to power in 1989 has kept verging on genocide in its general treatment of the national question in Sudan*. GoS policy in the South and in the Nuba Mountains could conceivably have been called genocide, and some authors were not shy about using the word.[66] The practice of genocide or quasi-genocide in Sudan has never been a deliberate well-thought out policy but rather a spontaneous tool used for keeping together a "country" which is under minority Arab domination and which is in fact one of the last multi-national empires on the planet. From such a vantage point the murderous counter-insurgency in Darfur was "rational" and its final explosion into massive ethnic destruction was due largely to two facts: unlike the Southern struggle the Darfur rebellion was culturally too close for comfort and threatened the Centre of the system, not its Periphery; also it occurred at a time when the GoS, after failing to destroy the SPLA, was trying to embrace it into sweet impotence, a delicate operation by no means assured of success.

In Naivasha the GoS was trying to co-opt an old and dangerous enemy into its system of government without surrendering anything vital and with the hope of then making the co-opted enemy impotent. This presupposed a constant and sustained game of double-talk. The press naively reflected this in some of its pieces, for example when it could write after the signing of the "almost final but not quite comprehensive" document in Naivasha: "In any case the Ministry of Defence, of the Interior or of Energy will not be offered to the SPLA in the next government."[67] Animal Resources or Youth and Sports had traditionally been the innocuous niches set aside for Southern ministers in Khartoum. But getting the whole of the SPLA into government and de-fanging it at the same time would not be easy. Each of the negotiating parties in Naivasha was hoping to cheat the other. Nobody—except perhaps the international community—believed in a long-term honest coalition government of such disparate partners. The SPLA was hoping that its arrival in Khartoum would launch a democratising movement whose dynamics would engulf the regime and bring about its fall. The GoS was planning to hem in the Southern movement, buy it and slowly digest it, as Nimeiry had done thirty years earlier. Within such a context the Darfur insurrection was a catastrophe for the GoS first because the SPLA, once it arrived physically in Khartoum, would make repression much more difficult, and secondly because the Darfur insurrection looked like a perfect illustration of Garang's thesis on the revolutionary potential of marginalized "African" groups all over Sudan. If the GoS was to succeed in its handling of the SPLA, this presupposed that the Darfur danger, with its potential for spreading to large sections of the Black Muslim populations in Northern Sudan, would be "ended" root and branch.

The Southerners had always been a quasi-colonial people, out on the fringes of society, power, the economy, everything. Even if they could not be crushed they could be contained. For example, inter-marriage, always a criterion of social admixture, hardly ever happens between Southerners and Northerners.[68] Not so with the Westerners. The *awlad al-Gharb* may be poor relatives but they are part of the Northern family, hence their revolt made them much more dangerous for the survival of Central Arab power than any threat from the Southerners.[69] The Southerners were fighting from outside the house, the Westerners were fighting with one foot already inside the *hosh*.[70] The violence of the reaction was bound to be in direct proportion to the degree of fear felt at the Centre.

In September Minni Arku Minnawi, the SLM's Number Two, and Abdallah Abbakar, its military commander, had arrived in Abé-ché (Chad) to meet emissaries from GoS. By then the counter-insurgency campaign was in full swing and Chad was already host to about 65,000 Sudanese refugees. The situation of the IDPs inside Darfur had taken on the dimensions tragedy and the guerrillas wanted a truce in the hope that it would allow humanitarian aid to arrive before the rains. While the GoS wanted to dry the civilian population pond, the interest of the guerrillas was in protecting it. Death and flight were fast emptying it. A forty-five-day truce was signed which included a cantonment of the guerrilla forces after two weeks; this would have been tantamount to surrendering, since the GoS had no intention to disarm the *Janjaweed*. Therefore the "truce" could not hold since the local guerrilla fighting units never accepted the cantonment principle.[71] On 23 September, in an almost surrealistic statement, the UN Special Envoy for Sudan, Tom Vraalsen, announced that he was "increasingly optimistic that an agreement will be signed before too long" and that donor support to the involved parties would depend on them being seen as "positively, actively, proactively, implementing the agreements they have entered into".[72] He was of course referring to Naivasha and, like the rest of the international community, behaving as if Darfur did not exist. In its desire to look "normal" at all costs, the GoS even decided to free Hassan al-Turabi on 13 October, and Al-Tayeb "Sikha" declared calmly that "the ceasefire is largely respected in spite of a few violations".[73] During late October the parties to the Darfur conflict met again in Abéché, where the Chadian facilitators were being made increasingly nervous by the ever more frequent border violations by the *Janjaweed* and by their own army's tense reactions. The GoS declared that it "rejected the accusations according to which it had violated the September agreement and adopted a racial policy, encouraging the militias to attack civilians".[74] The SLM retorted sharply: "We don't trust the government .... we want neutral observers. [...] The GoS thinks it is just a small conflict and they just want to offer us development." On 4 November the SLM walked out of Abéché and the war continued.[75] Foreigners became anxious about this nasty peripheral conflict which threatened their grandiose plans for "peace in the Sudan". Andrew Natsios of USAID visited Darfur in late October and came back worried, declaring in Nairobi: "We don't want to have an end to the war and a new war starting in the West."[76]

The GoS then took measures which introduced genocidal proportions into the conflict by going deeper than the massacres themselves and targeting the very livelihood of the civilians who had survived the violence. It blocked the US Chargé d'Affaires and a USAID delegation from travelling to Nyala under the pretext that "they had not complied with the administrative regulations", and on 15 November it blocked a first shipment of food aid for Darfur arriving at Port Sudan from the United States on the pretext that the wheat and sorghum cargo "was genetically modified".[77] A few days later Ibrahim Mahmood Hamid, Minister of Humanitarian Affairs, declared that there was no food emergency in Darfur.[78] Death had moved to the administrative level. During December the GoS started to transfer increasing quantities of troops from the South after screening them so that most of those transferred would be Southerners, not Westerners. President George W. Bush had called Omar el-Beshir to inquire about the implementation of the "peace" (he meant Naivasha) and the Sudanese President had answered optimistically that "war in the South and in all the other areas" had come to an end.[79] Not a word was said about Darfur. A third round of SLM/GoS negotiations was quickly aborted in Abéché. The SLA had demanded that there should be a direct linkage between talking with them and the Naivasha talks; that the talks would have international observers; that an international committee would be set up to investigate war crimes; and that a military force would be set up to protect civilians.[80] The GoS lied in declaring that the rebels had demanded a percentage of the oil money, a separate army and self-determination for Darfur.[81] In fact what happened was that when the GoS delegates learned of the SLA demands, they refused to meet them and went home.[82]

On 28 December Vice-President Ali Osman Mohamed Taha and the Security Chief Abdallah Gosh gave a press conference in Khartoum at which they declared that the SPLA was involved in the insurrection; the Eritrean government was also involved; Ndjamena and Tripoli were innocent of wrongdoing even if Zaghawa tribesmen living in Libya and Chad were fighting on the rebel side; and Hassan al-Turabi and his party were implicated. These declarations were true and they could have been a welcome recognition of the basically political nature of the crisis. But three days later, in a completely confused and contradictory way, the Information Minister al-Zahwi Ibrahim Malik released a communiqué saying, "There is no rebellion in Darfur, just a local conflict among specific tribes. The government has never armed any militias. The propaganda in the West is trying to exaggerate what is happening."[83] Confusion was more than ever the order of the day because on 2 January President Omar el-Beshir went on television just after a particularly gruesome massacre in Sorrah, 15 km from Zalingei, in which 225 Fur peasants had been killed, and declared: "We will use all available means, the Army, the police, the mujahideen, the horsemen, to get rid of the rebellion."[84] Part of the reason why the violence reached genocidal proportions was the climate of complete contradiction and political infighting among the various cliques within the GoS. Ministers fought each other, the most preposterous declarations flew back and forth, and so much seemed improvised, creating an impression of confusion in many ways typical of the GoS style of government, i.e. partly unintended and partly deliberate. Contradictions are useful since they allow subsequent denial by contrasting one pronouncement with another—this is a factor which the international community finds very difficult to understand in its dealings with Khartoum. For Europeans extreme evil is associated with tragedy and tragedy is serious. Genocide or ethnic cleansing is a deadly serious business, and the fact that it could be carried out in haphazard conditions was unthinkable for the decorous international community. The grotesque is not part of its conceptual equipment, and only late in the day did foreigners begin to realize that the horror was far from coherent.[85]

Improvising a "final solution"

"The unity of the Sudan is in danger because London and Washington want to reproduce in Darfur the peace agreement signed with the South which schedules power- and wealth-sharing, self-determination and an international monitoring system." These lines, printed in January 2004 in a pro-government Sudanese newspaper,[86] are revealing about several issues. First, the fact that the "peace agreement signed with the South", far from being the great leap towards peace touted by the GoS and the international community, was in fact considered by Khartoum to be a dangerous threat. Then there is the part about "self-determination", which nobody ever mentioned in connection with Darfur, not even its guerrilla groups, but about which Northerners still feel bitter where the South is concerned. Then there are the points about sharing power and wealth and having an international monitoring system to verify it, which are presented as "dangerous". The very notion that the war might be due to the imbalance in power and wealth-sharing at the Centre is implicitly rejected, and mentioning it is seen as the spearhead of foreign intrusion. Such a paragraph is far from being a pure piece of government propaganda and it corresponds to rather broadly-held feelings among the northern riverine Arab population. Particularly since the US occupation of Iraq, anti-American and anti-Western feelings in the Muslim world have developed to such a point that any Western political initiative is seen as underpinned by dark and heinous political plotting. A commonly heard remark in Khartoum in late 2004 was "Why are those *khawadja* [Europeans] so interested in Darfur? What about Palestine? It is because there is oil. They want our oil." That the only companies holding oil exploration permits in Darfur are Japanese,[87] and that nobody from Khartoum ever goes there except on government business, is not even considered. The place is seen as remote and savage, but at the same time it is the sacred ground of the fatherland (*al-watan*) even—or perhaps especially—for the vast majority who have never set foot there. The same was already true of the South before it was believed to be rich in oil.[88]

The GoS actions in Darfur were atrocious violations of the most basic human rights, and the vast majority of the riverine Arab population never supported them. But the average *walad el-beled* today in Khartoum, Atbara or Wad Medani has a strong feeling that the intense foreign interest in the Darfur crisis has dubious motives. This is increased by a sense of the distance and "strangeness" of Darfur, which might be dissipated if the standard of non-Western media coverage of it were better.[89] There is suspicion of foreign "meddling" which has opened a whole field of possibility for the GoS to carry out policies of concentrated violence.

On 27 January the Naivasha peace talks were adjourned as the Sudanese Vice-President Ali Osman Mohamed Taha "went on the Hajj". The pilgrimage to Mecca can be completed in a few days, but on this occasion he and most of the GoS top leadership disappeared for weeks. Consultations were in process because a general offensive had started at the beginning of the month, at first with 25,000 regular soldiers involved but eventually with 40,000. Bombings occurred daily. Tinay, on the border with Chad, had completely emptied, the whole population having fled to Tinay-Chad, the twin town on the other side which was only separated from Sudan by a dry riverbed and now had 35,000 refugees. Bombs were falling on it and claimed three lives on the Chadian side of the border on 29 January. The only comment came from the presidential adviser Qutbi al-Mahdi who declared: "Insurgents suffered heavy losses in bombing raids that targeted camps along Sudan's border with Chad."[90] This was a preposterous claim since there were no guerrilla camps on the border and the bombing carried out by the Antonov, inaccurate at best, could not possibly be assessed on the ground. On 23 January Ali Osman had met Ahmed Ibrahim Diraige in Nairobi and the GoS negotiator Abdallah Masar had declared that it would lead to "the Fur moving away from the conflict".[91] The government itself, which was clumsily trying to manipulate the old Fur leader, undermined any such hope. Diraige put his personal weight behind a meeting arranged in Geneva by the Henri Dunant Foundation, a charitable foundation which had thought that a purely humanitarian meeting might be effective and enable the rebels and the GoS to start some kind of a dialogue. The rebels accepted. But at the last moment the GoS, betraying Diraige's trust, refused to go to Geneva and preferred to call for an impossible "meeting on reconciliation" in Khartoum. This marginalization of Ahmed Diraige blew the last line of communication the government still had with the Fur. The Under-Secretary of the Foreign Affairs Ministry Mutrif Siddiq explained his refusal to go to Geneva by saying that the meeting had been "politicised" and that the proposed conference in Khartoum would offer the true national and patriotic "unpoliticised" forum in which positive discussions could take place.

The killings continued unabated and masses of refugees and IDPs kept fleeing towards either Chad or the cities. UNHCR, which was yet to receive the first penny of an $10.3 million appeal for Darfur in September 2003 (a figure by then completely inadequate anyway) declared in early February: "We are now in a race against time." On 9 February President Omar el-Beshir was feeling satisfied about the results of his offensive which had achieved "an end of the military operations now that the Armed Forces are in full control of all the theatres of operations". He promised the rebels an amnesty and a "conference on development, peace and co-existence". Carried by his own rhetoric, Beshir promised "unimpeded access" in Darfur to UN agencies and NGOs, and Tom Vraalsen, ever the optimist, arrived in Khartoum on 12 February hailing the supposed "unimpeded access" as a breakthrough. But the "*breakthrough*" remained highly theoretical since Khartoum switched from straight access denial to much more refined forms of sabotage. Manipulating aid was very much an aspect of the destruction of Darfur.

The first food aid for the camps had finally arrived in Chad on 13 February, i.e. nine months after the first refugees had crossed the border. But the quantities were pitifully inadequate. Tom Vraalsen, somewhat crestfallen, had to admit that "aid workers are unable to reach the vast majority of IDPs, fighting has not stopped and the corridors for safe access are not open".[92] Worse, people who had talked to the USAID representative Roger Winter when he had gone to Darfur in mid-February were immediately arrested after his departure. Meanwhile the killings continued and on 17 February, as the "Peace Talks" re-started in Naivasha, eighty-one civilians were slaughtered in Shatayta. On 27 February an unknown number of civilians (between sixty-seven and eighty) were killed in Tawilah and 5,500 new IDPs fled to El-Fashir. On 2 March another massacre took place 15 km. from Nyala, where fifteen were killed and thirty injured. The UN Special Inter Agency Team which had arrived on an exploratory mission, reported that many IDPs refused to take whatever small amount of aid would be available because, without the benefit of armed protection, they were more likely to get killed by *Janjaweed* intent on grabbing the food; *Al-Hayat* twisted the report and wrote that the ordinary population "refused aid because they were afraid that they would be attacked by the rebels".[93] The US Government issued a communiqué saying it expected to see Darfur food production fall by 60 % within the year and Turabi organized a press conference where he denounced the government "*for being the cause of the present situation*"[94]. On 5 March 168 Fur peasants arrested in four villages of Wadi Saleh province were summarily shot in Delaij, 30 km. from Garsilla, in one of the best documented and most cold-blooded mass murders of the war. Cross-border raids and counter raids with Chad were getting ever more frequent as the Chadian Zaghawa sought to help their Sudanese cousins and as the *Janjaweed* looted at random. When Mukesh Kapila, the UN Humanitarian Coordinator for Sudan, declared that "the only difference between Rwanda and Darfur now are the numbers involved",[95] the GoS was incensed, the Ministry of Humanitarian Affairs calling his comment "a heap of lies"[96] and lodging a protest with the UN. Since Kapila was leaving the country he felt free to speak with a degree of candour rare among UN officials and he retorted that he did not "see any reason why the international community should not consider some sort of international court or mechanism to bring to trial the individuals who are masterminding or committing war crimes in Darfur. [...] There are no secrets: the individuals who are doing this are known."[97] One of the most horrible aspect of the situation was that the genocidal violence was by then unfolding in full view, on the orders of people whose names were known and who were still being received in international forums.

On 31 March Hassan al-Turabi was re-arrested after a GoS trumped-up accusation of trying to organize a coup. Turabi would probably gladly have done so if it had been within his capabilities, but there was no way he could have done it in the existing circumstances. The government promised that his trial would be public.[98]

On 8 April the GoS and the rebels agreed on yet another ceasefire for forty-five days. It was broken within hours of being signed. The UN was asking for a large fact-finding mission to be sent to

Darfur and Khartoum asked for more time "in order to prepare for it".[99] In a way the request was justified because the government had begun emptying the mass graves existing in various parts of the province and moving the bodies to Kordofan for incineration. Some of the *Janjaweed* were also being issued with army identity numbers, and those who had been killed in the fighting were retrospectively "regularized" as properly documented army casualties. Rather desultory attempts were also made at settling "Arabs" on some of the land vacated by the Fur.[100] When the UN team finally arrived, it was prevented from travelling to Wadi Saleh province where some of the worst and most recent atrocities had occurred. On 9 May the Chadian Minister of Defence declared: "My government has reached the limit of its patience when faced with the aggressions of the Sudanese militias and even of the regular Army."[101] A week later was a coup was attempted in Ndjamena, supposedly over army pay; this was partly true but the main problem was that Idris Deby's Zaghawa retainers no longer accepted the President's support of the Khartoum policies in Darfur. Lengthy negotiations took place and the coup was eventually said to have been "put down". In fact, if anybody was "put down" it was Idris Deby himself; to retain his presidential seat he capitulated to almost all the mutineers' demands.[102]

This power switch had consequences which have not yet been fully played out, but which have heavy consequences for the future, bearing in mind the thirty years of interlocking conflicts between Chad and Darfur.[103] In that climate of violence and media frenzy the signature of yet another protocol in Naivasha (this time on power-sharing) appeared almost as an anti-climax—a major magazine called it "a triumph marred by terror".[104] The terror was certainly present but the triumph would have to wait. Two former members of Clinton's administration wrote what had by then become an evidence: "*The Bush administration efforts to bring peace between*

Khartoum and Southern Sudan will be wasted if we allow the GoS to continue committing crimes. [...] With another genocide, any hard-won peace agreement will not be worth the paper it is signed on."[105] In a desperate bid to salvage some positive results from the mess, US Under-Secretary of State for African Affairs Charles Snyder threatened: "*Clearly the GoS has calculated that our desire to see a North-South peace accord might lead us to adopt a softer approach on Darfur. That was a major miscalculation.*"[106] Perhaps, but the conclusion was not so obvious, and Snyder carefully avoided mentioning the real backdrop, Iraq. Enmeshed in the disastrous Iraqi mess, the United States was trying to assert its strength but could only carry a very short stick.

Meanwhile an increased humanitarian presence had started to develop, profoundly affecting the situation. Open violence slowly receded, but without really ending. The GoS, now submitted to hard diplomatic pressure but feeling safe from military intervention, began to rely more on the parlous food and medical situation to finish off the job that the militias had started.

The government was keeping international activism to a minimum by playing on fears that it would walk out from the IGAD North-South peace process if too much pressure was applied. [...] The doors to large-scale humanitarian intervention were open only in May 2004, just as the rainy season was about to begin.[107]

This meant that the ethnic cleansing was now changing back into low-intensity counter-insurgency, and that in effect people would now die under a different label.

Foreign intervention and death by attrition[108]

Anti-Khartoum activist Eric Reeves set out the new rules of the game when he wrote: "This regime lies repeatedly, shamelessly, egregiously and without consequences. Why then should it not lie low and simply say what the international community wishes to hear and thereby be relieved from any responsibility to act?"[109] The international community had always insisted on dealing with the Darfur massacres essentially as a humanitarian emergency, pretending to believe that if humanitarian workers and organizations were allowed in the situation would somehow be solved. But the humanitarians found it hard to do their work when those they were trying to help lived in the IDP camps in constant fear, surrounded by the very same people who were responsible for their fate.

The *Janjaweed* were now increasingly incorporated into the army and police who, the GoS said, would "secure" the camps[110]. By then there were 1.2 million IDPs (with 800,000 living in camps), over 120,000 refugees in Chad and probably over a million other "war-affected persons"—those who could not live and produce their food away from their normal environment. This would give a minimum of 2.3 million people who could be expected to need food assistance. If we consider food requirements to be roughly 16,000 tons per million people, some 120,000 tons would have to be available to cover the rainy season of three-and-a-half months during which road transport would be unable to function. The World Food Programme could only plan on 52,000 tons and it was through that expected gap that the "genocide by attrition" could be expected to unfold.

Meanwhile the situation was so stark that real ethnic clashes began to develop, often between Arab tribes desperately struggling for means of survival.[111] This allowed for incredible sophistry on the part of the international community, as when the UN Under-Secretary for Humanitarian Affairs Jan Egeland declared: "*The same tribes are represented both among those who are cleansed and those who are cleansing.*"[112] The African Union accepted to send 300 troops to Darfur, but only with a mandate to protect a planned force of 132 observers. On 22 July the UN Security Council adopted its Resolution 1556 which gave the GoS till 30 August to disarm the *Janjaweed*. This was to be the first of a number of similar empty demands on the subject. It was of course impossible for the Khartoum authorities to rein in their hired killers in so short a time, and the very unrealistic nature of these demands allowed the government to complain of them in public[113] and shrug them off in private, with the tacit "understanding" of the "realists" within the international community. This complex game allowed the GoS to lie repeatedly with no consequences since the international community wanted none, pinning all its hopes on a successful conclusion to the Naivasha negotiations. When the French army was deployed on the Chad border to avoid infiltrations and help supply the refugee camps, a pro-government newspaper immediately wrote: "The French forces have been deployed at Ndjamena's request because of the fighting which has taken place inside the Sudanese refugee camps."[114] When Khartoum arrested and tried some alleged *Janjaweed* in Nyala, it was soon found that all were petty criminals, some of whom had been in jail for the last four years. None had ever been in the militia and one was the town's drunkard, jailed for violating the alcohol laws.[115] Jan Pronk who had signed a "Darfur Plan of Action" with Mustafa Osman Ismail on 6 August nevertheless saw "positive progress in implementing last month's agreement", citing the fact that there were now more "policemen" in the towns.

Giving his own interpretation of Pronk's "safe areas" concept which was part of the Darfur Plan of Action, the Interior Minister Abd-er-Rahim Mohamed Hussein announced a plan to regroup all IDPs in about eighteen "secure" locations, without explaining how the IDPs would survive there. And for his part President Beshir straight-facedly declared that the reason for the Darfur crisis was that "there is an agenda to seek petrol and gold in the region".[116] Meanwhile the rains had started, cutting the camps off from food supplies. The *Janjaweed* did not have to attack any more, death had by then, in the humanitarian lingo, become a statistic called "Crude Mortality Rate" (CMR)—this of course in places where the CMR could be monitored. As for the majority of the Darfur population who were out of reach of the aid agencies, they could die without benefit of the label.

Meanwhile "peace negotiations" on Darfur had started in Abuja. The GoS proposal was that the African Union would disarm the rebels while Khartoum would disarm the *Janjaweed*, a proposal which even the most wilfully blind members of the international community could not take seriously. To put a little pressure on the foreigners Khartoum's Minister of Information, Al-Zahawi Ibrahim Malik, declared that his government would not sign in Naivasha before the Darfur question was solved.[117] This of course was not true, but why not try? The GoS played on its own internal contradictions, real or supposed, like a master performer.

As Darfur's landlocked situation was becoming an aggravating factor in the crisis with the onset of the rains, the WFP became desperate. An effort was made to try bringing food supplies from Tripoli through the desert to circumvent the impossibility of operating either from Cameroon through Chad or from Port Sudan through Kordofan. A convoy of twenty trucks was assembled in Kufra with 440 tons of food, and managed to drive the 2,200 km. run in slightly less than a month, but this could not solve the problem of shrinking food supplies for the camps. Clashes between the guerrilla groups and the regular army and the *Janjaweed* multiplied in early September, while Khartoum announced that it had foiled a sabotage plot by Turabi's Mutammar ash-Shabiyi, which was supposed to have been carried out with the help of Eritrea. Thirty-three members of Turabi's party were arrested.[118] Amid contradictory assessments of the mortality in the IDP camps, the Abuja "peace talks" finally collapsed on 15 September and the European

Parliament declared that the Darfur situation was "tantamount to a genocide",[119] whatever that meant. Three days later the UN voted its Resolution no. 1564 demanding the end of human rights violations, recommending the deployment of more AU troops, and creating a "Commission of Inquiry" to determine whether genocide was taking place or not. The resolution was accompanied by various vague threats on an oil embargo and travel restrictions for members of the Khartoum government who would be identified as responsible for the Darfur horror. USAID's Andrew Natsios who had just come back from Darfur said that it was indeed genocide. All these declarations, statements and recommendations had no practical results whatever.[120]

Meanwhile President Omar el-Beshir had gone to Kordofan where new rebel groups had become increasingly active. In many ways Beshir's official visit to Kordofan was reminiscent of Vice-President Ali Osman Mohamed Taha's to Darfur in November 2002: soothing talk about Khartoum's interest in the area, promises,[121] and appeals for to peace and good ethnic relations. There again the feeling was that it was perhaps too late to resort to tired politicking when the feelings of the population were centred much more on economic neglect and political marginalization.

On 19 October the Red Cross released a report on the "agricultural collapse" of Darfur, saying that the situation was by now worse than that of the 1984 famine;[122] 22% of children aged under five in the IDP camps were found to be malnourished and by then the WFP had to feed almost 1.3 million displaced people, with the ICRC supplementing its effort by reaching another 100,000 in supposed "no-go" areas. In the report just mentioned, the ICRC had written that it was expecting the IDP number to arrive at two million by the end of the year. But in fact that figure had already been reached.

To make matters worse Khartoum was becoming more vocal about populations "returning home", in the knowledge that there were no homes for them to return to. The GoS launched a trial balloon in late October, saying that it had already repatriated 70,000 IDPs, which the international community briefly believed in the midst of so much confusion, and strongly protested. The alarm was premature but not without foundation. Three weeks later the GoS went a step further and actually stormed the El-Jeer camp near Nyala.[123] Bombarding the refugees with tear-gas, government forces invaded the camp and started to bulldoze the refugees' shacks; those who tried to resist were beaten and several women were raped. Soon "the aid workers had to leave the scene for their own safety" when the army started firing in the air. Two African Union officers who were on the spot to "protect the people" were threatened, had their cameras confiscated, and were obliged to leave. The whole episode only resulted in a "strong complaint", rather unlikely in itself to deter the GoS from further violence. The international community kept pinning high hopes on African Union action as fifty Nigerian and 237 Rwandese soldiers arrived, bringing total AU strength to 597. In a nice touch of spite the Sudanese government required all the African soldiers to undertake HIV tests.

As the pace of negotiations was quickening (Naivasha had restarted and a new conference had opened in Cairo between the government and the mostly Northern opposition, the National Democratic Alliance) the guerrillas heightened their pressure in a desperate bid to be taken seriously and force their way to the negotiation table. But their positions were far from coherent and the tensions between the JEM and the SLM were growing. The JEM was basically jockeying for power in Khartoum, in line with Turabi's global political agenda. It also, still in accordance with the Mutammar ash-Shabiyi radical line, steadily refused even to discuss the idea of a separation of religion and politics. The paradox was that that particular segment of the guerrillas appeared more radically "Islamist" than the government itself while the line followed by the SLM, which by then had joined the NDA and flaunted its ties with the SPLA, was resolutely secularist. The SLM also made it clear that its main agenda was the situation of Darfur and not taking power in Khartoum, even if it realized that a change of power at the Centre was probably the only way it could alter its attitude towards the Periphery. On the ground this translated itself into squabbles about tactics and the sharing of military supplies and booty, eventually developing into full-scale fighting between the two movements in Jebel Marra in early November.

Caught between its own indecision, the guerrillas who were raising the stakes, and the government which was now mastering the new rules of killing by attrition, the international community was reduced to a state of irritable and fruitless complaining. By mid-November the UNHCR had to withdraw its staff from South Darfur after the government simply refused to let them work when the aid workers protested at the GoS programme of forced relocations and tried to oppose it.[124] To solidify its Sudan policy the UN Security Council transferred itself to Nairobi and met on 17–19 November, voting Resolution 1574 which demanded "an immediate end to violence". This was nice but largely ineffectual. In fact the GoS now felt that as long as it showed "good faith" in Naivasha it could do what it wanted in Darfur.

The problem was that it was succeeding only too well. The massive amount of violence had led to a point where the society had almost ceased to function. Communities were not only at each other's throats, but they were quickly becoming incapable of regulating themselves on a day-to-day basis. The whole of Darfur was turning into a lawless refugee camp where social patterns were under severe strain. The *Janjaweed* had been delinquents and socially marginal people from the start, but the guerrillas were now increasingly losing control of themselves and bandit groups were quickly springing up. On 2 November Special Envoy Jan Pronk had warned that the whole province was descending into "total anarchy and warlordism". The GoS had re-started "peace conversations" with the guerrillas in Abuja during December, but it had launched a military offensive designed to clear the roads of all insurgents even while the talks were in progress, and these predictably came to a halt. The government stopped the offensive only long enough to sign the "comprehensive peace agreement" for which everyone had been waiting on 9 January 2005, thereby satisfying the main demand of the international community. But Darfur was pointedly left out of the agreement and the GoS offensive re-started in January, with massive loss of human life and further restriction of access to the affected populations because the roads had been cleared. A peace of sorts had been proclaimed for Southern Sudan, but it remained to be seen whether this would have any effect in the West.

5

THE WORLD AND THE DARFUR CRISIS

For the world at large Darfur was and remained the quintessential "African crisis": distant, esoteric, extremely violent, rooted in complex ethnic and historical factors which few understood, and devoid of any identifiable practical interest for the rich countries. Once the international media got hold of it, it became a "humanitarian crisis"—in other words, something that many "realist" politicians saw (without saying so) as just another insoluble problem. In the post-Cold War world such problems were passed on to the UN, but the UN did not know what to do with this one, even less so when it became a distinct possibility that this was another genocide. Fearing that it would have to intervene and that the developed world would encourage it to act without giving it the means to do so, the UN then passed on the catastrophe it could or would not handle to the care of the newly re-born African Union, formerly the Organisation of African Unity. For the continental organization wanting a new start this was a dangerous gift. "African solutions to African problems" had become the politically correct way of saying "We do not really care". Thus in many ways the hard reality of Darfur was still kept at arms' length, while statistics, press releases, UN resolutions and photo opportunities took centre-stage. But as in all globalized world crises, this recreation of the situation due to media attention and discussion at the UN acquired as much importance as the reality it was applied to, if not more, because whether real or not it deeply affected the initial reality.

Media coverage: surfing on the horror charts

At first the Darfur crisis went almost unnoticed by the media. In Sudan the media were concentrating on the North-South peace negotiations in Naivasha on which the foreign media sporadically reported. Even in Khartoum a few nomads shooting it up in distant Darfur did not draw much attention. After all, had not these people devoted themselves to fighting each other for many years—even, as some would add, for as long as anyone could remember? The school of explaining conflicts by "ancient tribal hatreds" is not the role preserve of Western journalists and has many adherents in Africa itself. An unconscious form of Sudanese cultural racism enabled the government (which in some ways believed its own propaganda) to dismiss the whole thing as "another instance of tribal conflict"; Or, when it reverted to the ideological approach of its early years, to describe the violence as an attempt by the SPLA rebels aided by the Americans and the Zionists to stir up trouble for a good Muslim regime. Understandably such musings did not even reach the international media for most of 2003.

The deteriorating situation in Darfur had been known to the wider world since around 1999, but only through specialized publications such as *Africa Confidential* or the *Indian Ocean Newsletter*. In Sudan itself the national press began to give some space to the activities of the "bandits" around the middle of 2003, and the word "*Janjaweed*" first appeared in September of that year[1] when the attack on the small town of Kadnir in Jebel Marra was reported. Inasmuch as any news on Sudan reached the international media, the reports remained fully focused on the North-South Naivasha talks and nobody picked up on the "evil horsemen" who had shot up yet another African village in a God-forsaken province at the centre of the continent. The Massalit Community in Exile[2] and Sudan Human Rights Organization[3] press releases found no takers. Even David Hoile, the GoS public relation lobbyist in London then busy trying to refute stories of government-sponsored slave raids in Southern Sudan,[4] had no need to disclaim any of the Darfur horrors since nobody was writing about them. Symmetrically the anti-Khartoum activist Eric Reeves still concentrated fully on his denunciations of the evils of GoS policy towards the South.[5] To his credit he was nevertheless the first foreign observer to pick up on what was by then ominously developing in Darfur,[6] but he did not succeed in drawing much attention to something that was still seen as a sideshow. Even the usually well-informed advocacy NGO Justice Africa did not mention Darfur in its October 2003 monthly brief. Some echoes of the Darfur situation slowly had found their way into the international press by November, when the Abéché peace negotiations between the then unknown guerrillas and the GoS were reported to be failing. The Deutsche Presse Agentur wrote indirectly about Darfur when it said that the US Chargé d'Affaires in Khartoum had been forbidden by the Sudanese government to travel to El-Fashir.[7] Agence France Press[8] also felt the wind and sent a dispatch. But the papers they wrote remained focused on the diplomatic problems and not on the actual violence in Darfur. And when the situation in Darfur proper became the focus of the dispatches it was described as a humanitarian problem, even when militia attacks were among its causes that were mentioned.[9] The big story remained the North-South peace prospects and not the tribal disturbances in the west of the country.

It was the advocacy NGOs which began picking up on Darfur, first Amnesty International[10] and then the International Crisis Group[11] and it is largely through them that the crisis began to come out of the shadows.

Given their interest in Chad, the French media were among the first to give a separate picture of the Darfur situation.[12] Then the first US article on the subject focused immediately on the "Black versus Arab" side of the problem,[13] an aspect which, even if justified, was going to obscure rather than clarify the essential elements in the following months because of its misleadingly "evident" explanatory power. By then the Voice of America had followed the BBC in covering the growing crisis, and press agencies had begun sending their reporters to eastern Chad.

But what actually "blew the ratings" was the interview given by the UN Human Rights Coordinator for Sudan, Mukesh Kapila, to the UN's own IRIN network in March. Kapila declared that Darfur was "the world's greatest humanitarian crisis" and that "the only difference between Rwanda and Darfur is now the numbers involved". He quoted a tentative figure of 10,000 casualties[14]—having worked in Rwanda at the time of the genocide there he knew what he was talking about. And although Rwanda itself had been neglected in its hour of need ten years before, it had by then become the baseline reference for absolute evil and the need to care. Newspapers went wild, and the *New York Times* started to write about "genocide".[15] The "angle" had been found: Darfur was a genocide and the Arabs were killing the Blacks. The journalists did not seem unduly concerned by the fact that the Arabs were often black, or that the "genocide" was strangely timed given Khartoum's diplomatic goals in Naivasha. Few people had ever heard of Darfur before; its history was a mystery nobody particularly wanted to plumb, but now there was a good story: the first genocide of the twenty-first century. Suddenly it was the Naivasha peace talks in which interest seemed to slacken as the blood flowed between the lines. Here was something really serious and happening *now*, not like the peace negotiations which had been dragging on for two years. Heart-wrenching images of children, rapes, horsemen—suddenly everyone was interested from the quality press[16] to the mass media[17] by way of the intellectual publications.[18] What is conventionally known as "world opinion" now cared about Darfur, even if the actual mechanics of what was happening remained obscure. But the moral outrage which was felt tended to overshadow, if not hide completely, the political nature of the problem. Some specialized articles started to disentangle the various lines of causality but soon got lost amid the loud humanitarian demands for action. "Action" was a big word, although no one went so far as to demand a military intervention. Iraq and its image of easy military success leading to political discomfiture was still too present on TV screens.

Moral indignation and its attendant media coverage kept rolling on till the end of 2004. Darfur was *the* humanitarian crisis and horror story of the year and writing about it was now obligatory. Then came the Asian tsunami on 26 December, and Darfur instantly vanished from the TV screens and the pages of newspapers. The media could handle only one emotion-laden story at a time, not two, and the tsunami was much more politically correct than Darfur; it was unpolitical, only emotional. Darfur had enjoyed its famous fifteen minutes of Warholian celebrity. It had even remained in the limelight for over six months which, for an African horror story was a lot, and if it was true that some sort of "peace" had been signed in Nairobi on 9 January 2005, the show was surely over.

But before we move back to reality as opposed to its media image, we have to answer one question about the Darfur coverage: why so much so late? The lateness is probably easiest to explain: Darfur was not expected to happen when it did, and it did not fit the common patterns of thinking about Sudan. Everyone knew that this was a religious war where wicked Muslims killed desperately struggling Christians. There had been over a million casualties, perhaps as many a million and a half, and we had accepted that. Peace was at last about to be achieved now that the evil Hassan al-Turabi had been replaced at the head of the country by the far from virtuous but acceptable Omar Hassan al-Beshir. And now this sudden Muslim-on-Muslim violence had surged to the forefront of world attention in a way that was completely unexpected and hardly explicable. This just at the time when the world, from charitable organizations to hard-boiled businessmen, was looking at Sudan as potentially the next profitable investment on the continent. This last point is probably what caused the intensity of the media coverage once it finally took off. There was a kind of delayed reaction, a substitute for disappointment. The media was preparing for a nice story: peace at last, returning refugees, selfless NGO and UN workers helping the destitute, Muslim-Christian coexistence and perhaps even reconciliation, a farewell to arms. In other words, an African success story. Now everything, even the way of interpreting the situation, was topsy-turvy, which is why the "genocide" angle soon became so important. Nobody denied that an enormous quantity of human beings had been killed, but was it or was it not genocide? Although it made little difference to the interested parties who continued to die without recourse to international legal concepts, the word became a question of the utmost relevance in the media. What was it that we were witnessing? Could it be that this was the real story, and not Naivasha? The world media remained suspended between the two and did not want to make a mistake. The spokesmen of the international community who are well-attuned to media reactions understood the nature of the problem and distilled their opinions in complex and often contradictory statements. Meanwhile humanitarian action was trying, as so often before in similar circumstances, to fill the gap between the media-raised expectations of public opinion and the prudent procrastination of the political and diplomatic segments of the international community.

Embattled humanitarianism

Given the immediately visible reality of violence and the murky complexity of its causes, Darfur was largely perceived as "a humanitarian crisis". And a humanitarian crisis calls for "humanitarianism" in order to face the situation. This is a topic which has been discussed at great length by such "French doctors" as Jean-Christophe Rufin or Rony Brauman, seasoned practitioners of humanitarian intervention in extreme situations, who knew what it could and what it could not achieve.[19] Ethiopia in 1985, Somalia in 1992 and Rwanda in 1994 are examples which immediately spring to mind. There the humanitarians were in fact supposed not to complement political action but themselves to be substitutes for what the politicians should have done. But then humanitarianism is consensual and "nice" but also non-committal: it is not the job of the humanitarians to analyse the causes of the disasters they are asked to deal with. This leaves the field free for a whole range of political manoeuvres and diplomatic moves while public opinions in rich countries is given the impression that something is being done without that "something" being political. In the telling words of an anonymous humanitarian aid worker, "We have seen at first hand what has gone on in Darfur. We have watched government planes and helicopters passing overhead to bomb villages, hours before the *Janjaweed* militias moved in to burn them. We have seen *Janjaweed* and government officials working together. [...] But the fact is that any aid agency speaking out would be immediately expelled from the Sudan."[20] It is this contradiction which has plagued humanitarian action in Darfur, as in all the major African crises of the last twenty years.

A humanitarian emergency in Darfur had become noticeable with the unleashing of the major counter-insurgency campaign in July 2003. By the end of the month there were 6,000 IDPs in Kutum fleeing the *Janjaweed* attacks, and refugees had started to cross the border into Chad. Then the summer months of 2003 witnessed a massive explosion in the numbers of people affected by the war and by mid-September the estimated number of IDPs had jumped to 400,000 and there were 70,000 refugees in Chad. The first reactions now began.[21] UNHCR asked for $10.3 million for what it said were 65,000 refugees in Chad, and Médecins Sans Frontières sounded the alarm for a "forgotten crisis". At mid-October the Swiss NGO Medair, one of the few operating inside Darfur at the time (most of the others were blocked at the border inside Chad, unable to get authorizations to go into Sudan), did a spot-check in the Mukjar area of West Darfur and found 32,000 IDPs herded in a tight space after 150 people had been killed and 225 injured in eighty-nine village attacks in the area since August. Living conditions were appalling. People had almost nothing to eat, and foraging for wild foods, which had been a life-saving device during the 1984 famine, was impossible because of *Janjaweed* activity outside. Women were afraid of being raped and men of being murdered. Water was a problem. People defecated on the ground because there were no implements to dig latrines and nowhere that they could be dug. Disease was rife.

On 14 November Mukesh Kapila, the outgoing UN-OCHA Coordinator for Sudan declared that the Darfur situation was "a tragedy" and deplored that Sudan was "producing refugees as it is making peace". The answer of the Sudanese Humanitarian Affairs Commissioner was that "the UN should concentrate on its field-work instead of issuing press statements".[22] Slowly the international community was waking up and Tom Vraalsen, the UN Special Envoy who had sobered up since his enthusiastic September statement, declared:

"The GoS presenting of the situation as steadily improving contrasts sharply with first-hand reports. [...] Delivery of humanitarian assistance is hampered by systematically denied access. Khartoum authorities claim there is unimpeded access but they greatly restrict access to the areas under their control while imposing blanket denial to all rebel-held areas. [...] As a consequence of growing insecurity and denied access, the humanitarian crisis has reached unprecedented proportions, with one million now war-affected."[23]

In El-Geneina the price of food was escalating, with a bag of *dura* reaching 7,000 dinars, up from 1,800 three months before.[24] While IDP numbers were pushing towards half a million, local authorities issued surrealistic statements, such as the one by Adam Idris al-Silaik, the acting Governor of Nyala (where 50,000 IDPs were piled up), who declared to IRIN on 10 December that: it was "*too difficult*" to send aid to the rebel-held areas; that the NGOs were "*our guests*" and would have to be protected from the *Janjaweed* who were "*just a bunch of thieves*"; and that the situation in South Darfur was anyway "*calm and under control*".

There was a new burst of border crossing in December with over 25,000 new refugees fleeing into Chad, bringing the number to over 100,000. But in a way the refugees in Chad were the lucky ones; they were relatively free from further *Janjaweed* attacks—but relatively only because the *Janjaweed* often crossed the border at night to attack the camps which had remained too close, such as the one in Tinay; they could forage, look for water and firewood and, most of all, they could depend on the kind hearts of the local Chadian population who fed them for months before the slow-moving international community could get its stuff on the ground. The local Zaghawa were poor but hospitable.[25] The refugees did not starve. However, it was much worse inside. There, in the *Janjaweed*-infested areas, the people tried to take shelter near the towns, but they did not always manage it and when they did the situation was grim: the authorities did nothing for them and in some cases even harassed them. In Nyala, for example, people were denied the right to dig latrines because the area on which they camped "was residential land" and they should not damage it by digging holes. And the international community, contained on the Chadian side of the border, it would remain absent for many more months. The *Janjaweed* kept close to the camps and the police were much too scared of them to intervene. Racketeering, violence and rape were rife. So were diseases, but luckily the feared "big ones" (measles and cholera) did not come, keeping the death-rates at a semi-moderate level. The IDPs in the most desperate situation were those trapped inside the rebel lines. They had lost all their belongings in their flight and had no food or medical deliveries whatever. Even now we have only the most approximate idea of the death-rate in such communities.

The "unimpeded access" promised by President Omar el-Beshir was largely a mockery. For example travel permits for Darfur would be issued to NGO workers but made valid only for three days; then the beneficiaries were told that they had to give seventy-two hours' pre-flight notice before going, meaning that their permits would have expired by the time they were to be used. When they protested the Ministry of the Interior answered: "That is your problem, not ours." Permits were capriciously given or with-held. One American worker was successively denied permits to travel to Darfur by car and then by plane. When he lost his temper and said he would go with a camel he was told without a smile that this too required a permit. Medicines that had been unloaded in Port Sudan were held up in Khartoum, the official excuse being that they should be lab-tested before use in the camps in case some were expired or dangerous. Once teams got to Darfur, they were often penned up in the big towns and not allowed to travel outside "because it was too dangerous". The pretence of "unimpeded access" drove the humanitarian community to extremes of frustration, Refugees International declaring: "There is absolutely no access to any place. Things are not changing and if they are changing, they are changing for the worse." The GoS was channelling all its diplomatic energies into preventing outside help from arriving. When the US government offered its mediation for at least facilitating humanitarian deliveries, Najib al-Kheir, the Secretary of State for Foreign Affairs, replied with brutal sophistry: "*The have a right to propose and we have a right to decide. The US proposal does not conform to our vision, which considers that the conflict is a matter regarding only the sons of Darfur.*"[26] The sophistry could reach amazing levels of cynicism, as when the Minister of Humanitarian Affairs retorted to a complaint by the head of the Red Cross:[27] "*The government is under no obligation to cooperate with ICRC because it never signed the annexes to the Geneva Convention which would oblige it to cooperate with NGOs in case of conflict.*"[28] And Qutbi al-Mahdi, the President's Adviser on Political Affairs, proudly declared: "The solution to the Darfur conflict will be purely Sudanese."[29] The *Janjaweed* were then deeply engaged in a "purely Sudanese" solution to the Darfur conflict and Khartoum was trying its best to delay any nosing around in what they were doing. The GoS probably knew that it could not stick permanently to that position of denial and refusal, but it probably also hoped that by gaining time it could create an irreversible situation so that foreign intervention could only deal with the results rather than be able to prevent them.

By mid-April USAID reported an alarming growth of Global Acute Malnutrition Rates among the IDP population which the UN now estimated at one million. The burden of the situation was largely dumped by the political entities on the lap of the humanitarians, and this "division of labour" was happening even within the confines of the UN. Just as the World Food Programme was appealing for $98 million for Darfur, the UN Human Rights Team which was visiting Darfur for the first time at almost the same moment displayed an overcautious approach to its mandate.[30] The feeling seemed to be that humanitarianism should be allowed to play its consensual and diplomatically protective role. The GoS did not shrink from the most preposterous statements, as when the Foreign Minister Mustafa Osman Ismail declared: "I can assure you that all those who have been killed, whether militia, rebels, soldiers or civilians caught in the fighting, do not reach one thousand."[31] Never mind the obviously underestimated figure. But notice the clever use of "civilians caught in the fighting": this was a *war* and civilians could only die as "collateral damage". Massacres were purely a product of foreign propaganda. Bertrand Ramcharan, acting UN Commissioner for Human Rights, reached a fairly high level of sophistry when he declared: "I condemn the GoS but I do not think it is responsible."[32] If this was the kind of support they could expect from their political counterparts, the humanitarians were working in a field largely barren of any acceptance of reality.

And their task was not made any more easy by persistent underfunding. In early June a high-level donor meeting in Geneva had appealed for $236 million for Darfur but only $126 million had been pledged.[33] Logistical means were inadequate, and with its 140 trucks WFP had only a capacity for transporting about 8,000 tons of food a month, i.e. enough to feed about 500,000 people. A minimum of three times that number were affected by the emergency. UNHCR which had initially requested $20.8 million at the beginning of the year, ratcheted up this figure to $55.8 million by June 2004. OCHA which had requested $54 million in March 2004 brought this figure up to $166 million by September. This budgetary mushrooming reflected the wild growth of the affected population. Refugees in Chad who had long been described as numbering about 100,000 were suddenly said to be 200,000. IDPs shot up to 1.2 million. The "war-affected" population, a vaguely defined group taken to mean "anybody who suffered from the war", was thought to have reached over two millions. There was indeed growing "humanitarian access" to many of the IDP camps. But what did it mean in practice? "The same militias who carried out the initial attacks [forcing the villagers to flee] now control the camp's periphery, virtually imprisoning the people who live in constant fear. The men risk being killed if they leave and women have been beaten and raped looking for wood or water. In the past nine weeks MSF teams have treated 132 victims of such violence."[34] The situation in the IDP camps was so hard that many who could manage it undertook the long journey to Khartoum where they hoped to find a modicum of peace. But even there security was far from assured. By mid-2004 there were tens of thousands of "spontaneously resettled" IDPs in the Khartoum area and they were often targeted for further dislocation. In early July the Swiss NGO Medair denounced the demolition of the Wadi-el-Bashir and Omdurman-as-Salam shantytowns on the outskirts of the capital while more people were still arriving.

Forced relocation of the IDPs was mooted as a "return of the IDPs to their places of origin", a proposal that would have been catastrophic if ever carried out because there was no way people could live in the destroyed villages, and any dispersal of the IDP camps would make it impossible for the humanitarian agencies to keep feeding them in distant locations. The humanitarians were thus caught between two possibilities: keeping the camps where they were or dispering their populations, one being bad and the other worse. Securing and improving the camps was the only (imperfect) short-term answer.

This problem was typical of the management of the crisis. The humanitarians were asked to venture into what was really political decision-making (with potentially enormous humanitarian consequences) without being given a solid doctrine from which to decide or any assurance that help would be forthcoming if things went wrong. They were first in the line of fire, with no political back-up. The GoS was fully aware of this quandary and played on it to the hilt. *Janjaweed* exactions had slowed down, changing from a massive murder campaign to random harassment, but the camps and facilities which supported them had never been dismantled.[35] Khartoum's tactic was to let the militia harass the camps, harass the humanitarian workers and harass the guerrillas. The resulting confusion and violence had a number of consequences which all played into the hands of the authorities. First, the insecurity was such that IDPs kept fleeing from the villages to the "secure" locations, thereby dangerously overloading the humanitarian "ship". Second, the "secure" locations were insecure enough to keep the refugee populations penned up in the camps, making their survival very difficult without full humanitarian support. In other words the local survival mechanisms which had proved so essential during the 1984 famine were now prevented from coming into play. Third, the guerrillas were overloaded with their own IDPs, thereby losing some of their combat effectiveness. And finally, insecurity on the roads progressively reached a level where, even when the rains stopped in late 2004, trucking supplies to the camps became increasingly difficult simply because transport companies either did not want to tender for the contracts or else asked such enormous prices that transport costs became prohibitive.[36]

The costs of the Darfur emergency were escalating. By late July 2004 the amounts already spent were massive. The 2004–5 previsions were even higher. UN agencies had asked for $722 million specifically for Darfur, but only $288 million had been firmly pledged. The WFP, which gave 39% of its budget to Darfur, was hardest hit. Once a key preoccupation, the Chad refugee camps were slowly becoming almost a sideshow. They too were underfunded: the OCHA needed $166 million, but had only $80 million pledged and even less disbursed, and the WFP had increased its planned expenses to $42 million and UNHCR to $105 million. Since preliminary estimates of needs for the South in case peace was finally signed in Naivasha had stood at $246 million,[37] the whole humanitarian system for the Sudan was by then dangerously overstretched. By late 2004 UN financing needs for 2005 in the Sudan would rise

Organization	Chad refugees budget	Darfur budget	Total
	(in US dollars, calculated since September 2003)		
FAO	362,000	2,042,000	2,404,000
UNHCR	39,167,000	3,300,000	42,467,000
UNICEF	2,960,000	16,647,000	19,608,000
WFP	23,196,000	138,385,000	161,580,000
WHO	17,290	6,524,000	6,541,000
UN sub-total	65,752,000	174,582,000	240,335,000
NGO sub-total	11,707,000	42,573,000	54,280,000
Grand total	85,675,000	301,013,000	386,688,000

Source: UN/OCHA. *Funding Overview for the Darfur Crisis*, Khartoum, 27 July 2004. Totals do not balance exactly because of other funding sources.

to $1.5 billion, an amount which was unlikely to be raised in one year.

The combination of rising costs and growing insecurity slowly brought about a new situation. Throughout the second half of 2004 the proportions of IDPs and war-affected persons who could be reached by humanitarian help regularly declined, thereby leading to a steady increase in estimated mortality rates.[38] The campaign of destruction waged against Darfur began to change shape as death by the gun was slowly replaced by death through attrition. The government kept destroying the civilian population, while pretending at the same time to cooperate with the international community. This was a clever approach since there seemed to be little that the world was prepared to do to stop the massacre provided it was progressive and respected certain norms and regulations.

"Shuffling papers while Africans die"[39]: *the international community and the Darfur crisis*

US diplomacy: between engagement and electioneering.   Washington was embarrassed by the Darfur crisis, not least because it did not fit well within the two main camps in the State Department and on Capitol Hill, the "realists" and the "Garang lobby". The "realists" were found mostly in the State Department, the CIA and the DIA. They argued that, given the useful role that Khartoum was playing in the war on terrorism by supplying information on its erstwhile friends, the GoS should at least be helped even if perhaps not fully supported, especially if it showed any signs of cooperation at Naivasha. The "Garang lobby" was mostly found in Congress and at USAID where it tried its best to ensure support for anti-Khartoum legislation such as the Sudan Peace Act[40] (which had never been enacted) or the "Comprehensive Peace in Sudan Act" which would finally be voted into law, but not implemented, in December 2004. On 1 June 2004 the members of Congress who sympathized with the SPLA sent President Bush a list of twenty-three names of *Janjaweed* supporters, controllers and commanders who were either members of the GoS or closely linked to it. The message was clear: do something about these people. President Bush seemed to have been embarrassed by the implicit demand, all the more because supporters of the anti-Khartoum legislation tended to be more "on the left" (in so far as this political category has relevance in US politics) within both parties and within the fairly tight Black Caucus. President Bush could not be expected to care too much about "the left", but unfortunately for him there was a core group of anti-Khartoum activists at the opposite end of the political spectrum, from where he drew most of his electoral support. Many fundamentalist Protestant organizations had rallied to the anti-Khartoum lobby activated by Nina Shea. Then by mid-2004 vocal Jewish groups such as the Committee for the Holocaust Memorial in Washington had joined in the indignant chorus of protests about Darfur. The President thus found himself under pressure from an array of public opinion elements too wide to be ignored during an election year. But since the "realists" in the intelligence community kept insisting that Khartoum was too important to be harshly treated, these contradictory pressures led the White House to compromise on all fronts—supporting the Naivasha negotiations; not putting too much practical pressure on Khartoum but nevertheless passing legislation which could be used as a sword of Damocles in case of non-compliance; be vocal on Darfur; put a fair amount of money on its humanitarian aspect[41]; and do nothing at the military level. This author was assured that Secretary of State Colin Powell had practically been ordered to use the term "genocide" during this high profile 9 September 2004 testimony to the Senate Committee on Foreign Relations but that he also been advised to add in the same breath that this did not oblige the United States to undertake any sort of drastic action, such as a military intervention[42]. Thus President Bush tried to be all things to all men on the Sudan/Darfur question. Never mind that the result was predictably confused. What mattered was that attractive promises could be handed around without any sort of firm commitment being made. Predictably the interest level of US diplomacy on the Sudan question dropped sharply as soon as President Bush was re-elected.

The European Union: many voices into one won't go.   In its usual way of treating diplomatic matters, the European Union presented a spectacle of complete lack of resolve and coordination over the Sudan problem in general and the Darfur question in particular. The French only cared about protecting Idris Deby's regime in Chad from possible destabilization; the British blindly followed Washington's lead, only finding this somewhat difficult since Washington was not very clear about which direction it wished to take; the Scandinavian countries and the Netherlands gave large sums of money and remained silent; Germany made anti-GoS noises which it never backed up with any sort of action and gave only limited cash; and the

Italians remained bewildered. The result was a purely humanitarian approach to the crisis, with the EU and its member states giving $142 million (out of $301 million, i.e. more in total than the United States) without coming up with anything meaningful in terms of policy. Alan Goulty, the British Special Envoy for Sudan, only managed a depressingly candid statement of impotence: "*Humanitarian intervention in Darfur would be very expensive, fraught with difficulties and hard to set up in a hurry.*"[43] Since money was already coming into Darfur (with Britain the largest European contributor) Goulty obviously meant "military" and not purely humanitarian intervention. Everyone knew that a military operation was the only form of intervention that could have any drastic effect on the situation. But Brussels was quite incapable of mustering the energy to do in distant Darfur what it had failed to do without American or NATO prompting in neighbouring Bosnia or Kosovo a few years earlier. Even on the question of deciding on the nature of what was happening in Darfur, the Union could not manage to speak with any clearly recognizable voice, its Parliament only declaring in September that what was going on was "tantamount to genocide"[44]. During the several Darfur "ceasefire" or "peace" talks in Abéché or Abuja the Europeans pushed for a "no fly zone" above Darfur; but the problem was that even when it was accepted, they did strictly nothing to try to enforce it.

The United Nations: minding the shop. The UN was in a terrible position regarding the Darfur crisis for a number of reasons. First, it was deeply involved in the Naivasha process where it had to boost the IGAD capacity and resolve in what ended up being a saga of endless procrastination and obfuscation. Khartoum kept playing Darfur against Naivasha in order to win at both levels or, if a choice had to be made, at least to keep Darfur out of the military reach of the international community. Second, the UN was at the forefront of the humanitarian effort both in Southern Sudan (through OLS) and in Darfur. Third, Kofi Annan knew that the US administration hated him (and the UN in general) and would do anything in its power to make the world body and its Secretary-General take potentially fatal false moves. Fourth, the Arab/Black African split which was implicit in the Darfur crisis had many echoes inside the UN; and finally, the EU member states and America kept pushing the world body to act as if they were not themselves responsible for it. Kofi Annan knew that the December 1948 genocide Convention only obliged the member states to "*refer*" such a matter to the UN but that once the world body had accepted the challenge it had become mandatory for it to act. Therefore his permanent nightmare over Darfur was that the member states would corner him into saying "genocide", thereby forcing him to act, and then fail to give him the necessary financial, military and political means to do so. For the United Nations which had been shaken by the United States by passing it on the Iraq question, such a debacle would have been a catastrophe. In many ways the UN striving after 2002 to maintain its credibility and its Secretary-General wanted to avoid both US traps and EU passivity.

Caught on the horns of so many dilemmas Kofi Annan tried to act without upsetting things, to scold without being threatening, and to help without intruding too much. The result was that he appeared weak and irresolute at a time when the United States and some of his own staff were insisting on more "action", even if it was no more than symbolic.[45] In June 2004, after he had been booed by demonstrators in Harvard Square,[46] he declared: "Based on reports I have received I cannot at this stage call it genocide or ethnic cleansing yet." This was the worst of both worlds: he had uttered the big taboo words, but prevaricated over their relevance.[47] The pressure kept building up on the UN to come up with some radical solution. And the more the pressure built up the more the Secretary-

General resisted it, because he knew only too well that those who were applying it had no real intention of doing anything. When in early July 2004 he signed a common communiqué with Khartoum's Foreign Minister Mustafa Osman Ismail promising (not for the first time) to "disarm the *Janjaweed*" he remarked: "We can't go and say 'Send in the cavalry' and then not be able to go through with it."[48] This was tantamount to admitting that whatever he signed, nobody should take it seriously. The more the crisis developed, the less the UN seemed capable of doing anything political about it, even though at the humanitarian level it carried over 60 % of the financial burden. In many ways this situation came to demonstrate the UN's practical limitations in crisis over which the heavyweight member states do not want to act. Blaming the UN was easy for those who were responsible for its inaction, and passing the buck to the African Union was another favourite resort to sophistry.

The Report of the UN Commission of Inquiry on the Darfur Violence was the latest but perhaps not the final example of the world's body and the US each acting their parts in a coordinated show of egregious disingenuousness.[49] The report documented violations of international human rights by "people who might have acted with genocidal intentions"; yet the situation was not a genocide[50] although it was definitely "war crimes". But the United States did not like the International Criminal Court (ICC) because it feared that some of its own human rights violations, particularly in Iraq, might make it liable to prosecution, and it therefore did not favour the UN suggestion that the Darfur war crimes should be brought to the ICC, suggesting instead that a special tribunal might be set up in Arusha on the model of the Rwanda tribunal. Off the record everyone worried about naming names in an eventual prosecution because the perpetrators of the Darfur war crimes were the same people who, according to the 9 January 2005 "Peace Agreement", were now supposed to implement the Nairobi decision and turn Sudan into a brave new world of peace and prosperity. Nevertheless, the appended list of fifty-one individuals deemed to be responsible for the Darfur war crimes would later have a major—and unexpected—effect.

The African Union: a make-or-break test. Since the old OAU had decided to shed its skin and be reborn as the African Union (AU), it had known that it would be by its competence in conflict management that the world, from its member states to the broader international community, would judge it. Darfur was the first major crisis to face the organization since its transformation, and its Commission chairman Alpha Konare and the AU chairman in 2004–5, President Obasanjo of Nigeria, knew that the moment of truth had come. But the financial provisions under which the AU operated were highly unrealistic. Its 2003 budget had been a meagre $43 million and out of this the member states had neglected to pay $26 million. This did not prevent Konare from requesting $1.7 billion for a "strategic plan" for the AU, which was to have its own peace fund, a pan-African Parliament (based in South Africa), a court of justice and even a standing army. When the dreaming stopped, the Addis Ababa-based organization finally settled for a budget of $158 million, with $63 million financed by obligatory payments and another $95 million by "voluntary contributions". In the short term the estimated cost of a peacekeeping operation in Darfur—nearly $250 million—had to be financed entirely by foreign donors. In many ways they were only too glad to do so: Brussels promised $110 million and others, from Washington to the UN, pledged the rest. Konare went to Darfur in June on a fact-finding mission and the AU gave its conclusions on 6 July: the organization would send 132 observers to Western Sudan, with 300 troops whose mandate would be restricted to protecting the observers. It also declared that in its opinion there was no ethnic cleansing in Darfur. This was to be a recurrent problem for the AU: in many ways it had not stopped being the "Heads of States Trade Union" which President Julius Nyerere of Tanzania had denounced in 1978.[51] Afraid of Darfur's potential for splintering the organization between Arabs and Black Africans, Konare tried his best to minimize the racial angle of the crisis. Worse, he systematically refused to condemn Khartoum or even to put the responsibility for the massacres squarely on the *Janjaweed*. For the AU Darfur remained a case of mass-murder without any known perpetrators, and Khartoum was even discreetly advised on how to "handle the Whites".[52]

Obasanjo had offered 2,000 Nigerian troops,[53] but only a fraction of them were going to be sent as part of the AU contingent. Khartoum's Minister of the Interior Abd-er-Rahim Mohamed Hussein, one of the two or three most powerful figures in the government, retorted, "We will not tolerate the presence of any foreign troops, whatever their nationality."[54] In the GoS usual style this meant "We will accept foreign troops; all what matters is their nationality and their mandate." Khartoum would be satisfied on both accounts, leading it to accept what it had at first so vociferously rejected. The troops would all be African, their mandate limited to watching the tragedy unfold. This double limitation—no Western troops, since the death of any in action could spark serious international trouble, and no peace-making mandate (peace-*keeping* alone being acceptable)—was satisfactory both for the Western countries, which were being let off the hook easily, and for Khartoum which was getting an impotent and probably mute witness to its "good faith". As for the AU, it was also satisfied: it had been allowed to play in the big boys' league and would not have to pay for the privilege. "Africa" would be at the forefront of the Darfur crisis and any accusations of impotence or limitation of means could be beamed back at the donors.[55] In a way not completely unlike that of the UN, the AU had been scheduled for a "Mission Impossible" type of situation. It was supposed to substitute itself to the coalition of the unwilling, to stop what it was only mandated to observe, to operate on a shoestring and to keep the pretence of serious international involvement for its tight-fisted sponsors. Predictably all it achieved was a token presence.

At this point, after quickly reviewing the policies of the "usual cast of suspects", we have to integrate an interesting comment made by Hugo Slim in his thoughtful analysis of the international response to the Darfur crisis:

There is a paradox in the blame game around any discussion of international responsibility for and response to massive human rights violations. This is quite simply that the moment international public and NGO attention turns to the question of response ...the potential responders can find themselves under heavier fire than the original violators. [...] A strange inversion of responsibility can take place which tends to transfer primary moral responsibility from perpetrators to responders. States are castigated and lobbied about their failures to respond effectively—often with little real attention to what is actually possible.[56]

Slim is certainly right, but he forgets to explain the reason for what he criticizes. For one thing the "responders" are close by and can be addressed directly by Western public opinion, while the perpetrators are far away and tend not to care much about what foreigners think as long as those foreigners do not carry guns. It is the perpetrators' job, so to speak, to kill, while it is the "responders" job to stop them. The question of moral responsibility in the international community hinges on what it stands for. If all that the international community can come up with is that it has not killed anybody, it becomes a statement of peevish irresponsibility. A particularly pathetic example of such an attitude was given by then UN Security Council President Ambassador John Danforth in early November 2004:

"The problem in Darfur is that people are killing, raping, pillaging and removing people from one place to another without their permission. And

I don't think that it is right to say that suddenly the blame should be shifted from the people doing these terrible things to people living half way around the world. I just don't agree with that at all."[57]

"Primary" guilt is clear, but "secondary" guilt is more complex. Great wealth and power give its holders certain responsibilities, if the world "collective morality" is to have any meaning. Ambassador Danforth was in effect saying, "We didn't kill anybody so why are you holding us responsible?" Criminals are criminals, he says, and even as witnesses to their crimes we bear no responsibility for them. This constitutes a regression of civilization because most civilized countries have laws obliging a person who sees a crime being committed to try to stop it by any means available.

It is actually interesting to see that, in line with that claim to irresponsibility, we generally fail to name the perpetrators because naming them would make us fully cognizant of the facts and increase our moral obligation to act. The list of perpetrators complied by a number of US Senators has not been made public;[58] nor (at the time of writing) has the list of fifty-one names compiled by the UN and appended to Resolution 1593 in April 2005. Diplomatic niceties are just another way of saying that we do not care and that we do not intend to act seriously; for the perpetrators any move to the contrary would have signalled a resolve potentially dangerous for the perpetrators; they are fully aware of this because on a trip to Khartoum in December 2004 this author found that under a pretence of "who-the-hell-cares?" several of the people who could be potential targets for the type of legal action Mukesh Kapila had in mind were extremely nervous. Waiting for the unveiling of the now notorious "list of 51" even began to destabilize the GoS during April 2005.

Aggressive labelling and primary guilt attribution are part and parcel of a realistic response. The example of Afghanistan and even more of Iraq are cases in point, proving that when the political will is there (and this because we and not some exotic far-away human beings have been the victims), the means, financial, military and diplomatic, do suddenly materialize. What Hugo Slim validly points out is only one aspect of a complex political/moral game. The shift in guilt that he mentions is in fact a form of escapist scapegoating. We criticize our own institutions because doing so is non-committal, and after we have finished criticizing them we can go back to sleep because no commitment to action has been made other than putting a bit more cash on the table. So criticizing our response should be seen not as a cowardly act of passing the buck but as part of an integrated approach where "secondary" and "primary" forms of guilt should be articulated with each other and not regarded as alternatives.

Was there a genocide in Darfur or not?

The numbers.   The number of victims is definitely not a key factor in deciding if large-scale killings constitute a genocide or not. However, numbers are relevant first in themselves (the magnitude of what the targeted group has suffered) and secondly because of their real or potential impact on world opinion. In the case of Darfur these numbers have been both extremely difficult to compute and, as is usual in such situations, have been the object of fierce differences of opinion.

Any discussion of the numbers of deaths, displaced individuals, refugees and war-affected population in Darfur since February 2003 must start with a short history of how these numbers were arrived at and disseminated. First of all, no clear numbers were given for the Darfur crisis till January 2004, making everything that had taken place previously the object either of neglect or of highly speculative assessments. Up till January 2004 very vague numbers floated around with victims usually estimated at 3,000, but then the UN finally came out with "official" figures of 110,000 refugees in

Chad, 600,000 IDPs inside Darfur and one million "war-affected" people.[59] At the same time the NGO Sudan Focal Point, protesting against the underestimation of the number of deaths, threw in a figure of 30,000 casualties which was only an informed guess, but definitely much closer to the truth than the "official" 3,000 which had been quoted for months. As already mentioned, Muskesh Kapila raised a few eyebrows when he came out with his own estimate of 10,000 victims, a figure immediately denounced by Radio Khartoum as "a heap of lies".[60] By May the UN estimates for the refugees in Chad, suddenly jumped to 200,000 and for the "war-affected" to 2.2 million, including the 700,000 who were in the IDP camps.[61]

Working from partial area estimates by various NGOs, USAID then compiled a rough death-rate for the IDP population of about 4,000 for every week in May. This showed a marked increase, because in January the same compilation had shown only 1,000 a week. This very crude estimate gave between 40,000 and 50,000 deaths since the beginning of the year for the IDP population only, which, if added to the probable 2003 figure, would signify around 80,000 deaths. This was still vague, but it was far above the "official" figure of 10,000 now accepted since Mukesh Kapila's interview.

The first serious mortality survey was carried out by personnel from the French NGO Médecins Sans Frontières (MSF) between April and June 2004 in four IDP camp sites (Zalingei, Mornay, Niertiti and El-Geneina) which together sheltered 215,400 people.[62] MSF personnel insisted, in a very ethical and scientific way, that these results should not be extrapolated to the whole of Darfur, arguing that nobody could tell if similar results would be found elsewhere. But in the absence of other similarly detailed studies we will have to neglect this disclaimer and try to deduce an overall view from their partial but excellent work. First of all, the MSF study provides us for the fist time with an estimate of violent deaths in the pre-camp period of these IDPs' lives: people's answers indicated that about 5% of their number had been killed before they were able to reach (relative) safety. If we add to these deaths those caused by disease, lack of food and water on the way, and exhaustion, we arrive at a Crude Mortality Rate (CMR) of 7.56 per 10,000 a day. The camp period CMR fell sharply, and violent deaths dropped from a majority cause to a small proportion. Disease then became the main cause. But the new CMR, at an average of 2.35 for the four sites, remained definitely higher than the internationally accepted benchmark for an emergency, i.e. one per 10,000 a day. Counting on "only" four months of attacks and flight, we can estimate the number of deaths at around 150,000 for the whole "war-affected" population up to June 2004. If this CMR was any indication of the situation of the war population at large,[63] the growing numbers of "war-affected" and IDPs lead to staggering conclusions about the total human losses. By June 2004 the UN had escalated its estimates to 1.2 million IDPs, 200,000 refugees and 2.3 million war-affected, including by then 800,000 in "registered" IDP camps. If we apply MSF's CMR findings to this population, it meant that around 16,000 people were dying every month, i.e. a grand total of perhaps 180,000 deaths by the end of the rainy season (September 2004). In fact these figures are probably conservative since other attempts at a partial study point to an even larger number of deaths by violence before arrival at the camps. The Centre for International Justice (CIJ) working on a commission from the US State Department interviewed a systematically randomised population of 1,136 refugees in camps in Chad in May–June 2004. It found that 61% of the refugees reported seeing at least one member of their family killed before their eyes. Since the rough average family size is five people and since around 2 million people were affected by the conflict, this means 400,000 families. 61% of 400,000 is 244,000, an even higher figure. If violent deaths numbered even half of that we would be faced with a total death-toll of 210,000 and not 180,000 by September 2004.

At this point we have to go back to the "official" figures because the discrepancy is so large. In September 2004 the UN, while still augmenting its war-affected and IDP estimates,[64] started to quote a total casualty figure of "50,000", later (November 2004) raised to "70,000". No explanation was usually given for using these figures, but they were in fact derived from a very partial WHO report which compiled, very conservatively,[65] the mortality of accessible IDP camps between April and September 2004. So this 50,000–70,000 "total casualty figure" excluded deaths from all causes between February 2003 and April 2004, violent deaths after April 2004, deaths among the inaccessible population of internally displaced people, and any deaths occurring after September 2004. The routine repetition of this 70,000 figure by all the media is a shocking indication of the absolute lack of independent thinking or research by the press. In the case of the Darfur crisis mortality figures, journalists have just lazily copied each other and reproduced obsolete data without verification.

By October 2004 the UN had still augmented its estimates of the various populations at risk, and the "inaccessible" IDPs were now reported to number 500,000. If we use the CMR compiled by USAID for populations without any outside help, i.e. around 10 per 10,000 a day, we would then have to add another 75,000 deaths between April and October. Let us assume an "easier" security situation for this population which largely lives in rebel-controlled area and we could say that their foraging capacity would be much better than those in aided but *Janjaweed*-infested camps. Let us assume that this would sharply diminish the number of deaths and put it at only 30,000. Which would give us around another additional 100,000 deaths between April and October 2004. But by December 2004 the UN had ratcheted up its IDP figure to 2 million, and food distribution figures started to fall due to the growing insecurity caused by the repeated GoS offensives. 1.5 million people were accessed in December 2004 but only 900,000 in January 2005, even as IDP numbers kept relentlessly going up.[66] Rough estimates on such a basis, admittedly poor but still the best we have, would give us a casualty figure ranging between 280,000 and 310,000 at the beginning of 2005. The uncertainty is large, but this is the less bad of estimates under the present circumstances and we will stand by that number, uncertain as it may be.[67]

The semantics. These constitute a fundamental aspect of the problem, not only for the heart of the matter but perhaps even more for the way it has been dealt with by the international community. Basically there are four types of explanations given to the Darfur violence.

The first is that it was an explosion of tribal conflicts exacerbated by drought. This was usually (but not always) a GoS explanation. Secondly, it is explained as a counter-insurgency campaign gone badly wrong because the GoS used inappropriate means to fight back the JEM and SLM insurrection. This is roughly the position of the Darfur specialist Alex deWaal and a number of Western governments. De Waal does not use the argument to exonerate Khartoum. However, the Western governments adopting this position usually minimize the responsibility of the GoS, preferring to talk of "errors". A third explanation is that it was a deliberate campaign of "ethnic cleansing", with the GoS trying to displace or eliminate "African" tribes in order to replace them by "Arab" ones which it feels would be more supportive of "Arab" rule in Khartoum. Finally, genocide began to be mentioned as an explanation in early 2004 by more militant members of the international community and was given a strong boost by Mukesh Kapila's interview in March. This hypothesis was supported by evidence of systematic racial killings. It failed to explain why Khartoum would have picked such an obviously wrong moment.

The "ethnic conflict" explanation has to be looked at technically, not ideologically. We have seen, in Chapters 2 and 3, that ethnic tensions and problems did indeed exist in Darfur for a long time, though not along the lines of the present conflict. This is an essential point which makes Darfur not unlike Rwanda. Tensions between Tutsi and Hutu did not begin with the poorly coordinated attempts at democratisation in 1990 or even with the confused Belgian decolonisation in the 1950s. They were already present when the first Europeans arrived in the 1890s. However they had never been globalized in the way that happened during the genocide. Ethnic tensions can slip into violence, but they use local weaponry, do not present a relentless and systematic character, and do not involve large-scale administrative co-operation from the administration. When Darfur villages were bombed by Antonov aircraft and strafed by combat helicopters, this was not the work of spontaneously violent local nomads. When the *Janjaweed* were organized into coordinated military units and assigned to camps they shared with the regular army, it was not possible to characterize what was happening as "spontaneous violence". Ethnic tensions in Darfur were and still are real, and recurring droughts have made them worse. But they of themselves were not sufficient to unleash the violence we have seen. They were the raw material, not the cause.

Nevertheless the GoS systematically resorted to this and other similar "explanations" in order to deny its involvement in the massacres. The problems of Darfur were caused by "bandits, not rebels"[68]; in any case they were "just a little gang, incapable of standing up to the regular army"[69]; as for the *Janjaweed* they were "a bunch of thieves", just like the rebels.[70] Actually the rebels and the *Janjaweed* were the same thing.[71] There was "no rebellion in Darfur, just a conflict among specific tribes. The government has not armed any militia. The propaganda in the West is trying to exaggerate what is happening."[72] A list of such quotations would be almost endless.

If one discounts these unlikely "explanations", then what of the "counter-insurgency gone wrong"? In many ways this is true, but is it the whole picture and, specifically, is it an "excuse" of some kind? Technically, as we have seen earlier, Darfur is a bad case of poorly conceived counter-insurgency carried out with completely inadequate means. We will not return to a discussion of whether or not a "clean" counter-insurgency is possible; the likelihood is that it is not if a guerrilla movement has arisen from deep-seated economic, social and cultural grievances. But beyond this question of "counter-insurgency gone wrong" there is another point which causes the problem to slip into another dimension. As we have seen, the consequences of the 1984 famine were exploited and made worse by the Libyan and Mahdist obsession with "Arabism" in Darfur in the 1980s. The impact of the Chadian war was not merely some kind of natural catastrophe which fell upon Darfur from the heavens; it was a deliberate policy engineered by Prime Minister Sadiq al-Mahdi and the "Guide" of the Libyan Arab Jamahiriya, Colonel Muammar Gaddafi. In many ways the 1980s were a period of permanent counter-insurgency when the "African" tribes in Darfur were looked upon as the enemy. The fact that the pace of the violence slowed down somewhat during the 1990s did not change that basic outlook. The state of ethnic relations resulting from the frantic ideological manipulation of that period remained a permanent threat to non-Arabs in the province. Thus any armed movement initiated by the non-Arab tribes of Darfur was like a red rag waved before the eyes of an excited bull. Here again the parallel with Rwanda is striking. When Tutsi rebels entered Rwanda in October 1990 they probably did not realize the degree of danger they were creating for the other Tutsi living inside the country. In an atmosphere charged with racism an armed rebellion by the "inferior" group[73] is fraught with enormous danger for the civilians of that group. Counter-insurgency in Darfur could perhaps only have gone wrong. This was not "counter-insurgency" organized by a government trying to restore law and order; it was an answer with arms by a racially and culturally dominant group to the insurrection of a racially and culturally subject group. The hope that repression could be limited to combatants was completely unrealistic.

The two other explanations, "ethnic cleansing" and "genocide", are closely related. As a rough differentiation we could take "ethnic cleansing" to mean massive killings of a certain section of the population in order to frighten the survivors away and occupy their land but without the intent of killing them all. "Genocide" is more difficult to define. The December 1948 International Convention on the Prevention and Punishment of Crimes of Genocide says that what constitutes genocide is "deliberately inflicting on the group conditions of life calculated to bring about its physical destruction *in whole or in part*".[74] I personally have used another definition of the word in my book on the Rwandese genocide,[75] namely a coordinated attempt to destroy a racially, religiously or politically predefined group in its entirety. I am attached to the notion of an attempt at *total* obliteration because it has a number of consequences which seem to be specific of a "true" genocide. First, the numbers tend to be enormous because the purge is thorough. Second, there is no escape. In the case of a racially defined group, the reason is obvious, but if the group is religiously defined no conversions will be allowed. And if it is politically defined no form of submission will save its members.[76] Finally, the targeted group will retain for many years after the traumatic events a form of collective paranoia which will make even its children live with an easily aroused fear. This is evident among the Armenians, the Jews and the Tutsi. But it is present also in less obviously acute forms in groups such as the North American Indians, French Protestants and Northern Irish Catholics. It is this "fractured consciousness" which makes future reconciliation extremely difficult.[77]

If we use the December 1948 definition it is obvious that Darfur is a genocide, but if we use the definition I proposed in my book on Rwanda it is not. At the immediate existential level this makes no difference; the horror experienced by the targeted group remains the same, no matter which word we use. But this does not absolve us from trying to understand the nature of what is happening. Unfortunately, whether the "big-G word" is used or not seems to make such a difference. It is in fact a measure of the jaded cynicism of our times that we seem to think that the killing of 250,000 people in a genocide is more serious a greater tragedy and more deserving of our attention than that of 250,000 people in non-genocidal massacres. The reason seems to be the overriding role of the media coupled with the mass-consumption need for brands and labels. Things are not seen in their reality but in their capacity to create brand images, to warrant a "big story", to mobilize TV time high in rhetoric. "Genocide" is big because it carries the Nazi label, which sells well. "Ethnic cleansing" is next-best (though far behind) because it goes with Bosnia, which was the last big-story European massacre. But simple killing is boring, especially in Africa.

For Darfur the only reasonable position when faced with such sensationalism and verbal inflation is that adopted by ICG President Gareth Evans[78] or USAID Director Roger Winter,[79] who drew attention to the horror without entering into the semantic quarrel over whether or not it was genocide. The term "ethnic cleansing" was first used in connection with Darfur in a BBC commentary on 13 November 2003 and it soon expanded into the accusation of genocide. The difference between the proponents of the "ethnic cleansing" view of Darfur and those who insisted that it was a "genocide" largely had to do with the size of the killings:

The current phrase of choice among diplomats and UN officials is "ethnic cleansing"; but given the nature and scale of human destruction and the clear racism animating attacks systematically directed against civilians from the African tribal groups, the appropriate term is "genocide".[80]

The notion of "ethnic cleansing", implying that the GoS had been trying to displace African tribes in order to give their land to "Arabs", is not backed by any evidence other than the shouts hurled at the victims by the perpetrators themselves. Although they (the perpetrators) might have hoped for such an outcome of the massacres, it is doubtful that a policy of that kind had been clearly thought out in Khartoum. This does not exclude the possibility that some in the GoS might have wished for that outcome, but the few instances of "Arabs" settling on the land abandoned by African peasants do not seem very convincing. The "Arabs" are mostly nomads who do not seem much interested in becoming agriculturalists.

As for the most prominent user of the word "genocide" in connection with Darfur, the former US Secretary of State Colin Powell seems to have based himself on the December 1948 definition of the word when he said on 9 September 2004 that in his opinion Darfur was a genocide.[81] Other spokesmen for world opinion danced a strange ballet around the "big-G word":[82] President George W. Bush declared: "Our conclusion is that a genocide is underway in Darfur." His electoral opponent John Kerry concurred: it was "the second genocide in ten years". The British Minister of State for Foreign Affairs Chris Mullin was more prudent, merely saying that a genocide "might have taken place". The spokesman for the French Foreign Ministry limited himself to saying that there had been "massive violations of human rights", while Walter Lindner, for the German Foreign Affairs Ministry, said that this was "a humanitarian tragedy...with a potential for genocide". In the end none of them went beyond talk. The UN, the AU and the humanitarians were left holding the bloody babies.

This leaves open the question of "intent" which was at the centre of the UN Commission of Inquiry's decision not to call Darfur a genocide. The report apparently wrote that there was "not sufficient evidence to indicate that Khartoum had a state policy intended to exterminate a particular racial or ethnic group", a definition that moved away from that of December 1948, but which in itself is acceptable. However, the semantic play ended up being an evasion of reality. The notion that this was probably not a "genocide" in the most strict sense of the word seemed to satisfy the Commission that things were not really too bad. But conclusions about "war crimes" could, if actually carried over into IPC indictments, for once have serious consequences.

6

CONCLUSION

DARFUR AND THE GLOBAL SUDAN CRISIS

The Darfur horror is still unfolding at the time this book is going to press. Its further developments are unpredictable, but they can be reasonably guessed at. Media coverage will vary depending on the level of violence and on other competing subjects. Indignation will be voiced and diplomatic manoeuvring will take place while the GoS will continue to procrastinate, lie and obfuscate in its usual fashion. Whatever something practical will be attempted at the international penal level remains to be seen. And the UN and the AU will continue to be shock-absorbers between the raw African reality and the international community dreamworld. Thus whether or not a radical change occurs in the situation of Darfur will depend on the global evolution of the situation in Sudan itself. As is usual in the post-Cold War environment real developments will remain internal because the post-historical world no longer has any reasons beyond its media-driven humanitarianism for seriously intervening in obscure distant conflicts.

Which in turn begs the question of how to put the Darfur horror in its general Sudanese context. The Sudanese themselves call their country *al-laham ras*, "a sheep's head" because the cooked head of a sheep, a delicacy in Sudanese cooking, is composed many different types of meat with radically differing texture, aspect and taste. For many years this quip was not reflected in global political and ideo-logical reality. A concerted effort was made by the British and later by the post-1956 Sudanese governments to treat the country as pri-marily Arab with exotic side appendages. This fiction was obsti-nately promoted during the Cold War both by the West and by the Communists, who each went to great lengths for their own purpo-ses to respect the feelings of the Arab world. The first Sudanese North-South war was dealt with within those parameters up till 1972. The outside word then almost completely forgot Sudan till 1983 when the SPLA alliance with a dying but ultra-militant neo-Stalinist Ethiopia as its eastern neighbour briefly posed a threat to Western interests in the Horn of Africa. At that time Darfur existed only marginally on the intellectual map of the Sudanese themselves and not at all on that of the *khawadja*.

The 1984 famine caused a flicker of interest because it could be linked with a global Sahelian problem and with the starvation in Ethiopia mediatized by a rock band. This interest was brief and it died out when pictures of the famine ceased to appear. But intern-ally Darfur had put itself on the map of Sudan beyond simply offering a captive electorate for the Umma party. Still there was nevertheless a massive contrast in the recognition status of South-ern Sudan and Darfur. The perception of Southern Sudan was mostly wrong, but it was at least perceived. In the media Darfur was just a dusty springboard for Chadian warlords who periodically jumped all the way to Ndjamena, either with the support or in op-position to Colonel Gaddafi. Not a very interesting place, except to the French government and the CIA.

After the Soviet/Ethiopian collapse in the Cold War the SPLA was able to shed its Communist image and it was reincarnated as the expression of a Christian survival guerrilla. The symmetrical devel-opments of radical Islam and of radical Protestantism during the 1990s tended to harden this initially blurred image. Meanwhile nobody was much interested in the slow development of violence in Darfur into an endemic situation. It was considered by the few people who knew about it as a typical African "ethnic" conflict with a low danger potential. The contrast with the South was reinforced by the spectacular quasi-genocidal policies carried out by the Sudanese government in that region. Radical Muslims had taken power in Khartoum in July 1989 and the Southern situation began to be seen as largely of their making and, increasingly, as an example of Muslim-Christian conflict, with radical Islam the prime motivating factor. That the war had been started by the catastrophic policies of the staunchly pro-Western President Nimeiry and made intractable by another friend of the West, the democratically-elected Prime Minister Sadiq al-Mahdi, tended to be glossed over. The essentially racial-cultural nature of the war—and hence its potential for spreading to other areas of the *laham ras*—was mostly overlooked.

One element which could have alerted foreign observers to the true nature of the Sudanese conflict was the genocidal violence carried out by the Khartoum regime in the Nuba Mountains after 1992. There, after duly proclaiming a *jihad*, it bombed and deported thousands of civilians, penning them up in concentration camps and selling them as slave labour to the large Arab-owned farms in Kordofan. The fact that many victims of this massive violence were Muslims was largely overlooked. Mosques were bombed, Muslims were deported or killed along with their Christian and "pagan" brethren, and the SPLA began to penetrate the area to defend the population. Its local commander, Yussif Kuwa, was a Muslim.

By then the SPLA had also begun to penetrate other "marginal" areas of the Sudan, particularly the southern part of Blue Nile province. The East, populated by Beja tribes similar to those living in Eritrea, had also begun to move. And Darfur continued obstinately to fight its own low-intensity civil war. Southern Blue Nile, the Beja country and Darfur were all completely Muslim, which made the "radical Islam" explanation difficult to sustain. So what was the real logic of the war if it was not religious? The answer was blunt and was related to a word which Nazism, the demise of colonialism and the development of scientific anthropology have marginalized into intellectual exile and political opprobrium: the word "race".

The problem with race is that, contrary to the notions developed by nineteenth-century pseudo-science, the word has no scientific meaning. Hence the extremely naïve notion that once its scientific relevance is disproved, it will fall into disuse. "Race" is first and foremost a perceived construct, based on simple anthropological markers and, even more, on perceived cultural values inseparable from them. We saw in Chapter 1 how intricate and complex the real cultural and ethnic makeup of Darfur is. It is evident that trying to superimpose on that mosaic simple notions such as "Arab" or "African" is not a very productive endeavour. But, as we saw in Chapter 3, this is nevertheless what happened. How was it done? Largely by pathological persuasion. Chapter 2 tried to demonstrate how Darfur had remained a poor and neglected appendage of its distant Nile Valley masters, whether they were British or *awlad al-beled* Arabs. When the hope and promise of independence came to nothing, somebody had to be made responsible. And suddenly in the 1980s Colonel Gaddafi and Prime Minister Sadiq al-Mahdi gave an answer: Darfur was poor and backward because it was insufficiently Arabized. It had missed out in the great adhesion to the Muslim *umma* because its Islam was primitive and insufficiently Arabic. The 1984 famine brutally sharpened the nomad/sedentary dichotomy, and now this dichotomy received another coextensive dimension, that of "Arab" versus "African", the first good, the second bad. This marked the beginning of years of low-intensity racial conflict and harassment, with the "Arab" Centre almost automatically siding against the "African" Periphery.

The situation was pregnant with the potential for enormous destruction because it fitted only too well within the broader context of racial prejudice in the Sudan. The "Arabs" in the Sudan are unsure about the purity of their Arab credentials, which tends to make them all the more touchy about these being respected. The South and its barbaric denizens had always been considered as a colony ripe for exploitation. But by virtue of being Muslims the other non-Arabs of the West and East had acquired a kind of tolerable status in the eyes of the ruling minority at the Centre. This "privileged" status was put into question during the 1980s when the new war in the South and the military successes of the SPLA seriously alarmed the ruling group. "Race" thus became a new and acknowledged dimension in the war. When Western soldiers and NCOs mutinied at the Bahari barracks in September 1985, their revolt was immediately dubbed a "racist plot".[1] In a paradoxical semantic twist, the uprising of the "African" *awlad al-Gharb* had become "racist" because it objectively served the interests of the SPLA. The globalization of "race" above and beyond the previously existing concepts of religion and tribe cut two ways: for the "Arabs" there was the fear of seeing all the non-Arabs coming together in a coherent challenge to their privileges; but for the non-Arabs this fear began to define a new form of consciousness which Colonel Garang's ideology of a "New Sudan" tended to reinforce. The SPLA's "marginalized" people tended to be roughly the Muslim non-Arabs, that hitherto silent third of the Sudanese national equation.[2] By the late 1980s, when the Muslim Brothers took power, they were keenly aware of the inherent danger of the racial pattern and desperately tried to emphasize the religious factor in order to look at the situation from the more favourable angle. The Darfur insurrection, indirectly provoked by the accommodation they had been forced to seek with the Southern Christians, suddenly shifted the whole paradigm. A large chunk of the Muslim North had decided to act not according to its religious identity but rather in line with its racial origins. The attempt by the Nile Valley Arabs to have their cake politically and eat it economically was suddenly falling short of its objective.

Since the Muslim Brothers' regime knew that it was weak and politically unstable the danger was great, in fact much greater than that posed by the South. Khartoum had had a long history of manipulating its Southern quasi-colony, from breaking its 1955 promises of federalism to the empty rhetoric of the 1965 Round Table Conference, and from absorbing the Anya Nya movement after 1972 to unilaterally dismantling the Addis Ababa Agreement in 1980.[3] The Northern political class had had full confidence that it would always be able to fool its "African" citizens, the "slaves". But the Muslim peripheries were something else. Nobody was so sure. There was the question of intermarriage, of a shared religious community, of cultural proximity. The *awlad al-gharb* were half out, but they were also half in. They threatened the Centre from much closer. And what about the possibility of an alliance with the "slaves"? After all the North owed its political and economic hegemony to its capacity to mobilize the other third of the country in the name of Islam, even if it never paid the bill when it became due. But what if the "slaves" could bring about its very opposite; a "racial" alliance? This would be the end of "our" Sudan, of the *awlad al-beled* Sudan.

The reaction to such a possibility was bound to be brutal, hence the counter-insurgency "going wrong". It could not go "right" given the fear motivating it. Which is why there is such ambiguity around the word "genocide". The Southern war had been of genocidal proportions. The Nuba Mountains *Jihad* had been another quasi-genocide. Now Darfur was going to be yet another. In none of these cases did we have a Sudanese equivalent to the Wannsee Conference,[4] with all the top brass of the regime sitting down at a table and cold-bloodedly deciding on the annihilation of a racial group. There was no need to. The decision-makers understood each other without having to plan and plot. They knew what they had, they knew what they stood to lose, and beyond their ceaseless political squabbles they largely felt of one mind. From that point of view the various regimes in Khartoum were as one and the Muslim Brothers were no worse (or no better) than the others. The danger had to be dealt with and the ruling group could not afford to be too choosy about the means. Since Darfur had been in a state of protracted racial civil war since the mid-1980s, the tools were readily available; they merely needed to be upgraded. It was done, and the rest is now history.

The question now is basically whether or not this will succeed. The Sudanese government had hoped to be able to crush the Darfur insurrection before it would have to enter into any form of power-sharing arrangement with the SPLA because such a deal would enormously complicate the repression. Since January 2005 it has become too late and Colonel Garang can be counted upon to keep the Darfur wound festering. For him the prolongation of the Western insurrection is a guarantee that his Northern "partners" will have a harder time trying to manipulate him than if their hands were free. It is at present impossible to know whether the *awlad al-beled* will manage to do what they did after 1972. Their efforts at keeping power will now become much more arduous. Will Sudan remain the centralized "Arab" country it has been since independence? This is now increasingly dubious and is the real question—not whether the country will be "Islamized" or not. Sudan is and will remain a country with a Muslim majority. But will the state reflect the presence of an "African" majority or not? If it does, what form will this take? Arriving at an answer will be slow and probably painful. One can reasonably doubt whether the political system defined by the "Comprehensive Peace Agreement" signed at Naivasha on 9 January 2005 will be the appropriate tool to enable such a task to be undertaken, at least in its present form where Darfur remains completely excluded.

NOTES

Chapter 1   *Independent Darfur: Land, People, History*

1. The best overall introduction to Darfur can be found in Rex O'Fahey, *State and Society in Darfur*, London, Hurst, 1980. Its bibliography is an essential starting point for any deeper study of the land and its people, even if it has to be completed by a number of works published in the last twenty-five years.

2. For a global overview replacing Darfur in "the Sudan" see M. Horowitz, "A Reconsideration of the 'Eastern Sudan'", *Cahiers d'Etudes Africaines*, vol. 7, no. 3 (1967), pp. 381–98.

3. In 1994 the Sudanese government divided Darfur into three states—Northern, Southern and Western. This was part of a more general administrative reorganisation which divided the nine states of the Sudan into 26 and its 18 provinces into 72. The result was a form of centralized pseudo-federalism combining the problems of both systems.

4. Late 18th-century travellers such as the French Vivant Denon and the British G. B. Browne first described this legendary itinerary. W. B. K. Shaw describes the road and its history in "Darb el Araba'in" *Sudan Notes and Records*, vol. XII (1929), pp. 63–71.

5. About 50 km. from East to West and 110 km. from North to South.

6. Similar in this to the geologically very different but historically not dissimilar Nuba Mountains of Southern Kordofan.

7. Non permanent watercourses.

8. The *haraz* is a local tree which produces large fruit pods, unfit for human consumption but excellent cattle fodder.

9. The name «Baggara» («cowherds») is a collective name used to describe a variety of cattle-raising tribes of "Arab" origin who live in Southern Darfur and Kordofan. They are nomads and their grazing areas range into the Southern Sudan province of Bahr-el-Ghazal and at times as far south as the Central African Republic.

10. This means before 1874 i.e. before the Turco-Egyptian occupation which, as we will see, preceded the British colonisation by nearly forty years.

11. Although not precisely known, it must stand today at around six millions.

12. Darfur has little to offer to the outside world and little money with which to purchase its products. Since at the best of times barely 80% of food needs are locally produced, food security is often perilously close to survival.

13. Depending on the criteria used to distinguish the various groups from each other, authors consider that Darfur is populated by a minimum of 36 to a maximum of 150 "tribes". These arguable distinctions tend to put on the same footing groups numbering a few thousands and others in the million range. Self-perceptions, outsider perceptions and neighbouring people's perceptions often vary considerably as to who is who.

14. In classical Arabic the word means "blue" (from "*azraq*"), but in local Sudanese Arabic this is used to mean "black", i.e. "African".

15. K. M. Barbour, *The Republic of the Sudan: a Regional Geography*, University of London Press, 1961, p. 80.

16. This was described by R.S. O'Fahey in his key article "Fur and Fertit: the history of a frontier" in J. Mack and P. Robertshaw (eds), *Culture History in the Southern Sudan: Archaeology, Linguistics, Ethnohistory*, Nairobi. British Institute for Eastern Africa, 1982.

17. We place the name "Fur" between inverted commas since this presently homogeneous community is the product of a complex process of aggregation to which we will return.

18. This is globally true, but some groups, like the Habbaniya, took to agriculture in the early 1900s.

19. To make things even more intractable for the outside observer, the word "Fellata" has been in common use since the Condominium period to describe recent West African migrants who have settled all over the Sudan where they perform mostly menial jobs. This is illustrated by a common Sudanese proverb of the colonial period: "the British have taken away our slaves but God has given us the Fellata."

20. The role of the *awlad al-Bahar fuqara* was essential in this process.

21. For a detailed development of this period see R.S. O'Fahey and J. Spaulding: *Kingdoms of the Sudan*, London: Methuen, 1974.

22. «Keyra» was the name used at the time, and later came to describe the aristocracy of the Fur Sultanate. Today many Fur will still refer to themselves as "Keyra" rather than as "Fur".

23. Many nevertheless became islamized later.

24. R. S. O'Fahey, *State and Society in Darfur*, op. cit., p. 76.

25. This dichotomy between "the domain of Islam" and "the domain of war" is a fundamental feature of traditional Muslim political culture. The *kafir* ("heathen") world of the *dar al-harb* is a legal hunting-ground either for conversion of the pagans or for their enslavement.

26. A Fur traditional song says: "the Fertit are all slaves even if they walk free."

27. Even if all court documents were written in Arabic, the kingdom never lost its practice of bilingualism, and court titles were expressed in *Furawi*. Ordinary people have retained their language to this day, even if spoken Sudanese Arabic ("aamiya sudaniyya") has vastly grown in use since the nineteenth century.

28. L. Kapteijns and J. Spaulding, *After the Millennium: Diplomatic Correspondence from Wadaï and Darfur on the Eve of the Colonial Conquest (1885–1916)*, East Lansing: Michigan State University Press, 1988. [document no. 81]

29. The letter was written at an undefined date during the Mahdiyya (see next section).

30. The role of the sacred *nahas* (copper drums) closely parallels that of the sacred drums in the Great Lakes monarchies.

31. Gian Battista Messedaglia, "Le Dar For pendant la gestion de feu le Général Gordon Pacha", *Bulletin de la Société Khédivale de Géographie*, vol, III, no. 1 (1888), pp. 41–61.

32. The Fur Sultans had an enormous number of children, the record probably going to Ali Dinar (1898–1916) who had 120 sons and around 150 daughters.

33. Sing. *Faris* meaning «horseman» but definitely with the European connotation of the word «knight». Epic poetry was sung and man-to-man challenges followed by single combat were frequent when the war involved worthy opponents i.e. other *fursan* from Dar Masalit or Wadaï.

34. They were bought from Germany via Egypt and the *darb al- 'arbain* trade route.

35. The period of Darfurian dominion over Kordofan (1785–1821) was remembered in later years as a golden age, particularly when contrasted with the rapacious economic and tax policies of the Turco-Egyptian regime which followed (see next section).

36. Like many «capitals» in traditional kingdoms based on a peasant subsistence economy, these towns had to be moved every few years as the court progressively devoured all local resources. El-Fashir, with its broader commercial economic base, managed to survive in one place.

37. *Umm Kwakiyya* (lit. "the mother of banditry") was the name given in Darfur to the period going from the conquest of Zubeyr Rahman Mansur in 1874 to the fall of the Mahdiyya and the restoration of the Sultanate in 1898.

38. The clumsy term "Turco-Egyptian" has to be used because at the time, though largely independent from Istanbul, Egypt was nominally a province of the Ottoman Empire. Muhammad Ali was only the Khedive (Viceroy) of Egypt and owed allegiance to his Turkish overlord. Native Egyptians took very little part in the conquest and occupation of "Sudan". Muhamad Ali was an ethnic Albanian and out of twenty-three Governors of Sudan during the period of what the Sudanese call "*Turkiyya*", "the time of the Turks" (1821–85) none was an Egyptian Arab and only five were ethnic Turks. All the others were "Ottomans"—Circassians, Kurds, Greeks or Albanians. The standard work on this period is R. Hill, *Egypt in the Sudan*, Oxford University Press, 1959.

39. Khartoum did not exist at the time. It was founded in 1824 by the Turco-Egyptians to become the capital of their newly conquered territory.

40. The *casus belli* was provided by the betrayal of the Rizzeyqat. This Arab tribe which was nominally under the control of the Fur Sultan had signed a trading agreement with Zubeyr to allow him to trade northward. In 1873 they broke this agreement and started plundering his caravans. Zubeyr held the Sultan responsible for this breach of faith by people he could hardly control.

41. He was eventually allowed back by the British in 1898, but by then he was a tame old man.

42. P. M. Holt, *The Mahdist State in the Sudan (1881–1898)*, Oxford: Clarendon Press, 1958, p. 21.

43. Killing in the process the famous Colonel Charles Gordon, a former employee of the Turco-Egyptian regime in the Sudan, who had been sent to Khartoum by the British to organize its evacuation. But Gordon was strong-headed and independent and chose instead to fight it out, with disastrous results. Gordon's mission had been initiated from London because shortly after the beginning of the Mahdist revolt (in 1882) the British had occupied Egypt to repossess its unpaid debts to various European banks, and thus found themselves the rather embarrassed heirs to its African empire.

44. After the fall of Khartoum the Mahdi had ordered the "heathen" Turco-Egyptian city to be abandoned and created another capital at Omdurman on the opposite shore of the Nile.

45. In fact Abdullahi wanted Western fighters near him to help him control the political competition of the *Ashraf*, the riverine Arabs who had been close to the *Mahdi* himself.

46. Nobody ever knew where he was born, but he seems to have been from a tribe following the Sanussiya, i.e. on the border between today's Chad and Libya.

47. The Mahdists had the ambition to conquer Mecca one day and did not allow passage to Islam's holy cities in the meantime.

48. Martin Daly, *Empire on the Nile: the Anglo-Egyptian Sudan*, vol. 1: *1898–1934*, Cambridge University Press, 1986, 172.

49. A combination of religious school, travellers' hostel, monastery and fortress. The *zawiya* of the Senussiyya brotherhood drew a network of strongpoints extending from Libya down to the northern part of today's Central African Republic, constituting a kind of quasi-state across the Sahara.

50. This was a regional obsession for the Foreign Office leading, *inter alia*, to the deposition of the supposedly pro-Turkish Ethiopian Emperor Lij Yassu in 1916 through the agency of Ras Tafari Makonen, the future Emperor Haile Selassie, who favoured the Allies.

51. The Turks were indeed actively courting the Senussiyya brotherhood with which they had had long-standing ties since their days in pre-Italian Tripolitania. But the reasoning of the British government was crudely wrong since, as we saw, Ali Dinar had no sympathy whatever with the Sanussiyya.

52. Martin Daly, *op. cit.* p. 177.

Chapter 2 *Darfur and Khartoum (1916–1985): An Unhappy Relationship*

1. Following the British occupation of Egypt in 1882, the country became *de facto* a Protectorate. In its position as "tutor" to Egypt, Britain had to be mindful of Cairo's sensitivities and it used the pretext of the former Turco-Egyptian occupation of the Sudan to occupy it "in the name of Egypt". But even though a number of Egyptian administrators were sent to the Sudan, Egypt remained very much the junior partner in the Condominium arrangement. After the 1924 mutinies which were supported by Egyptian nationalists, Cairo's functionaries were largely removed from the Sudan.

2. See R.O. Collins, "The Sudan Political Service: a Portrait of the Imperialists", *African Affairs*, no. 284 (1972).

3. M. W. Daly, *Empire on the Nile: the Anglo-Egyptian Sudan (1898–1934)*, Cambridge University Press, 1986, p. 87.

4. Wilfrid Thesiger, *A Life of my Choice*, London, 1987, p. 201.

5. Francis Deng and Martin Daly, *Bonds of Silk: the Human Factor in the British Administration of the Sudan*, East Lansing: University of Michigan Press, 1989.

6. Darfur, with its 500,000 square km., was run by about a dozen administrators.

7. This was the prayer book compiled by the historical Mahdi during his revolt. After 1898 it became a rallying symbol for the neo-Mahdist movement.

8. In the middle of the Nile, about 100 kilometres upstream from Khartoum.

9. In *The Dual Mandate in British Tropical Africa*, London: Frank Cass (repr.), 1965.

10. Some tribes, particularly among the nomadic ones, were left out of the *Dar* allocation. It was they who felt the most bitter against *dar*-based sedentary peasants after the 1984 famine (see below and Chapter 3).

11. Martin Daly, *op.cit.*, vol. 1, p. 383.

12. At least, in Dongola, there were government schools.

13. 'Note by the Director of Education on the Government Plan to for educational development', 16 February 1946. SAD 658/6. *AR* 1939 to 1946. Quoted in Martin Daly, *op.cit.*, vol. 2, p. 108.

14. Martin Daly, *op. cit.*, vol. 2, p. 312.

15. James Morton, 'Tribal administration or no administration: the choice in Western Sudan', *Sudan Studies*, no. 11, January 1992.

16. This is the expression used in the Arabic documents of the Sudan Political Service. In the strict sense of the term it means "administration of the people", with the term "people" used in implicit contrast with other forms of administration which could have come from "outside".

17. C. H. Harvie and J. G. Cleve, *The National Income of Sudan*, Khartoum: Department of Statistics, 1959.

18. This last crop is an amazing choice in view of the quantities of water sugarcane cultivation requires.

19. Raphaël Koba Badal, *Origins of the Underdevelopment of the Southern Sudan: British Administrative Neglect*, University of Khartoum, Development Studies and Research Centre, 1983.

20. H. L. Greenwood, 'Escape in the Grass', *Sudan Notes and Records*, vol. XIV (1941), pp. 189–96. The author was a member of the Sudan Political Service.

21. It is interesting to note that the members of the Sudan Political Service assigned to the South were often of more modest social origin than those posted to the North.

22. The South was deemed too backward to take part. Provision was made for the establishment of a countrywide Council for a later unspecified date.

23. The Graduates Congress had been founded in February 1938 as the first modern nationalist organization. Its membership was theoretically non-sectarian i.e. not reflecting the main Katmiyya/Mahdist split of Sudanese politics but in practice sectarianism ran rife in its midst.

24. Sayid Ali al-Mirghani was so offended by the dominant influence of the Mahdists in the Advisory Council that he had withdrawn from it.

25. J. W. Robertson, "Note on the amendment of the ordinance to secure Khatmia participation", 2 November 1949. Quoted in Muddathir Abd-er-

Rahim, *Imperialism and Nationalism in the Sudan*, Oxford: Clarendon Press, 1969, p. 189.

26. In Darfur the results were the opposite of the national ones, with *Umma* winning in six of the eleven provincial constituencies and only two going to the Unionists. The others went to independents.

27. They were right: al-Azhari led the first post-independence cabinet and managed to escape from his party's commitment to union with Egypt.

28. It was finished in 1959 under the military dictatorship of Ibrahim Abboud.

29. The doubling of the constituencies for the province was largely due to the fact that Mahdists had managed to get the Fellata registered for voting, even when they were not Sudanese. For the Umma this was a tremendous coup which played a far from negligible role in their countrywide victory.

30. Peter Bechtold, *Politics in the Sudan: Parliamentary and Military Rule in an Emerging African Nation*, New York: Praeger, 1976, pp. 197–8.

31. This was due to the Army having agreed with both the Mahdists and the Khatmiyya that their interests would be preserved. The state became a kind of enterprise (in the economic sense) where the three partners shared the pie. It was losing sight of that basic proposition and increasingly relying on arrogant and shortsighted officers who later brought discredit to the regime.

32. This separate voting college was a throwback to the British period. People with university degrees, officers above a certain rank and high-level civil servants voted separately a second time. They elected fifteen MPs in 1965, a number disproportionate to the size of their electorate.

33. The ICF was an openly Muslim fundamentalist party regrouping some minor Muslim *turuq* under the aegis of the Muslim Brotherhood. It fielded a number of candidates and won three seats in the territorial constituencies (apart from Darfur the two others were in Kassala and Khartoum) plus two more in the Graduate constituencies.

34. The Mahdists were reputed to have an 8,000-strong militia and periodically flaunted that fact in the face of the more peaceful and less militant Unionists.

35. Gabriel Warburg, *Islam, Sectarianism and Politics in Sudan since the Mahdiyya*, London: Hurst, 2003, p. 148.

36. That factor is absolutely essential. The whole "Riverine Arab" political élite is a huge network of intermarried families. Hassan al-Turabi, for example, is married to a sister of Sadiq al-Mahdi. The term of *awlad al-Beled* (sons of the country) used to describe them implies that non-members of that élite are second-class citizens.

37. Sayed Abd-er-Rahman's son Siddiq had died in 1961, only two years after his father. His death opened a crisis of succession and created a split between the

leadership of the Ansar quasi-*tariqa* and the more secularly oriented leadership of the Umma party.

38. The Imam al-Hadi's mother was a Darfurian Baggara. This led many local "Arabs" to support him but not all. For other "Arabs" more keen on racial/cultural "purity", Sadiq was better because he was "*a pure Ashraf*", i.e. not tainted by the second-class Arabism of the Baggara. (interview with Ahmed Ibrahim Diraige, London, October 2004)

39. During the Abboud dictatorship there was not a single Cabinet Minister from Darfur.

40. Robert Buijtenhuijs, *Le FROLINAT et les révoltes populaires du Tchad (1965–1976)*, The Hague: Mouton, 1978.

41. The 1960s saw a steadily growing anti-Arab insurgency in Sudan's southern provinces.

42. J. Millard Burr and R.O. Collins, *Africa's Thirty Years War: Libya, Chad and the Sudan (1963–1993)*, Boulder, CO: Westview Press, 1999, p. 61. This book gives the best detailed account of the complex conflict.

43. Robert Buijtenhuijs, *Le FROLINAT et les guerres civiles du Tchad (1977–1984)*, Paris: Karthala, 1987, p. 108.

44. In January 1935 Italy and France had signed a treaty in Rome defining the border between Libya and Chad. But the treaty had been denounced by Mussolini (December 1938) who claimed a much bigger slice of territory. What Gaddafi did was to revive the old 1938 Fascist claim. See Bernard Lanne, *Tchad-Libyed: La querelle des frontières*, Paris: Karthala, 1982, for a detailed account.

45. This is all the more paradoxical since he later adopted a diametrically opposite stance after 2000 and his long exile in the cold of international diplomacy following the Lockerbie outrage. Furious at the "treason" of his Arab peers he decided that he was "an African", that he would have nothing to do with the Arab world and he actively supported the creation of the new African Union, even trying to get it relocated in Tripoli. But this was thirty years later, and in the 1970s and 1980s the mercurial Libyan leader was crudely anti-Black.

46. J. M. Burr and R.O. Collins, *op. cit.*, p. 84.

47. He had made the same offer to Anwar as-Sadat, only to be turned down by the Egyptians as well.

48. Sadiq had managed to organize a broad opposition front in Libya, the so-called Front for National Salvation, which brought together the Muslim Brothers of the Islamic Charter Front (ICF), the two branches of the Unionists (the secular NUP and the religious PDP), and even Father Philip Gabboush's Nuba

Mountain Group who was the Black Christian guarantee of this very Arab and Muslim movement.

49. The Front's militia was entirely recruited in Darfur by the *Tajammu al-Arabi* and its combatants were all "Arabs" although its leader, An-Nur Saad, was an "African" Berti.

50. This account of the coup attempt and following repression is based on several conversations with former Darfur governor Ahmed Ibrahim Diraige, with interviews of *Failaka al-Islamiya* fighters in the 1980s and with ordinary citizens of Omdurman who witnessed the events of July 1976.

51. Gaddafi systematically denounced the southern-dominated Chadian government as an arm of the CIA.

52. Alex DeWaal, *Famine that Kills: Darfur 1984–1985*, Oxford: Clarendon Press, 1989, p. 50.

53. The situation had dramatically changed in Chad when President Malloum had co-opted Hissen Habre as Prime Minister before he himself resigned. By late 1979 Ndjamena was in political and military chaos and Habre was fighting for political survival against a direct Libyan invasion. The Libyans had attacked in April 1979 and Habre had kept his Darfur rear bases both as a logistical support system and as a political insurance policy. This was a wise precaution because by late 1980 the Libyan army forced him out of Ndjamena and back into Sudan.

54. The Takrouri are a small community of Chadian-born Nigerians. Ali al-Hajj was born in Darfur and he was an ICF member. His nomination was the only one Nimeiry objected to.

55. The best known were the "Jebel Mara Scheme" and the "Western Savannah Project". Often visited by ministers and foreign dignitaries, these "pilot projects" were only experimental.

56. *Hafir* are deep reservoirs dug into the earth, usually at a low point of the ground. They are at the centre of a star-like network of small channels so as to collect surface water during the rains. But they fill very quickly with silt and have to be maintained at regular intervals in order to keep their storage capacity.

57. Diraige was regularly kept informed by State Security of the broad developments of Hissen Habre's war but he had no control over the Chadian bases. In June 1982 Hissen finally won and took Ndjamena. Nimeiry immediately lost all interest in Darfur. (Interview with Ahmed Ibrahim Diraige, London, October 2004)

58. *Africa Economic Digest*, 23 November 1984.

59. *Africa Confidential*, vol. 25, no. 23, 14 November 1984.

60. *African Business*, February 1985.

61. The United States negotiated a reprieve, but Khartoum was finally suspended a year later when it could not pay $250 million in arrears.

62. *Le Monde*, 3 April 1985.

63. During the riots people battled the police under large signs, not yet taken down, proclaiming "Welcome Vice-President Bush".

64. Although somewhat self-righteous, the works of Mansour Khalid (see Bibliography) best convey the appalling moral and political disaster incarnated by the Sudanese political "élite".

65. Several interviews with a wide variety of Sudanese political actors between 1985 and 2004 have yielded figures between $18 million and $35 million for the Libyan pre-electoral payoff to Sadiq.

Chapter 3 *From Marginalization to Revolt: Manipulated "Arabism" and "Racial" Anarchy, 1985–2003*

1. *The Economist*, 20 July 1985. Osman Abdallah had abruptly cancelled a previously planned visit to Cairo in order to go to Tripoli.

2. *Africa Confidential*, vol. 26, no. 13, 19 June 1985.

3. *The Economist*, 30 November 1985.

4. *The Economist*, 29 March 1986.

5. Author's interviews in both Khartoum and El-Fashir, May 1986.

6. Of the five others one was won by an independent candidate, two had gone to the Unionists and two to the newly-formed National Islamic Front (NIF), the latest reincarnation of Turabi's radical Islamist movement.

7. The Unionists' DUP had won 64 seats and Turabi's NIF 51. Since 37 of the South's 67 constituencies had not been able to vote because of the war, and since the secularist Northern parties had only eleven seats, this gave a massive majority (81% in terms of seats) to the religious-based parties. These results were deceptive since the NIF had got 23 seats (out of 28) from the restricted Graduates' College with a number of votes which would have won it three seats in the general college.

8. "Famine that kills" (as opposed to a simple food scarcity), which gave its title to Alex deWaal's already quoted book.

9. Alex deWaal, *op. cit.*, pp. 87–90.

10. Author's interviews in Khartoum and London, May and September 1986.

11. *Africa Confidential*, vol. 27, no. 21, 15 October 1986.

12. Although it flew in the face of reality, the denial was reiterated by Sudanese Army Chief of Staff, General Abd-el-Aziz Siddiq in January 1987 (*al-Bayan*, 17 January 1987). A week later another large convoy of sixty Libyan trucks arrived at El-Fashir (*Sudan Times*, 27 January 1987).

13. Mindful of their security, the *Murahleen* tended to select SPLA-free areas to carry out their raids, paying their Dinka informers with stolen cattle (*Sudan Times*, 1 February 1987).

14. *Africa Confidential*, vol. 28, no. 4, 18 February 1987.

15. The "Council of State" was a five-man collective presidency which, in the absence of a constitution, side-stepped the problem of choosing a head of state. Each of the five members was successively "President" of the country.

16. *Le Monde*, 14 February 1987.

17. *Le Monde*, 24 February 1987.

18. Agence France Presse dispatch, Khartoum, 28 February 1987.

19. *Le Monde*, 10 March 1987.

20. *Sudan Times*, 27 March 1987.

21. *Africa Confidential*, vol. 28, no. 7, 1 April 1987.

22. All were destroyed in combat or accidents within a year.

23. Interview with Jean Audibert, Special Adviser for African Affairs to President Mitterrand, Paris, 24 April 1987.

24. See Suleiman Ali Baldo and Ushari Mahmood, *The el-dien massacre and slavery in the Sudan*, Khartoum, privately printed, 1987. This courageous document, written by two Arab intellectuals, rocked cultural Sudanese complacency to its foundations.

25. These were the forces of Chadian dissident Acheikh ibn-Omar from the Salamat "Arab" tribe, who had joined the pro-Libyan camp, supplanting the former GUNT boss Gukkuni Weddeye.

26. By this he of course meant the "Arab" tribes. It is interesting to note that the Zaghawa, later described as some of the main victims of the "Arab" militias in 2003–4, were at that time on the other side. Interview in London with DDF activists, November 1987.

27. *Afrique Défense*, December 1987.

28. *Le Monde*, 1 December 1987.

29. Bakri Adil (Minister of Education. Baggara Humr), Fadlallah Burma Nasir (State Minister for Defence. Missiriya), Musa Adam Madibo (Minister for Energy, an ed-Da'ien Rizzeyqat)

30. Interview with Ahmed Ibrahim Diraige. London. December 1987.

31. See Reuters dispatch (10 December 1987), *Libération* (22 December 1987).

32. Eva Dadrian, 'Danger in Darfur', *New African*, January 1988. The figure of 3,000 was a very conservative one.

33. Interview with Umma Political Bureau member Joseph Sabbagh, Khartoum, January 1988.

34. The base was off-limits to the Sudanese, including the military (interview with Bichar Idris Haggar. Paris. August 1987).

35. Interview with a young DDF activist, Abdallah Adam Khatir, Khartoum, January 1988.

36. Interview with Dr Idris Mohamed Ali, London, March 1988.

37. Industry, Communications, *Zakat* (Islamic taxation), Commerce and Justice. It was Hassan al-Turabi himself who took up the last of these appointments.

38. 'Sudan: the Wild West', *Africa Confidential*, vol. 29, no. 11, 27 May 1988.

39. *The New African*, August 1988.

40. Interview with Ahmed Diraige, London, July 1988. Hissen Habre was still not convinced of the wisdom of backing the "African" tribes in Darfur to counter-balance the Libyan support for the "Arab" ones.

41. In the South, particularly in Bahr-el-Ghazal, the food emergency was much worse, killing between 200,000 and 250,000 people.

42. *Libération*, 9 December 1988, and interview with Jean Audibert, President Mitterrand's Special Adviser on African Affairs, Paris, 28 December 1988.

43. Interview with a Sudanese army officer, Khartoum, February 1989.

44. By the spring of 1989 there were six different coups getting organized and out of those five groups of plotters had travelled to Addis Ababa to confer with the SPLA and sound out its potential attitude in case Sadiq al-Mahdi should be overthrown (interview with Deng Alor, Addis Ababa, May 1989)

45. They were the FANT top officers who had been responsible for Chad's latest string of victories against Libya and whose daring and military knowledge were almost legendary. But their tribe had become embroiled in a quarrel with Habre's Anakaza about selling the guns taken from the Libyans during the FANT's recent victorious campaign. The "customers" competing to buy the guns were the Fur and "Arab" militias from Darfur.

46. *Le Monde*, 15 April 1989.

47. 'Darfur's Secret War', *Indian Ocean Newsletter*, 15 April 1989.

48. *Le Monde*, 11 May 1989.

49. *Africa Confidential*, vol. 30, no. 15, 28 July 1989.

50. *Sudan Times*, 21 May 1989.

51. The putschists admitted neither to being NIF nor to having carried out their coup to stop the peace process. But the Islamist press, the only one still

allowed to appear, made no bones about it (see *as-Sudan al-Hadith* of 23 May 1990 for a detailed account of the coup motivations).

52. The French journalist Jean Gueyras coined the clever formula of "a masked junta" to describe the new NIF-inspired military regime (see *Le Monde*, 23/24 July 1989). The NIF officers' main fear was that Cairo would organize a counter-coup, probably with Nimeiryist help.

53. *Indian Ocean Newsletter*, 25 November 1989.

54. *Le Monde*, 9 December 1989.

55. *The Forgotten War in Darfur Flares Again*, Africa Watch, London, April 1990.

56. *Le Monde*, 13 November 1990.

57. «Technicals» are Toyota Land Cruisers whose top has been sawn off to allow their passengers to jump out more easily. They have a large weapon (a single 105-mm. recoilless gun or twin 23-mm. ZUG automatic cannons) mounted in the back. A light machine-gun such as the Russian 7.62 mm. Dashaka is often mounted for a gunner sitting next to the driver. Following the Chadian wars of the 1970s and 1980s they later became ubiquitous in the Somalia conflict, where they are still used today. They are the modern equivalent of the camel-riders who fought in the *ghazzua* of old. Their use later spread to Darfur, in the hands of both the *Janjaweed* and the guerrillas.

58. *Le Figaro*, 20 November 1990.

59. This was the object of a negotiation between secret services in Paris and Washington. The French DGSE had been closely involved in the planning and support of Deby's *Blitzkrieg*, and their man Paul Fontbonne who accompanied the rebel forces all the way to Ndjamena remained with Deby as a close personal adviser. The CIA negotiated directly with Paris to be allowed to exfiltrate "its" Libyans without fighting (confidential interview, Paris, December 1990).

60. Khartoum had short-sightedly exported excess sorghum during 1989–90 to acquire hard currency.

61. The danger of famine in the Sudan was global (see *Sudan: Nationwide Famine*, London: Africa Watch, November 1990) but Darfur was the worst-hit region.

62. Agence France Presse, Nairobi, 2 November 1990.

63. See *Africa Economic Digest* (5 November 1990) and *Africa Analysis* (23 November 1990).

64. SUNA, Khartoum, 14 October 1991.

65. *Sudan Democratic Gazette*, November 1991.

66. *al-Hayat*, 15 November 1991.

67. A source of outside support which had been highly supportive of Garang's anti-secessionist policy because Menguistu who was fighting against the seces-

sionist Eritrean movement favoured a unitary and "revolutionary" solution to Sudan's civil war.

68. For a clear analysis of the 1991 SPLA split (which was not healed till 2002 and still festers under the surface at the time of writing in early 2005) see Douglas Johnson, *The Root Causes of Sudan's Civil Wars*, Oxford: James Currey, 2003, Chapter 7.

69. Nasir is a town in Eastern Upper Nile where the splinter group had its main base.

70. SUNA, Khartoum, 15 November 1991.

71. Letter from Daud Bolad to a friend living abroad, shown to the author by the recipient, London, March 1992.

72. This account of Daud Bolad's miscarried adventure is based on interviews in London in March 1992 with several Darfuri actors and witnesses to the events.

73. Vice-Governor Ahmad Ibrahim at-Taher had declared in November 1991 (SUNA, Khartoum, 4 November 1991) that the government had managed to confiscate 16,000 guns since the end of the Chadian war. Even if the figure was probably inflated, this gives an idea of the magnitude of the problem.

74. For a discussion of Sudanese Federalism see Ann Lesch, *op. cit.*, pp. 125–8.

75. Many of the poorest states failed to reach that level, and in 1995 the central government had to create a special fund to assist them because they could not pay the local salaries.

76. See the document issued by the Massalit Community in Exile (12 September 1999, www.towardfreedom.com) and Douglas Johnson, *op. cit.*, pp. 140–1. The Massalit document bore the ominous title "Not yet ready for Prime Time Genocide".

77. For a particularly frank and naive development of that view, see Abbas Mekki, *The Sudan Question (1884–1951)*, London: Faber and Faber, 1952.

78. In racial terms, this meant very little. The "Arabs" of the Sudan are not "Arabs" by blood but semito-cushitic culturally arabized Creoles who are close cousins of the other people of the Horn, the Abyssinians and the Somali. The "false consciousness" which alienates the peripheral Muslim minorities starts right at the Centre, with the "Arabs" themselves. In an ironical twist of fate, the Rashaida tribe, who are probably the only "pure" Arabs living in the Sudan (they came from Saudi Arabia in the nineteenth century and did not intermarry much locally) enjoy a very low status on the scale of social prestige in the Sudan.

79. That name is in itself such an admission of racial/cultural prejudice that it is amusing to see the interested parties still using it unselfconsciously. It implies

that they (and only they) are the "real" inhabitants of the Sudan, and that all the others with their varieties of *rottana* and bizarre customs are amusing appendages which can be tolerated but never taken quite seriously.

80. See next chapter.

81. This is the eloquent title of a book by Francis Deng (*War of Visions: Conflict of Identities in the Sudan*, Washington, DC: Brookings Institution Press, 1995), which is a fundamental text but nevertheless falls too much into the North-South dichotomy view, ironically probably because the author had denied that fundamental gap for many years before reaching his intellectual Road to Damascus.

82. For a more detailed treatment of the interactions between the racial, cultural and religious prejudices in Sudan see Gérard Prunier, "Race, Religion and Culture in the Sudan", *Les Annales d'Ethiopie*, vol. 21 (2005).

83. Two pertinent (if very different) cases are the over-representation of Breton peasants in the French army during the First World War or the over-representation of Black Americans in the US army during the Vietnam conflict.

Chapter 4   *Fear at the Centre: From Counter-insurgency to Quasi-genocide (2003–2005)*

1. Turabi had considerable influence over the *Quwaat ad-Difaa ash-Shabiya* militia, which could conceivably have stood up to the Army.

2. Apparently technical, this change was in fact essential: Turabi had introduced his notion of *tawaali* (litt. "in line with") organizations according to which he intended to "franchise" a number of parties as long as they were "in line with" the principles of the *inqaz*. Several of his associates feared: a) that the GoS would not manage to control the consequences of such a move b) that Turabi would extend an inordinate level of influence over the *tawali* parties; or both. The new law brought everything back under centralized control.

3. Gabriel Warburg, *Islam, Sectarianism and Politics in Sudan since the Mahdiyya*, London: Hurst, 2003, p. 207.

4. Increasingly the Islamist movement looked like a possible vehicle for social promotion, and as such attracted careerists on a fast track including a number of former Communists like Ahmed Suleiman and Yassin Omar al-Imam. Ideological or religious purity was not the main concern of this new wave of recruits.

5. The "new personnel" he was lining up for this change of the guard was made up of either very young men who still had a whole career to make like Mahbub

abd-es-Salam or on the contrary of old party hacks like Ali al-Haj or Ibrahim as-Sanussi who retained an absolute personal loyalty to the "Guide".

6. After twenty years of hopes and failures, the pipeline between the Western Upper Nile oilfields and Port Sudan had finally been completed in 1999.

7. The influential "Islamic" banker Abd-er-Rahim Hamdi remained in his camp.

8. IRIN dispatch, 11 May 2000.

9. *Sudan Democratic Gazette*, no. 122 (August 2000).

10. *Mideast Mirror*, 4 August 2000.

11. In practice it came under fierce surveillance from the police and secret services, and its cadres were harassed.

12. Interview with a high-ranking SPLA cadre. Name, date and place withheld by request.

13. It would have been theoretically easier to acquire weapons from Chad. But the close relationship existing at the time between Idris Deby and the Khartoum government precluded such a solution.

14. Although unproved, the accusation could be true: faced with increasing militia attacks, the "African" tribes were beginning to share their means of defence and the government accused the Massalit of having created a "Darfur Liberation Front". It might have existed on paper but it is unlikely that it had a practical existence at that point.

15. The Sudan Peace Talks had moved to that pleasant Kenyan lakeside resort in 2003.

16. They were of course not the first attempt at a negotiated settlement of the then eighteen years old conflict. For a summary of the earlier unsuccessful attempts see Ann Lesch, *The Sudan: Contested National Identities, op. cit.*, Chapter 10, aptly called "The Impasse in Negotiations". Now for the first time things seemed serious.

17. This wrong interpretation of the power struggle within the Islamist regime became so prevalent that even such an experienced observer of Sudanese affairs as John Ryle condoned it in his otherwise excellent "Disaster in Darfur" (*New York Review of Books*, 12 August 2004). During an exchange of e-mails following the publication he readily admitted that he had been inadvertently influenced by the predominant view.

18. Never mind that at the time it would have been very difficult to charge Osama bin Laden with a coherent offence in front of a US court.

19. SPLA leader John Garang later candidly acknowledged as much when he declared: "The peace agreement was reached not necessarily because the parties wanted to but because they were forced to by a set of pressures." (Interview with Voice of America. 30 May 2004)

20. As we see later, crushing the Darfur insurrection before the SPLA could enter into a Transitional Government with the GoS became a priority for Khartoum during 2003.

21. On 13 November 2003 in a BBC media release.

22. In the general euphoria about "peace" few observers seemed to notice that this "important document" failed to mention the armed militias used by the GoS in the South or the question of any coordination between GoS and SPLA forces in case anything went wrong.

23. In an assessment of the Wealth-Sharing Agreement he released on 27 January 2004.

24. In a telling illustration that perhaps Naivasha was not what it was touted to be, Sudanese Vice-President Ali Osman Mohamed Taha announced that the "global" document signed to coordinate the six previously-signed "partial" documents was still not the "comprehensive" final peace document and that he would have to go back to Naivasha to start a new negotiation for the "true" final document (*Al-Hayat*, 2 June 2004).

25. *Ar-Ray Al-Am*. 3 November 2002.

26. There were 160 km. of tarmac roads in Darfur at the time, built by the World Bank in the 1970s. Ali Osman was alluding to the notorious project of the so-called "Inqaz road" which President Beshir had touted earlier (see *al-bayan*. 26 June 2001) and for which $55 m in special taxes had been levied although no road was built. It later transpired, during a violent exchange in Parliament between Transport Minister al-Hadi Bushra and Vice-President Ali Osman Mohamed Taha, that the money had been embezzled right from under the Minister's nose by the "Autonomous Committee for the Inqaz Road" led by Ali al-Haj.

27. *Alwan*, 30 December 2002.

28. *As-Sahafa*, 29 January 2003. Mubarak al-Fadl al-Mahdi, nephew of the former Prime Minister Sadiq al-Mahdi who had defected from Umma, had created his own scissionist Party, the "Reformed Umma", and joined the government to become Diplomatic Adviser to the President.

29. See Chapter 3, footnote 57.

30. Khalid Abu Ahmed, *Darfur Watergate and Disaster (Regime Lying Politics)*. This naïve piece written in August 2004 by a *walad al-beled* journalist who had worked in Darfur in 1993–6 is available on www.sudanjem.com. In spite of its naivety (or perhaps because of it) it gives an interesting if confused view of the Darfur events as seen by a sympathetic outsider.

31. *Alwan*, 27 February 2003. The "new armed group" had called itself the Darfur Liberation Front. A couple of weeks later it changed its name to "Sudan Liberation Army" (SLA), thereby staking a larger political claim.

32. IRIN press dispatch, 27 February 2003.

33. *Al-Khartoum*, 4 March 2003.

34. He soon after organized the well-attended "Union of the Marginalized Majority" conference in Germany (April 2003) which seemed to aspire at uniting all non-Arab populations against Khartoum.

35. In an article dealing more generally with the Sudan situation, Roland Marchal says that this section is the Kobe who are linked with the tiny "sultanate" of Tinay on the Chadian border. ("Le Soudan d'un conflit à l'autre", *Etudes du CERI*, no. 105 [September 2004])

36. All the journalists who went to Darfur noticed that the youngest rebel soldiers were eighteen or nineteen.

37. International Crisis Group, *Darfur Rising: Sudan's New Crisis*, 25 March 2004, p. 19.

38. Sharif Harir is a Zaghawa who had for years been a university teacher in Norway. During the mid 1990s he quit his job to animate the Sudan Federal Party (SFP) in collaboration with former Darfur Governor Ahmed Ibrahim Diraige and he settled in Asmara when his party became a member of the NDA. He joined the SLM in 2004, becoming one of its few *bona fide* intellectuals. He and Diraige parted ways when he tried to get the SFP to merge with the SLM.

39. *Alwan*, 12 March 2003. Ibrahim Suleiman, Governor of North Darfur, had been one of the few officials to realize that things were deeply wrong and he had started negotiating with a number of pro-SLA people even before the insurrection had broken out in the open. Hiding behind a screen of extremist rhetoric (the guerrilla was all a product of Israel, the SPLA and the United States) he in fact tried to keep channels of communications open. He and a few others like him were rudely undercut by the regime extremists and he was fired in early May 2003.

40. Paradoxically Ali Masar was a former supporter of the extremist *Tajammu Al-Arabi*. He was well placed to know how deep the polarisation had reached.

41. *Ash-Sharq Al-Awsat*, 20 July 2003.

42. One cannot discount a certain amount of ethnic pique towards these two upstart *awlad al-Gharb* who presumed that they could do better than their *walad el-beled* boss.

43. It seems that Abdallah Abbakar, a famous Chadian commander who had fought in the 1990 anti-Hissene Habri war and later rebelled against Idris Deby, led the force which attacked Fashir.

44. Interview with Charles Snyder, head of the US State Department Sudan Unit, Washington, DC, October 2004.

45. Including a number of Darfur *Mutammar* MPs.

46. This name had started to be used as early as 1988 to refer to "Arab" militiamen on horseback. "*Peshmerga*", "*mujahideen*" and simply "*fursan*" (horsemen) have also been used. But never the older "*murahleen*", this showing that the Baggara groups, who made up the *Murahleen*, were poorly represented, if at all, among the *Janjaweed*.

47. The notorious "Arabist" militant Sheikh Musa Hilal of the Jalul Arabs was released from detention in Port Sudan on orders of Vice-President Ali Osman Mohamed Taha and sent back to Darfur with orders to start recruiting. He had been gaoled on murder charges.

48. Hence the limited presence of Baggara tribesmen whose strong Mahdist leanings made them wary of a militia which, unlike the Murahleen of the 1980s, was not Mahdist-inspired. On the opposite members of "African" tribes which were trying to get "arabized", such as the Gimr, often joined in.

49. See Human Rights Watch, *Darfur Destroyed: Ethnic cleansing by Government and Militia Forces in Western Sudan*, May 2004, pp. 45–9.

50. *Sudan Tribune*, 28 November 2004.

51. See Human Rights Watch, *Darfur Documents Confirm Government Policy of Militia Support*, July 2004.

52. *Ar-Ray Al-Am*, 3 June 2003.

53. He had even been a resolute proponent of the strong arm method in dealing with the Darfur insurrection because he knew that some of his personal enemies, such as Abdallah Abbakar, were involved on the side of the rebels. (Interview with Ali Hassan Taj-ed-Din. Khartoum, January 2005)

54. In theory the Constitution does not allow Deby to run for a third mandate. But few doubt that he will work his way around that legal hurdle.

55. Personal communication, Addis Ababa, March 2004.

56. *Al-Adwaa*, 25 July.

57. This appropriate characterization of the way the Darfur horror developed was first used by Alex DeWaal in "Counter-Insurgency on the Cheap", *London Review of Books*, vol. 26, no. 15 (5 August 2004).

58. The following account is derived from the many interviews both with refugees in Chad and with IDPs inside Darfur. The most authoritative report was the one issued by the US Government: *Documenting Atrocities in Darfur* (September 2004), the product of 1,136 random refugee interviews.

59. The helicopter gunships were Mil Mi-17s, apparently bought in Kazakhstan, and the MiGs were either old Russian Mig-19 and 23 models or else the more recent Shenyang versions acquired from China, partly in payment for oil exports.

60. Killing the donkeys had a dual purpose: because these were the only means of transport the villagers had, it would prevent the survivors from running away with their property, if they still had some. The donkeys' bodies were then crammed into the wells in order to poison them. At times, wells could be blown up with dynamite. Dead human bodies and/or chemicals (fertilizers) were also used to poison the wells.

61. On the use of rape see Amnesty International, *Darfur: Rape as a Weapon of War: Sexual Violence and its Consequences* (July 2004), and Amnesty International, *Surviving Rape in Darfur* (August 2004). The fact that female victims were not sold off as slaves probably has to do with a vague remaining sense of religious taboo which prohibits the selling of Muslims as slaves. This would have made it difficult for the militiamen to find prospective buyers, contrary to the Southern situation where buying Black "pagans" had such a long cultural tradition that finding buyers was no problem.

62. The following accounts have been extracted from Amnesty International, *Darfur: Too Many People Killed for no Reason* (February 2004). They could have been taken from any other such report.

63. This is why the oft-repeated example of the "successful anti-insurgency campaign" against the Malaysian guerrillas carried out by the British in the 1950s is not really pertinent. The "Malaysian" guerrillas were in fact ethnic Chinese and they were a minority in the country, particularly in the rural regions where they tried to operate. The British forces were able slowly to isolate them because their pool of civilian support was too small and largely urban.

64. Due to both its pragmatic need for support as a minority party and its ideological faith in radical political Islam, the NIF (later Mutammar) has probably been less racist than the traditional sectarian-based parties. When the present author, who had been *persona non grata* for a number of years after the Islamist coup, was finally allowed to return to Sudan in 1993 he was greeted by an old friend with this desolate comment: "*These people are the end of the country. Now all you see everywhere are abid* ("slaves", i.e. Blacks) *and halabi*" (whites of Arab or Turco-Egyptian origins who are also looked down upon in Sudan). The complaint alluded to a very real fact, i.e. the promotion of non *awlad al-beled* elements in Sudan's civil service.

65. For an analysis of the motivations and tactics of the 1989 coup, see Gerard Prunier, "Les Frères et l'armée", *Les Cahiers de l'Orient*, no. 27 (Third Quarter 1992).

66. See J. M. Burr, *Quantifying Genocide in the Southern Sudan (1983–1993)*, Washington, DC, US Committee for Refugees, 1993, and African Rights, *Facing Genocide: the Nuba of Sudan*, London, 1995.

67. *As-Sahafa*, 10 June 2004.

68. Religion is not the main cause. In Ethiopia, for example, there are frequent Christian-Muslim marriages in which neither partner converts to the religion of the other.

69. The only Western actor to notice that fundamental point was the highly experienced US Under-Secretary of State for African Affairs Charlie Snyder who declared: "The rebellion in Darfur represents a much more serious threat for the GoS than the SPLA." (*alwan* 15 May 2004)

70. That inner courtyard of the house, scene of so much of the home and social life in Sudan.

71. In any case the JEM leader Khalil Ibrahim refused the truce signed by the SLM on 5 September. As a minority movement, the JEM took systematically more radical positions than its more broadly-based ally.

72. IRIN Press dispatch entitled "UN Preparing for Peace Accord", 23 September 2003.

73. *Al-Anbaa*, 14 October 2003.

74. *Al-Adwaa*, 28 October 2003.

75. Ali Osman Mohamed Taha declared that Turabi's agents had "infiltrated the delegation in Abeche and deliberately caused the agreement to abort". Even at that point fighting Turabi remained the regime's obsession.

76. IRIN Press dispatch, 31 October 2003.

77. *Al-Ayam*, 16 November 2003. The pretext was not only lame; it was false: the cereals were not genetically modified.

78. *Al-Anbaa*, 20 November 2003.

79. Reuters, 9 December 2003.

80. United Nations internal memorandum, 18 December 2003.

81. *As-Sahafa*, 17 December 2003.

82. Confidential information from Government of Chad sources, Addis Ababa, December 2003.

83. IRIN press dispatch, 31 December 2003.

84. IRIN press dispatch, 5 January 2004.

85. The first timid sign of recognition came from the respected *Oxford Analytica* online information site which on 17 September 2004 produced a brief called "Sudan: Ruling party fractiousness worsens conflict".

86. *Al-Anbaa*, 13 January 2004.

87. Block 12 (500,000 km.²) goes from South Kordofan to North Darfur. It has been allocated to Japan National Oil Corporation (a Japanese government company) and the semi-public Impex. None of the two have done the nec-

essary seismic exploratory work and therefore have no idea whether or not there is oil in Darfur.

88. Oil exploration only began in 1979. But Northern nationalist feelings towards the South were already in evidence as early as the 1950s, when independence was being negotiated, even if probably less than 1% of the Northern population had ever physically been there.

89. The GoS is actually well aware of this and it fears, even at the limited level of media exposure in today's Sudan, what could be called a "Viet Nam war effect". When the rather anti-Western and pro-Arab TV station al-Jazeera dared to film a documentary on Darfur in early 2004, its Khartoum office was immediately closed, its equipment seized and its local staff prosecuted. I personally saw the film and found it rather innocuous but this was not the feeling of the Sudanese Ministry of Information.

90. Agence France Presse dispatch, 27 January 2004.

91. *Alwan*, 27 January 2004.

92. Interview with Reuters, 18 February 2004.

93. *Al-Hayat*, 2 March 2004. This type of ambiguous reporting, where the *Janjaweed* and the rebels were lumped together into one category of "armed bandits", was common in Khartoum newspapers.

94. IRIN press dispatch, 3 March 2004.

95. He mentioned 10,000 casualties, a considerable underestimate.

96. Radio Khartoum, 19 March 2004.

97. Reuters, 26 March 2004.

98. *As-Sahafa*, 6 April 2004. The accusations against the old Islamist leader were rather fantastic, ranging from attempting to sabotage a power plant to having had the intention of "reopening the bars". Turabi was never formally charged, but kept in jail without trial.

99. *As-Sahafa*, 18 April 2004.

100. This poses the question, often asked, of whether the whole operation was motivated by an attempt as ethnic cleansing and population relocation. We discuss the problem at more length in Chapter 5. But even if plans have existed to do this, they were sketchy at best and hard to implement given the nature of the intended beneficiaries who would have to be turned into peasants.

101. *Al-Adwaa*, 10 May 2004.

102. Firing his CoS, replacing him by another general close to the Darfur rebels, putting as new Director of Security a first cousin of Khalil Ibrahim. See *TTU* newsletter [Paris] 27 May 2004 for details.

103. During 2004 the GoS started to support the Alliance Nationale de Résistance (ANR), the Libya-based Chadian rebel movement led by Colonel Mahamat Abbo Sileck, and gave it rear bases in Wadi Saleh province. In October 2004 at least one prominent *Janjaweed* leader flew to Paris to recruit Chadian exiles there. (Confidential interview, Paris, October 2004).

104. *The Economist*, 29 May 2004.

105. Susan Rice and Gail Smith, Op Ed piece, *Washington Post*, 30 May 2004.

106. IRIN press dispatch, 16 June 2004.

107. International Crisis Group, *Sudan's Dual Crises: Refocusing on IGAD*, Brussels, October 2004.

108. The purely humanitarian aspects of the situation is treated in more detail in Chapter 5. This section concentrates rather on the way the humanitarian intervention in Darfur affected the political and military parameters of the repression.

109. 21 June 2004. This was in response to a recent statement by Vice-President Ali Osman Mohamed Taha who had accused the media of "exaggeration" and the West from having "fabricated" the Darfur crisis (Agence France Presse, Cairo, 16 June 2004).

110. This author talked to a former IDP who had fled to Khartoum after he went to the police near his camp to complain about his daughter being raped, only to find that the "policeman" who stood to receive his complaint was the very same *Janjaweed* officer who had killed several members of is family when he fled his village (interview, Khartoum, December 2004).

111. *Ar-Ray Al-Am*, 5 July 2004. What the Sudanese paper described were clashes between sections of the Rizzeyqat and the Birgid near ed-Da'ien.

112. IRIN dispatch, 5 July 2004.

113. This is what Foreign Minister Mustafa Osman Ismail promptly did on 3 August when he complained that the thirty days allowed by Resolution 1556 were too short.

114. *Akhbar Al-Yom*, 4 August 2004.

115. *New York Times*, dispatch from Nyala, 6 August 2004.

116. Reuters, Khartoum, 12 August 2004.

117. *Alwaan*, 31 August 2004.

118. Sudanese Security "discovered" another coup attempt by the same group of suspects two weeks later and arrested some more people including some who were not at all part of Turabi's movement (see *Ar-Ray Al-Am*, 25 September 2004). Ibrahim Suleiman, the former governor of North Darfur then living in exile in Britain, was accused of being behind the plot.

119. *The Standard*, 16 September 2004.

120. Apart from the absence of implementation of these Resolutions in the face of systematic obfuscation by Khartoum there was also the problem that some of the threats were empty since they could not have been implemented whatever had been the wish of the international community. See for example on the question of the apparently tempting oil sanctions the sharp retort contained in the short CSIS paper, *The Threat of International Sanctions on Sudan's Oil Sector: How Feasible? What likely Impacts?*, Washington, DC, December 2004 (written by Nelly Swilla).

121. In that case the promise of a 'West Kordofan Development Committee'. Not only was the Committee never created but the state of West Kordofan was abolished and its civil administration disbanded. See *akhbar al-Yom*, 11 October 2004.

122. This comparison with the 1984 situation was made again in the 7 January 2005 report of UN Special Representative Jan Pronk where he described the condition of agriculture in Darfur at the end of 2004 as 'similar to that preceding the 1984 famine'.

123. IRIN dispatch, 11 November 2004.

124. IRIN dispatch, 12 November 2004.

Chapter 5 *The World and the Darfur Crisis*

1. In an article in *al-Ayyam* dated 3 September 2003.

2. MCE USA, 9 September 2003, communiqué.

3. SHRO (Canada Branch), 10 September communiqué.

4. See *Freedom House on Sudan: Shrill, Contentious and Unreliable*, www.espac.org, 19 September 2003.

5. See *Khartoum Muscling up on Security Issues at Naivasha*, www.listserv.emory.edu/archives/sudan-l.html, 23 September 2003.

6. *The Face of War in Darfur (Sudan): Many Tens of Thousands Flee Khartoum's Campaign of Aerial Bombardment and Militia Attack*, www.listeserv.emory.edu/archives/sudan-l.html, 8 October 2003. Note that the author had to add "Sudan" between parenthesis for fear that it would not be known where Darfur was.

7. DPA press dispatch, Khartoum, 9 November 2003.

8. Agence France Presse dispatch, Khartoum, 10 November 2003.

9. See Agence France Presse dispatch, Khartoum, 14 November 2003, titled "Alarming Food Crisis in Western Sudan".

10. Amnesty International, *The Looming Crisis in Darfur*, London, July 2003.

11. ICG media release, *The Other War in Sudan*, Brussels, December 2003.

12. See the one-page spread in *Le Monde* dated 20 January 2004 under the title "Khartoum Crushes the Darfur Rebellion with Fire and Sword"—note the allusion here to Carl Rudolph von Slatin's nineteenth-century classic *Fire and Sword in the Sudan* (London, 1896).

13. "Tamur Burma Idriss, 31, said he lost his uncle and grandfather. He heard the gunmen say: "You blacks we are going to exterminate you". He fled into Chad that night." *New York Times*, 17 January 2004.

14. IRIN dispatch, 22 March 2004.

15. *New York Times*, Op Ed column, 31 March 2004.

16. "Sudan can't wait", *The Economist*, 31 July 2004, and Samantha Power, "Dying in Darfur", *The New Yorker*, 29 August 2004.

17. "The tragedy of Sudan", *Time*, 4 October 2004.

18. John Ryle, "Disaster in Darfur", *New York Review of Books*, 12 August 2004.

19. See J. C. Rufin, *Le piège humanitaire*, Paris, 1986, and R. Brauman, *Devant le mal. Rwanda, un génocide en direct*, Paris: Arléa, 1994.

20. *The Telegraph*, 8 August 2004.

21. This meant that the emergency actually became news. Without media attention a humanitarian emergency does not exist, a fact well-known by emergency NGOs which both loathe and court the press.

22. IRIN, 14 November 2003.

23. Associated Press, 9 December 2003.

24. The same bag had cost 800 dinars before the war.

25. That hospitality had its limits and by mid-2004 it had begun to wear thin. By early 2005, given the receding water table, it had almost disappeared.

26. *Al-Anbaa*, 4 March 2004.

27. Its Swiss Director, Jakob Kellenberger, had declared on returning from Darfur: "ICRC is not at present in a position to carry out meaningful humanitarian operations."

28. *Al-Anbaa*, 8 March 2004.

29. *Al-Azmina*, 15 March 2004.

30. The UN team met a survivor of a recent massacre where 136 men had been shot with a bullet in the head at Garsila, south of Zalingei, in Wadi Saleh province at mid-April. The Team did not press the local authorities to accompany the man to the mass grave he wanted to show them.

31. Interview with the Voice of America, 28 April 2004.

32. Associated Press, 8 May 2004.

33. It should be remembered that "pledged" does not mean disbursement. There can be months, even years, between the pledging of sums and their being actually paid out.

34. MSF press release about the Mornay camp where 75,000 were living, 21 June 2004. A few days later Ibrahim Ahmed Omar, Secretary General of the ruling party, pledged to disarm the *Janjaweed* (*Al-Ayyam*, 24 June 2004). Nothing of the sort was even remotely attempted.

35. It has been argued that, even with the best of intentions, it would have been difficult for the government to disarm its killers. This is true, but Khartoum made no effort to dismantle the camps which served as their logistical bases (see Human Rights Watch release dated 27 August 2004, giving a list of the sixteen *Janjaweed* camps operating with full GoS support).

36. Interview with a WFP manager, Khartoum, December 2004.

37. This was soon found to be largely underestimated.

38. For a discussion of the numbers involved, see the last section of this chapter.

39. "Stronger, faster action is needed to save the people of Darfur", *The Economist*, 7 August 2004.

40. Public Law 107–245 (21 October 2002).

41. Washington was by far the biggest contributor in the Darfur humanitarian emergency, having given $111 m. out of $301 m. during the September 2003–July 2004 period. For comparison, Japan had given $1.68 m. and Saudi Arabia $1 m.

42. Confidential interview with a high-ranking member of the US administration, Washington, October 2004.

43. In an interview with *The Telegraph*, 31 May 2004.

44. *The Standard*, 16 September 2004.

45. From July 2004 onwards there was tremendous internal pressure for "action" at the UN, partly to try and please the US but also because a phenomenon of "bandwagon hopping" developed when UN personnel began to say to themselves "My God, this is BIG". (Interview with a high-ranking UN person, Addis Ababa, January 2005)

46. The UN Secretary General had gone to Harvard to be awarded an honorary doctorate. The demonstrators hooted and shouted at him to "Go to Darfur instead of Harvard".

47. What made it even worse was that Jan Egeland, the UN Under Secretary for Humanitarian Affairs, had used the expression "ethnic cleansing" as early as 4 April. It was difficult for the Secretary General to argue that the "reports received" did not include that of his own Under Secretary for Humanitarian Affairs.

48. Agence France Press, New York, 3 July 2004.

49. See Maggie Farley, "Sudan Report Cites Crimes against Humanity", *Los Angeles Times*, 29 January 2005.

50. We come back to this point in the last section of the present chapter.

51. This was at the time when Tanzania had been invaded by the Ugandan dictator Idi Amin Dada and the OAU had refused any condemnation of the act or any practical help for Dar-es-Salaam.

52. Interviews with AU personnel, Addis Ababa, October 2004 to January 2005.

53. Reuters, Lagos, 6 August 2004.

54. Interview in *ash-Sharq al-Awsat*, 6 August 2004. The retort prompted the director of Human Rights Watch Africa, Peter Takirambudde, to comment that Khartoum could not be serious about wanting to quiet things down in Darfur because otherwise it would have welcomed outside help. The point was correct but it had no impact.

55. By the beginning of 2005 the AU had about 1,000 men (observers and soldiers combined) deployed in Darfur. In spite of constant administrative and logistical harassment by the GoS authorities, they did what could be termed a commendable job given their financial and mandate constraints.

56. Hugo Slim, "Dithering over Darfur: a Preliminary review of the International Response", *International Affairs*, vol. 80, no. 5 (October 2004), page 827.

57. UN press release, New York, 4 November 2004.

58. Although it is available from the Congressional Research Service in Washington.

59. Reuters and Agence France Presse 23 February 2004. These numbers are essential to calculate the number of deaths due to disease and malnutrition.

60. On 22 March 2004.

61. The discrepancy between the camp population and the total IDP numbers was made up of the estimated numbers of inaccessible IDPs, i.e. those who were either in rebel-held areas or in government-held areas but unreachable for food distribution.

62. See the result in MSF: "Violence and Mortality in West Darfur (2003–2004): Epidemiological Evidence from Four Surveys", *The Lancet*, 1 October 2004.

63. It is likely to be so, since these figures concern camps with full humanitarian access. Populations that are inaccessible are more than likely to have had an even higher CMR.

64. They had reached 1.45 m. and 1.75 m. respectively.

65. We say "conservative" because the WHO survey not only limited itself to the accessible IDP camps, but even in those camps took account only of the people who had food registration cards, i.e. only 78% of the actual numbers.

66. IRIN, Nairobi, 29 January 2005.

67. A completely independent assessment by Dr Jan Coerbergh at the same time ("Sudan: Genocide has killed more than the Tsunami", *Parliamentary Brief*,

vol. 9, no. 7, February 2005, pp. 5–7) arrives at a figure of 306,000 excess deaths. In March 2005 Jan Egeland seemed suddenly to cave in to factual pressure and admitted that total casualties could amount to "200,000 or even 300,000". By then, since IDP camp deaths kept taking place, the figure could conceivably have reached 350,000.

68. Ahmed Dirdeiry, GoS spokesman for the Naivasha Peace Talks. IRIN interview, Nairobi, 27 February 2003.

69. GoS Minister for Information el-Zahawi Ibrahim Malik, *al-Khartoum*, 13 March 2003.

70. Adam Idris al-Silaik, acting Governor of Nyala, in an IRIN interview, 11 December 2003.

71. "The rebels in Darfur are part and parcel of the Janjaweed ....In any case the whole thing is entirely tribal." Information Minister el-Zahawi Ibrahim Malik interviewed by IRIN, 1 September 2004.

72. Information Minister el-Zahawi Ibrahim Malik, IRIN interview, 31 December 2003.

73. The word "inferior" has to be taken here as meaning "out of power", "not in control of the government".

74. Article 2, section C. The emphasis is mine.

75. Gérard Prunier, *The Rwanda Crisis: History of a Genocide*, London: Hurst, 1995.

76. Such as was the case for the Trotskyites in the Soviet Union after 1927 or the Communists in post-1933 Germany.

77. The intractable nature of the Israeli-Palestinian conflict and of the Rwandese problem are two cases in point.

78. See his Op Ed piece in the *International Herald Tribune*, 14 May 2004.

79. See his testimony to the Africa Subcommittee of the US House of Representatives Committee on International Relations investigating violence in Darfur, 11 March 2004.

80. Eric Reeves' testimony to the Africa Subcommittee of the US House of Representatives Committee on International Relations investigating violence in Darfur, 11 March 2004.

81. In his testimony to the US Senate Commission on Foreign Relations Powell added immediately that this determination of genocide "dictated no new action", a surprising but technically correct statement because the 1948 UN Convention only asks any government knowing of a genocide to refer the matter to the UN. It is then up to the UN, and the UN alone, to undertake the proper action.

82. An interesting sample of official verbal acrobatics was seen in the article by Christopher Ayad, "*Querelle sémantique autour du "genocide"au Darfour*", *Libération* (Paris), 15 September 2004.

Chapter 6 *Conclusion: Darfur and the Global Sudan Crisis*

1. Author's own observations. At the time a nice old lady in Omdurman who was in a state of panic asked the author: "Do you think the slaves are all going to come and kill us in our homes?". She was reacting to a leaflet then manufactured by Provisional Government strongman Osman Abdallah, threatening just that.

2. Religiously Sudan is made up of two unequal halves (25% Christian and 75% Muslim). But racially the two halves have the opposite inequality, with the "Arabs" representing perhaps 40% and the "Africans" 60%.

3. From that point of view the title of former Vice-President Abel Alier's memoirs *Southern Sudan: Too Many Agreements Dishonoured* (Exeter: Ithaca Press, 1990) is particularly telling.

4. Convened by the Nazi leaders in early 1942, the Wannsee conference defined the modalities of the "*Endlösung*" (final solution) to the "Jewish question".

BIBLIOGRAPHY

This bibliography does not intend to be exhaustive, either about Darfur or, even less, about the multi-layered crisis which Sudan has been under going since 1983. Its purpose is to direct the reader who might be interested in seeking further understanding of the present crisis in Darfur to three types of printed material:

— general works about the Sudan which have an overall relevance to the crisis;
— historical or ethnological works about Darfur;
— documents directly linked to the present crisis.

In addition, more limited bibliographical references of a specific nature can be found in the relevant chapters. Since the Darfur crisis in its presen extreme form is recent and still evolving, a number of relevant web-site have been included in a separate section at the end of the "paper" bibliography.

General Works

Abdel Salam Sidahmed, *Politics and Islam in Contemporary Sudan*, Richmond (Surrey). Curzon Press, 1997.

Barbour, K.M., *The Republic of the Sudan: A Regional Geography*, University of London Press, 1961.

Bechtold, P., *Politics in the Sudan: Parliamentary and Military Rule in an Emerging African Nation*, New York: Praeger, 1976.

Burr, J.M., and R.O. Collins, *Revolutionary Sudan: Hassan al-Turabi and the Islamist State (1989–2000)*, Leiden: E.J. Brill, 2003.

Daly, M.W., *Empire on the Nile: the Anglo-Egyptian-Sudan (1898–1934)*, Cambridge University Press, 1986.

————, *Imperial Sudan: the Anglo-Egyptian Condominium (1934–1956)*, Cambridge University Press, 1991.

Deng, F.M., *War of Visions: Conflict of Identities in the Sudan*, Washington, DC: Brookings Institution Press, 1995.

Holt, P.M., and M. Daly, *The History of the Sudan*, London: Weidenfeld and Nicolson, 1979.

Horowitz, M.M., "A reconsideration of the Eastern Sudan", *Cahiers d'Etudes Africaines*, vol. VII, no. 3 (1967), pp. 381–98.

Johnson, D.H., *The Root Causes of Sudan's Civil Wars*, Oxford: James Currey, 2003.

Jok Madut Jok, *War and Slavery in the Sudan*, Philadelphia: University of Pennsylvania Press, 2001.

Khalid, Mansour, *The Government they Deserve: the Role of the Elites in Sudan's Political Evolution*, London: Kegan Paul International, 1990.

————, *an-Nukhba as-Sudaniya wa Idman al-Fashel*, 2 vols, Cairo: Dar al-Amin li'l Nasr wa'l Tanziya, 1993.

————, *War and Peace in the Sudan: a Tale of Two Countries*, London: Kegan Paul International, 2003.

Lesch, A. M., *The Sudan: Contested National Identities*, Bloomington: Indiana University Press/Oxford: James Currey, 1998.

Muddathir abd al-Rahim, *Imperialism and Nationalism in the Sudan*, Oxford: Clarendon Press, 1969.

Prunier, G., "Race, Religion and Culture in the Sudan", *Les Annales d'Ethiopie*, vol. 21 (2005).

Warburg, G., *Islam, Sectarianism and Politics in Sudan since the Mahdiyya*, London: Hurst, 2003.

Yusuf Fadl Hasan, *The Arabs and the Sudan*, Edinburgh University Press, 1967.

———— (ed.), *Sudan in Africa*, Khartoum University Press, 1971.

History and ethnology of Darfur

Arkell, A.J., "The History of Darfur (1200–1700)", *Sudan Notes and Records*, vol. 32, no. 1 (1951), pp. 37–70; vol. 32, no. 2 (1951); pp. 207–38, vol. 33, no. 1 (1952), pp. 129–55, and vol. 33, no. 2 (1952), pp. 244–75.

Ahmed Suleiman al-Karsany, "The Establishment of Neo-Mahdism in the Western Sudan (1920–1936)", *African Affairs*, vol. 86, no. 344 (1987), pp. 385–404.

Braukämper, U., *Migration und Ethnischer Wandel: Untersuchungen aus der östlichen Sudanzone*, Stuttgart: Franz Steiner, 1992.

Cunnison, I., *The Baggara Arabs*, Oxford: Clarendon Press, 1966.

Haaland, G., "Nomadisation as an Economic Career among the Sedentaries in the Sudan Savannah Belt" in I. Cunnison and W. James (eds), *Essays in Sudan Ethnography*, London: Hurst, 1972, pp. 149–72.

Holt, P.M., *The Mahdist State in the Sudan*, Oxford: Clarendon Press, 1958.

Holy, L., *Neighbours and Kinsmen: a Study of the Berti People of Darfur*, London: Hurst, 1974.

————, "Cultivation as a long term strategy of survival: the Berti of Darfur" in D. Johnson and D. Anderson (eds), *The Ecology of Survival: Case Studies from Northeast African History*, London: Lester Crook, 1988, pp. 135–54.

Kapteijns, L., *Mahdist Faith and Sudanic Tradition: the History of the Masalit Sultanate (1870–1930)*, London: Routledge and Kegan Paul, 1985.

———— and J. Spaulding, *After the Millennium: Diplomatic Correspondence from Wadai and Dar Fur on the Eve of the Colonial Conquest (1885–1916)*, East Lansing: Michigan State University Press, 1988.

MacMichael, H.A., "The Tungur-Fur of Dar Furnung", *Sudan Notes and Records*, vol. 3 (1920), pp. 24–32.

Mohamed el-Tunisi, *Travels of an Arab Merchant in Soudan*, London: Chapman and Hall, 1854. An abridged translation of two volumes previously published in French as Mohammed Ibn Omar el-Tounsy, *Voyage au Darfour* (1845) and *Voyage au Ouadaï* (1851).

Nachtigal, G., *Sahara and Sudan*, vol. IV: *Wadai and Darfur*, London: Hurst, 1971. The material for this final volume of Nachtigal's exploration of the Sahel was collected in 1873–4 and published in the original German edition in 1889, four years after the author's death.

O'Fahey, R.S., "Slavery and the Slave Trade in Dar Fur", *Journal of African History*, vol. 14, no. 1 (1973), pp. 29–43.

————, *State and Society in Darfur*, London: Hurst, 1980.

————, and J.S. Spaulding, *Kingdoms of the Sudan*, London: Methuen, 1974. The part written by R. S. O'Fahey deals with the history of Darfur while Spaulding's part traces that of the Funj kingdom of Sennar.

Santandrea, S., *A Tribal History of Western Bahr-el-Ghazal*, Bologna: Editrice Missionaria Italiana, 1964.

Slatin, C.R. von, *Fire and Sword in the Sudan*, London, 1896.

Theobald, A.B., *Ali Dinar, last Sultan of Darfur (1898–1916)*, London: Longman, 1965.

Tubiana, M.J., and J. Tubiana, *The Zaghawa from an Ecological Perspective*, Rotterdam: Balkema, 1977.

Antecedents to the Darfur crisis

Abudullahi Osman al-Tom, "Black Book of Sudan: Imbalance of Power and Wealth in Sudan" (review article), *OSSREA Newsletter*, vol. XX, no. 3 (October 2002), pp. 14–25.

Adams, M., "The Baggara problem: attempts at modern change in Southern Darfur and Southern Kordofan", *Development and Change*, vol. 13 (1982), pp. 259–89.

Africa Watch, *The Forgotten War in Darfur Flares Again*, April 1990.

Anonymous: *al-Kitab al-Aswad* (the Black Book), n.p., n.d. (2000), no publisher. A partial English translation is available on www.sudanjem.com. See additional bibliographical reference under Abdullahi Osman al-Tom.

Buijtenhuijs, R., *Le FROLINAT et les révoltes populaires du Tchad (1965–1976)*, The Hague: Mouton, 1978.

————, *Le FROLINAT et les guerres civiles du Tchad (1977–1984)*, Paris: Karthala, 1987.

Burr, J. M., and R.O. Collins, *Africa Thirty Years War: Libya, Chad and the Sudan (1963–1993)*, Boulder, CO: Westview Press, 1994.

Bush, R., "Hunger in Sudan: the case of Darfur", *African Affairs*, vol. 87, no. 346 (January 1988), pp. 5–23.

De Waal, A., *Famine that kills: Darfur (Sudan) 1984–1985*, Oxford: Clarendon Press. 1989 (rev. edn 2004).

———— and Ahmed Hassan Abedel Salam, "Islamism, State Power and *Jihad* in Sudan", pp. 71–113 in Alex deWaal (ed.), *Islamism and its Enemies in the Horn of Africa*, London: Hurst, 2004.

Fouad N. Ibrahim, *Desertification in North Darfur*, Hamburg: Institut für Geographie und Wirtschaftgeographie der Universität Hamburg, 1980.

Mohamed Saleh and Sharif Harir, "Tribal Militias: the Genesis of National Disintegration" in Sharif Harir and Terje Tvedt (eds), *Shortcut to Decay: the Case of Sudan*, Uppsala: Nordiska Afrikainstitutet, 1994, pp. 186–203.

Mohamed Suleiman Adam, "Tribal conflicts in Darfur", *Sudan Studies*, no. 24 (June 2000), pp. 1–23.

Morton, J., "Tribal administration or no administration: the choice in Western Sudan", *Sudan Studies*, no. 11 (January 1992), pp. 26–47.

Oxfam, *Sudan: The Roots of the Famine*, London, January 1986.

Prunier, G., "Ecologie, structures ethniques et conflits politiques au Dar Fur" in H. Bleuchot, C. Delmet and D. Hopwood (eds), *Sudan: Identity, History, Ideology*, Reading: Ithaca Press, 1991, pp. 85–103.

Ruiz, H., *When Refugees Won't Go Home: The Dilemma of Chadians in Sudan*. Washington, DC: US Committee for Refugees, 1987.

Sharif Harir, "Racism in Islamic Disguise: Retreating Nationalism and Upsurging Ethnicity in Darfur" in H. Veber *et al., Never Drink from the Same Cup*, Proceedings of the Conference on Indigenous Peoples in Africa, CDR-IWIGH Document no. 74, Tune (Denmark), 1993, pp. 291–311.

———— and Terje Tvedt, "The 'Arab belt' versus the 'African belt': ethnic and political strife in Darfur and its cultural and regional factors" in *Sudan: Short Cut to Decay*, Uppsala: Nordiska Afrikainstitutet, 1994, pp. 144–85.

The present crisis in Darfur

Given the large media coverage and abundance of material from NGOs since late 2003, only the most significant publications are included here.

African Union, *Report of the Chairperson of the Commission on the Situation in Darfur, the Sudan*, Addis Ababa, October 2004.

Amnesty International, *Sudan: Looming Crisis in Darfur*, London, July 2003.

————, *Sudan: Empty Promises? Human Rights Violations in Government-Controlled Areas*, London, July 2003.

————, *Darfur: Too Many People Killed for No Reasons*, London, February 2004.

————, *Darfur: Incommunicado Detention, Torture and Special Courts*, London, June 2004.

————, *Sudan: At the Mercy of Killers: Destruction of Villages in Darfur*, London, July 2004.

————, *Darfur: Rape as a Weapon of War: Sexual Violence and its Consequences*, London, July 2004.

————, *Sudan: Arming the Perpetrators of Grave Abuses in Darfur*, London, November 2004.

Calabresi, M., S. Dealy and S. Faris, "The Tragedy of Sudan", *Time*, 4 October 2004.

Coerbergh, J., "Sudan: Genocide has killed more than the Tsunami", *Parliamentary Brief*, vol. 9, no. 7 (February 2005), pp. 5–7.

Collins, R.O., "Désastre au Darfour", *Politique Africaine*, no. 96 (December 2004).

Depoortere, E., F. Checchi *et al.*, "Violence and Mortality in West Darfur (2003–2004): Epidemiological evidence from four surveys" [MSF survey], *The Lancet*, October 2004.

DeWaal, A., "Counter-insurgency on the cheap", *London Review of Books*, vol. 26, no. 15 (5 August 2004).

————, "Tragedy in Darfur", *Boston Review*, November–December 2004.

Fowler, J., "In Sudan, staring genocide in the face", *Washington Post*, 6 June 2004.

Human Rights Watch Africa, *Darfur in Flames: Atrocities in Western Sudan*, Washington, DC, April 2004.

————, *Darfur Destroyed: Ethnic Cleansing by Government and Militia Forces in Western Sudan*, Washington, May 2004.

————, *Empty Promises? Continuing Abuses in Darfur, Sudan*, Washington, DC, August 2004.

————, *"If we return, we will be killed": Consolidation of Ethnic Cleansing in Darfur*, Washington, DC, November 2004.

International Crisis Group, *Sudan's Other Wars*, Brussels, June 2003.

————, *Sudan Endgame*, Brussels, July 2003.

————, *Darfur Rising: Sudan's New Crisis*, Brussels, March 2004.

————, *Sudan: Now or Never in Darfur*, Brussels, May 2004.

————, *Darfur Deadline: a New International Action Plan*, Brussels, August 2004.

————, *Sudan's Dual Crises: Refocusing on IGAD*, Brussels, October 2004.

Marchal, R., "Le Soudan. D'un conflit à l'autre", *Les Etudes du CERI*, no. 107/108, September 2004.

Médecins Sans Frontières, *Emergency in Darfur: No Relief in Sight*, June 2004.

————, *Persecution, Intimidation and Failure of Assistance in Darfur*, November 2004.

————, see Depoortere, E. *et al.* (2004).

Parliamentary Brief, *Genocide in Sudan*, special issue on Sudan with articles by Roderick Crawford, Julie Flint, Ali Ali Dinar, Gill Lusk, Patrick Smith, Kamel Labidi, Yoanes Ajawin, Eric Reeves, Douglas Johnson and Peter Verney, August 2004.

Power, S., "Remember Rwanda but take action in Darfur", *New York Times*, 6 April 2004.

————, "Dying in Darfur: can the ethnic cleansing in Sudan be stopped?", *The New Yorker*, 30 August 2004.

Reeves, E., *Current Data for Total Mortality from Violence, Malnutrition and Disease*, September 2004 (available on www.listserv.emory.edu/archives/sudan-l.html). See periodical updates on same site up to January 2005.

Ryle, J., "Disaster in Darfur", *New York Review of Books*, 12 August 2004.

Slim, H., "Dithering over Darfur: a Preliminary Review of the International Response", *International Affairs*, vol. 85, no. 5 (October 2004), pp. 811–28.

"Sudan can't Wait" (anonymous), *The Economist*, 31 July 2004.

Tijani Ateem, *An eyewitness account of the situation in Southern Darfur*, April 2004 (available on www.listserv.emory.edu/archives/sudan-l.html)

United Nations, *Report of the Office of the High Commission for Human Rights Mission to Chad (5–15 April 2004)*.

————, *90-Day Humanitarian Action Plan for Darfur*, June 2004.

———, *Resolution 1547*, New York, 11 June 2004.

———, *Resolution 1556*, New York, 30 July 2004.

———, *Report of the Secretary-General pursuant to paragraphs 6 and 13 to 16 of Security Council, Resolution 1556 (2004)*, 30 August 2004.

———, *Resolution 1564*, New York, 18 September 2004.

———, *Resolution 1574*, Nairobi, 19 November 2004.

———, *Report of the Secretary-General pursuant to paragraphs 6, 13 and 16 of Security Council Resolution 1556 (2004), paragraph 15 of Security Council Resolution 1564 (2004) and paragraph 17 of Security Council Resolution 1574 (2004)*, New York, 3 January 2005.

———, Resolution 1593, New York, 1 April 2005.

———, *Report of the Secretary-General pursuant to paragraphs 6, 13 and 16 of Security Council Resolution 1556 (2004), paragraph 15 of Security Council Resolution 1564 (2004) and paragraph 17 of Security Council Resolution 1574 (2004)*, New York, 7 January 2005.

United States Government, *Documenting Atrocities in Darfur*, Washington, DC: State Department, September 2004.

World Health Organization, *Retrospective Mortality Survey among the Internally Displaced Population, Greater Darfur, Sudan*, August 2004.

Relevant websites (not exhaustive)

www.hrw.org is the website of the advocacy NGO Human Rights Watch.

www.amnesty.org.uk is the Website of Amnesty International.

www.phrusa.org is the Website of Physicians for Human Rights, the first NGO to accuse the Sudanese government of genocide.

www.justiceafrica.org is the site of the advocacy group Justice Africa that has produced for several years a monthly report on peace efforts in Sudan.

www.sudanet.com is an information website on Sudan.

www.irinnews.org is the United Nations Information Website on Africa.

www.listserv.emory.edu/archives/sudan-l.html is a site where a variety of documents on Sudan can be found, including the past publications of the anti-Khartoum activist Eric Reeves.

www.tchad-info.net gives information about Chad and has material about the Chadian opposition in the Sudan.

www.sudanjem.com is the website of the JEM Darfur guerrilla movement.

www.darfurinfo.org has background material on Darfur.

www.msf.org the website of Médecins Sans Frontières. It has documents on the Darfur humanitarian situation.

www.usaid.gov/locations/sub-saharan_africa/sudan/cmr_darfur.pdf This site has statistics on IDP and mortality rates in refugee camps.

www.sudantribune.com is the website of an informative English-language Sudanese newspaper.

www.massaleit.info is the website of the Massalit community in exile.

www.espac.org displays documents and articles for the European-Sudanese Public Affairs Council (ESPAC), a London-based lobbying and public relations organization working for the Sudanese government.

INDEX

205